PICTURE AND GRAPHIC MANIPULATION

Center picture in box	Ctrl+Shift+M
Decrease size by 5%	Ctrl+Alt+Shift+<
Fit picture to box (maintain ratio)	Ctrl+Alt+Shift+F
Fit picture to box	Ctrl+Shift+F
Increase size by 5%	Ctrl+Alt+Shift+>
Move picture 1 point (nudge)	Arrow keys
Move picture $\frac{1}{10}$ point	Alt+Arrow keys

IMAGE CONTROL

High contrast	Ctrl+Shift+H
Higher resolution screen image	Shift+Open
Import at 36dpi (low res TIFF unch)	Shift (while importing)
Import at 72dpi (low res TIFF chkd)	Shift (while importing)
Import new picture	Ctrl+E
Negative	Ctrl+Shift+−
Normal contrast	Ctrl+Shift+N
Other contrast	Ctrl+Shift+C
Other screen	Ctrl+Shift+S
Posterized contrast	Ctrl+Shift+P
TIFF color to gray scale	Ctrl+Open
TIFF gray scale to line art	Ctrl+Open
TIFF line art to gray scale	Alt+Open

PICTURE BOX

Constrain to square or circle	Shift Alt+click
Maintain aspect ratio	Shift Alt+click
Maintain ratio of box and picture	Ctrl+Shift+Alt+click
Resize picture box	click handle
Scale picture with box	Ctrl+click

POLYGONS

Constrain line or handle	Shift+click
Create a handle	Ctrl+click on line
Delete a handle	Ctrl+click on handle
Delete runaround polygon	Ctrl+Shift+click
Suspend text reflow	Hold down spacebar

SELECTING TEXT

One entire line	triple click
One entire paragraph	quadruple click
One word	double click
Select all	Ctrl+A (or quintuple click)

SCREEN MAGNIFICATION

Between 100% and 200%	Ctrl+Alt+click (right mouse button)
Between 100% and Fit in Window	Ctrl+click
Close all document windows	Alt+click on close box
Zoom in/out	Ctrl+click (right mouse button)

FOR EVERY KIND OF COMPUTER USER, THERE IS A SYBEX BOOK.

All computer users learn in their own way. Some need straightforward and methodical explanations. Others are just too busy for this approach. But no matter what camp you fall into, SYBEX has a book that can help you get the most out of your computer and computer software while learning at your own pace.

Beginners generally want to start at the beginning. The **ABC's** series, with its step-by-step lessons in plain language, helps you build basic skills quickly. Or you might try our **Quick & Easy** series, the friendly, full-color guide.

The **Mastering** and **Understanding** series will tell you everything you need to know about a subject. They're perfect for intermediate and advanced computer users, yet they don't make the mistake of leaving beginners behind.

If you're a busy person and are already comfortable with computers, you can choose from two SYBEX series—**Up & Running** and **Running Start**. The **Up & Running** series gets you started in just 20 lessons. Or you can get two books in one, a step-by-step tutorial and an alphabetical reference, with our **Running Start** series.

Everyone who uses computer software can also use a computer software reference. SYBEX offers the gamut—from portable **Instant References** to comprehensive **Encyclopedias**, **Desktop References**, and **Bibles**.

SYBEX even offers special titles on subjects that don't neatly fit a category—like **Tips & Tricks**, the **Shareware Treasure Chests**, and a wide range of books for Macintosh computers and software.

SYBEX books are written by authors who are expert in their subjects. In fact, many make their living as professionals, consultants or teachers in the field of computer software. And their manuscripts are thoroughly reviewed by our technical and editorial staff for accuracy and ease-of-use.

So when you want answers about computers or any popular software package, just help yourself to SYBEX.

FOR A BROCHURE OF OUR PUBLICATIONS, PLEASE WRITE:

SYBEX Inc.
2021 Challenger Drive
Alameda, CA 94501
Tel: (510) 523-8233/(800) 227-2346 Telex: 336311
Fax: (510) 523-2373

SYBEX is committed to using natural resources wisely to preserve and improve our environment. As a leader in the computer book publishing industry, we are aware that over 40% of America's solid waste is paper. This is why we have been printing the text of books like this one on recycled paper since 1982.

This year our use of recycled paper will result in the saving of more than 15,300 trees. We will lower air pollution effluents by 54,000 pounds, save 6,300,000 gallons of water, and reduce landfill by 2,700 cubic yards.

In choosing a SYBEX book you are not only making a choice for the best in skills and information, you are also choosing to enhance the quality of life for all of us.

PAGE DESIGN WITH

QuarkXPress 3.1

FOR WINDOWS

PAGE DESIGN WITH

QuarkXPress® 3.1

FOR WINDOWS™

Patrick W. Fellers

SYBEX®

San Francisco • Paris • Düsseldorf • Soest

Acquisitions Editor: Dianne King
Developmental Editor: Kenyon Brown
Editor: David Krassner
Technical Editor: Peter Stokes
Book Designer and Chapter Art: Helen Bruno
Screen Graphics: John Corrigan
Page Layout and Typesetting: Len Gilbert
Proofreader/Production Assistant: Janet K. MacEachern
Indexer: Anne Leach
Cover Designer: Ingalls + Associates
Cover Illustration: Lynn Brofsky

Library of Congress Card Number: 92-82018
ISBN: 0-7821-1233-1

Manufactured in the United States of America
10 9 8 7 6 5 4 3 2 1

*This book is dedicated to
Mary Jane Fellers.
Thanks for the support!*

ACKNOWLEDGMENTS

want to acknowledge and thank the entire team at SYBEX who helped make this possible. Publishing is still a group activity and it's great to work with the best!

CONTENTS
AT A GLANCE

CONTENTS

PART

II

ASSEMBLING MULTIPLE PAGE DOCUMENTS

5 CREATING A MASTER PAGE 99

6 APPLYING A MASTER PAGE TO A DOCUMENT 113

P A R T

WORD PROCESSING

IMPORTING TEXT

TEXT FORMATTING

SPELLING AND DICTIONARIES 179

CREATING STYLE SHEETS 187

PART IV

TYPOGRAPHY

SIZE, FONT, AND LEADING 209

P A R T

PRINTING

POSTSCRIPT PRINTING 345

PRINTING FOR COLOR 361

QUARKXPRESS LIBRARY 409

INTRODUCTION

Many business leaders and educators proclaim that we are now in the midst of a second Renaissance. This second Renaissance embraces computer technology as a vehicle to distribute information and communications. Technological advances in this area over just the past few years have been astounding, and so has the pressure for people to keep pace!

As a practicing graphic designer and educator, I have had the pleasure of seeing the metamorphosis of preprint production activities as they have evolved from dedicated typesetting machines to the fantastic hardware and software of today. My first job as a typesetter was on one of the first CompuGraphic typesetting machines in the early 1970's. Then, to change type size on a line, you had to stop the machine and physically remove a lens and replace it with another to photograph a new size of the typeface. Twelve lenses were necessary to obtain the twelve basic type sizes. The font was in the form of a film strip. Employees were extremely careful when handling the $700.00 fonts.

Working on that equipment, one had to have knowledge of photography, typography, graphic design, and a bit of computer savvy. My studies in Industrial Design at The Ohio State University gave me just what was needed for the job. It was difficult to find someone with the skills to operate and maintain this type of equipment in a small shop environment. Early phototypesetting equipment was prone to breakdowns and the operator had to know what to fix and when to call for repairs.

Today, the technology seems light years ahead of that CompuGraphic typesetter I worked on nearly two decades ago. Now you can not only set variable sizes on one line but do so in .001 point intervals. You can even augment the typeface in several electronic variations simultaneously. Today, the price of a high-level desktop publishing software, such as QuarkXPress, is lower than that of early film fonts.

File compression and telecommunications make it easy to download a needed font over the telephone line from an on-line service. Electronic fonts of today cost pennies compared to the cost of their old filmstrip counterparts. Frequently, software applications bundle "free" fonts with their product to encourage sales.

Today, we use the desktop computer for a variety of tasks, including text input. Special desktop publishing software allows the user to see the text and graphics on the page as the layout would suggest. They call it WYSIWYG—What You See Is What You Get. I tell my students it should be called WYSIWYHF—What You See Is What You Hope For! Nothing's perfect yet.

The closest thing to *perfect* we have today is a state-of- the-art desktop computer, decked out in proper RAM, CD-ROM, DAT, HD, 10-BASE-T, and QuarkXPress software. To keep up with all the new acronyms is beyond hope.

Now, you can write copy, design the page, key the text, change type attributes, scan photos, position the print, proof, and color separate the job all through QuarkXPress. Is this Heaven…or Hell?

We've come so far in the past twenty years, since my work with the CompuGraphic machine, but one constant still remains. Exotic technology demands skilled people for proper operation.

As an Associate Professor at the college, I field many calls from printing firms and in-plant businesses. Many companies are taking the plunge toward QuarkXPress as their prepress software. These shop owners and department managers face the same problem, that is, they need skilled people to operate their QuarkXPress activities.

Today's problem with QuarkXPress is similar to those of twenty years ago. A company could afford typesetting equipment, but lacked skilled employees to operate and maintain their investment.

An obvious solution to the QuarkXPress training problem is to have people read the manuals! Unfortunately, this usually meets with little success. Manuals are traditionally written as reference, using a somewhat random access approach to information. Students of all ages learn best by having a mentor, presenting one technique after another, methodically building upon each skill level.

HOW THE BOOK IS ORGANIZED

Part I: Getting Started with QuarkXPress for Windows includes four chapters to get you started creating your first QuarkXPress document, to show you the anatomy of the program, and to explain the principles of document construction and page layout.

Part II: Assembling Multiple Page Documents contains two chapters to introduce you to the creation and use of master pages.

Part III: Word Processing consists of four chapters on the QuarkXPress word processor and other methods of putting text into your documents. Topics include importing and exporting text, formatting text, using spelling and dictionaries, and creating and using style sheets.

Part IV: Typography comprises four chapters that deal with the size, font, and leading of type. Also, this part covers kerning and leading, TrueType and PostScript fonts, and some advanced typographic maneuvers.

The three chapters of *Part V: Graphics and Pictures* introduce the world of graphic images. Included are discussions of manipulating pictures and graphics, combining text with graphics, and color concepts.

The final section of the book, *Part VI: Printing*, advises on the sometimes tricky task of printing out your work. There are chapters dealing with PostScript printing and printing in color. Because many XTensions are often concerned with printing or prepress operations, there is a chapter listing over a dozen XTensions currently available.

Finally, two appendices round out your QuarkXPress Odyssey, the first being a list of resources for the program, and the second a library of palettes and menus, just in case you forget what's where!

FEATURES AND CONVENTIONS OF THIS BOOK

At the beginning of each chapter, you'll find a *Fast Track,* which lists the most basic and useful commands covered in the chapter, explaining briefly how to use them and directing you to the pages they can be found on. The symbol ➤ has been used to indicate a menu command. The context you will usually see it in is *menu ➤ command*, as in File ➤ Save.

Finally, you will see three icons in this book next to the in-text notes. This list explains their meaning.

ICON	MEANING	CONTENT
	Note	General comments on Quark-XPress, including shortcuts and alternative methods.
	Tip	Advice on undocumented features of the program or hints on easy ways to perform actions
	Warning	Caveats advising you on common mistakes and problems with steps for avoiding pitfalls.

A FINAL WORD

I am on a constant lookout for QuarkXPress material presenting information properly matched with learning styles. Finally, I jumped into the market myself. This book is the culmination of my efforts. It is my attempt to help the sequential learner conquer a complex task. I feel confident that if you follow this book through from front to back, in sequence, you will gain a very good functional knowledge of QuarkXPress. Sure, you can also use the book as reference, but the ideal situation is to follow the chapters sequentially and build on your knowledge.

If you have any suggestions or comments, I invite you to E-mail my CompuServe address. I also would like to hear from all the freeware and shareware XTension developers (Mac and Windows). Contact me through CompuServe at 71202,3471.

—Patrick Fellers

Getting Started with QuarkXPress for Windows

1

CREATING YOUR FIRST QUARKXPRESS DOCUMENT

To place text in the automatic text box 16

select the Content tool from the Tool palette. Then click on the automatic text box created when you originated the document. You should have a cursor flashing in the top-left corner of the text box. This indicates you are ready to type in your text.

To alter text attributes such as font, size, etc. 19

highlight the text, using the Content tool. (Click and drag the mouse cursor over the text to highlight). Select the commands appropriate for change under the Style menu.

To adjust line spacing for text in your document 22

highlight all the text (click and drag), then move to the Style menu. Under this menu you have the option of Leading; it can be changed from the default (Auto) to the numerical leading of choice. Leading (line space) is usually measured in points.

To save the document to your hard drive 25

choose File ➤ Save. Locate the directory in which you wish to save the document, give it a name, click on the Enter button.

To give you a quick start in creating QuarkXPress documents, you will make a simple, one-page flyer. As you go through the tutorial you may have questions on QuarkXPress features, tools, and capabilities. Be patient, only basic information is given in *Chapter 1*. You will find more detail in later chapters. In this way, we will carefully guide you through QuarkXPress, building your knowledge and confidence.

CREATING YOUR FIRST QUARKXPRESS DOCUMENT

Begin QuarkXPress by finding and launching the application on your hard disk (or network). There are several ways to launch the program.

If you have not done any customization to the program since loading it, the application icon should be in its own program group under Windows. Find and open the QuarkXPress group on your drive. Inside you will find the original QuarkXPress application. Double-click the icon to launch the program (see Figure 1.1).

FIGURE 1.1
The QuarkXPress application icon is in the QuarkXPress group.

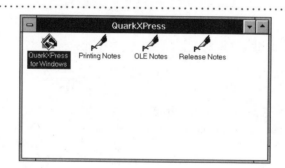

NOTE

If you did not accept the option of creating an automatic program group when installing QuarkXPress, you may have to use the File Manager to find the application.

Still another place to launch the application from would be a special program group, specifically dedicated to your frequently used applications. You can set up a special program group through the Program Manager and copy the frequently used programs or associated program icons into this group.

In a production environment, it may be awkward and time-consuming to launch programs from their program groups. In this case, you can take advantage of the Windows Startup Group. This group is designed to launch all applications within when you start Windows. It acts as an automatic launcher, so the user need not take the time or effort to search out the proper icon needed. As Windows is launched, it will search and launch any and all applications with icons contained within the Startup Group. You can still have full control over other Windows capabilities, but the applications within Startup launch first.

Of course, if you want real control, you will probably create a proper .BAT file and adjust the path, so that when you boot your computer, the Windows and QuarkXPress applications will launch. This is the "no hands" approach to getting directly to the application. Check your DOS operating manual or corner a nearby DOS fanatic for specifics on how to set up .BAT and path configurations.

In quick summary, you have several options as to where to launch the QuarkXPress application:

▸ First, with Windows running, the icon might already be in the QuarkXPress Program Group. This was an installation option. To launch the application from here, open the group and double-click on the QuarkXPress application icon.

▸ A second way, in Windows, is to create a specialty group of frequently used applications and copy the QuarkXPress icon into this group. In this way you are also easily in touch with other programs you may use with QuarkXPress, such as word processors or photo retouch programs (see Figure 1.2).

FIGURE 1.2

FIGURE 1.2

A special group of frequently used application icons can be housed together.

- Another location for the application icon is the Startup Group in Windows. This launches QuarkXPress upon Windows startup, and is the quickest way to launch applications within Windows (see Figure 1.3).

- The File Manager may be necessary to launch the application if no specific application icon or group has been created for QuarkXPress.

- Finally, the most direct approach is to use DOS configurations to place the Windows and QuarkXPress applications into automatic launch with a proper .BAT and path configuration.

NOTE

In Windows, you may have multiple application icons located in several program groups. This often occurs with different application setups in the Windows environments. It is OK and allows the user to launch from any of the icons, regardless of location.

FIGURE 1.3

Copy the QuarkXPress application icon into the Startup Group for quick launching within Windows.

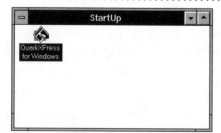

If you have any questions about positioning application icons or system approaches, reach for your DOS/Windows manuals. They are a great source of information.

The flyer you are about to create will demonstrate a few basic strategies for the QuarkXPress environment. You will

1. Start the application

2. Create a new document

3. Key in text material

4. Manipulate text

5. Save your work

6. And finally, print the document

The flyer is a one page promo for a bicycle retailer. It will be followed throughout the book by associated graphic applications in QuarkXPress, utilizing some of the tutorial files that came with your QuarkXPress program. Your first QuarkXPress document will look like the flyer shown here (see Figure 1.4).

STEP 1: LAUNCHING QUARKXPRESS

Launch the software using one of the procedures described above. The program takes several seconds to load all pertinent files, filters, and extensions, in addition to checking your system configuration and network status. If a copy of Quark-XPress with the same serial number is open on the network, you will get an error message. You can't open two copies of QuarkXPress with the same serial number at the same time. Similarly, when upgrading, you cannot simultaneously open two versions of QuarkXPress with the same serial number.

FIGURE 1.4
*Your first QuarkXPress
document will be a one
page flyer for Eddie
Merrik Bicycles.*

Eddie Merrik Spring Specials

NovaPed PR-12 Clipless Pedals
$149.95

Velloce Gel Saddles
$29.95

Scede MB3 Rims
$28.95

Sunlite Gamma Headsets
$39.95

Fujitaho Dura SK Brake Levers
$59.95

TIP
*The best way to run QuarkXPress is the same as the best way to
run any Windows application, that is, have a fast machine with a
lot of memory. If you don't have that option, make the machine
efficient by running only one application at a time. Multiple
applications loaded take up valuable memory and may slow down
or even stop your program from functioning.*

The first indication that the program has launched is the QuarkXPress logo (see Figure 1.5). This will disappear after a few seconds, but to hurry the process, just click the mouse once. The logo screen has information concerning the version number and the registered user name. The same screen also appears if you select the About QuarkXPress option under the Apple menu. For more information, see *Chapter 3*.

When the logo screen leaves, the work area appears to be transparent (see Figure 1.6). Before you open a document, there is no "work" area. You must create a work area through the use of New or Open options on the File menu.

To confirm a proper QuarkXPress launch, you should look for a few key signs. First, look for the *floating palettes*. One or more of these palettes may already show. To display or hide these palettes, use the Show/Hide options in the View menu. Shown options remain shown the next time QuarkXPress is open. For example, the Tools palette (see Figure 1.6) often remains shown, due to the nature of how QuarkXPress is used. It is positioned on the left side of the screen's work area by default, but may be repositioned by the user. The next time QuarkXPress is launched, the Tools palette will still show at the same location. The floating palettes consist of Tools, Measurements, Document Layout, Style Sheets, Colors, and Trap Information. These are all controlled from the View menu. The Library palette may be included, but it is located under the Utilities menu.

A second indicator of QuarkXPress activity is in the menu selection bar (also shown in Figure 1.6). The menu names differ from most other applications.

FIGURE 1.5
The QuarkXPress logo screen appears when you launch the application.

FIGURE 1.6

QuarkXPress as it appears properly launched, but without an open document work area.

NOTE

*You can **minimize** this application (a Windows capability), which keeps the program active, yet reduces the window to a small icon. Understand that minimized applications are still active and will take up memory, affecting other applications.*

Finally, you can determine which application is active by looking at the Task List (Ctrl+Esc). This allows you to see other launched applications (see Figure 1.7).

FIGURE 1.7

The Task List, a Windows utility, allows you to see and select from currently active applications.

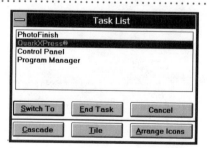

NOTE

If you are running concurrent applications, you can toggle between them using the Alt-Tab key combinations. This is a Windows function, not specific to QuarkXPress.

STEP 2: CREATING A NEW DOCUMENT

As with most Windows applications, you start a new document by selecting the New option from the File menu (noted hereafter as File ➤ New). You should learn to use the keyboard equivalents whenever available to speed operations. The keyboard equivalent for New is Ctrl+N. Once you've selected New, the New dialog box appears (see Figure 1.8). It includes options for Page Size, Margin Guides, Column Guides, as well as the Auto text box. Also, like most Windows dialog boxes, the New dialog box provides you the option of accepting your new settings (OK) or canceling them.

NOTE

Notice that some menu commands, such as New and Open, are followed by three periods (called ellipses). *These indicate that the command leads to a dialog box.*

FIGURE 1.8

The New dialog box under QuarkXPress. Your dialog box may not look identical to this image until changes are made as specified.

New

Page Size
- ● US Letter   ○ A4 Letter   ○ Tabloid
- ○ US Legal   ○ B5 Letter   ○ Other
- Width: 8.5"   Height: 11"

Column Guides
- Columns: 1
- Gutter Width: 0.167"

Margin Guides
- Top: 1"   Left: 1"
- Bottom: 1"   Right: 1"
- ☐ Facing Pages

☒ Automatic Text Box

[OK]   [Cancel]

A more comprehensive look at this dialog box appears later in the book, but for now, simply key in the following configuration:

Page Size: Letter (Click on the radio button for US Letter if it is not already chosen)

Top: 1″

Bottom: 1″

Left: 1″

Right: 1″

Columns: 1 (gutter width doesn't matter)

Automatic text box: checked

The dialog box may not have popped up looking like Figure 1.8, but with the changes just made, your dialog should look identical. Once you are satisfied that all the information is correct, accept this by clicking on the **OK** button.

NOTE
One quick way of accepting information in a dialog box is by pressing the Enter key. This acts as if you had clicked on the OK button.

When you're finished, click on the OK button. If you make a mistake and click on OK too soon, don't panic. Simply choose File ➤ New again and create another new document. Disregard any mistakes for now. You can close an erroneous document at any time.

Once you have clicked the OK button on the New dialog box, you're on your way! A new document work area appears on the screen (see Figure 1.9). This new document work area should be a full-size (100%) document page layout. Naturally, if you have a standard monitor, you won't be able to see the entire letter-size document on your screen. You can move around the page with the scroll bars. Resize the page by selecting from the View menu options.

FIGURE 1.9

The screen as it may appear when opening a new document under QuarkXPress.

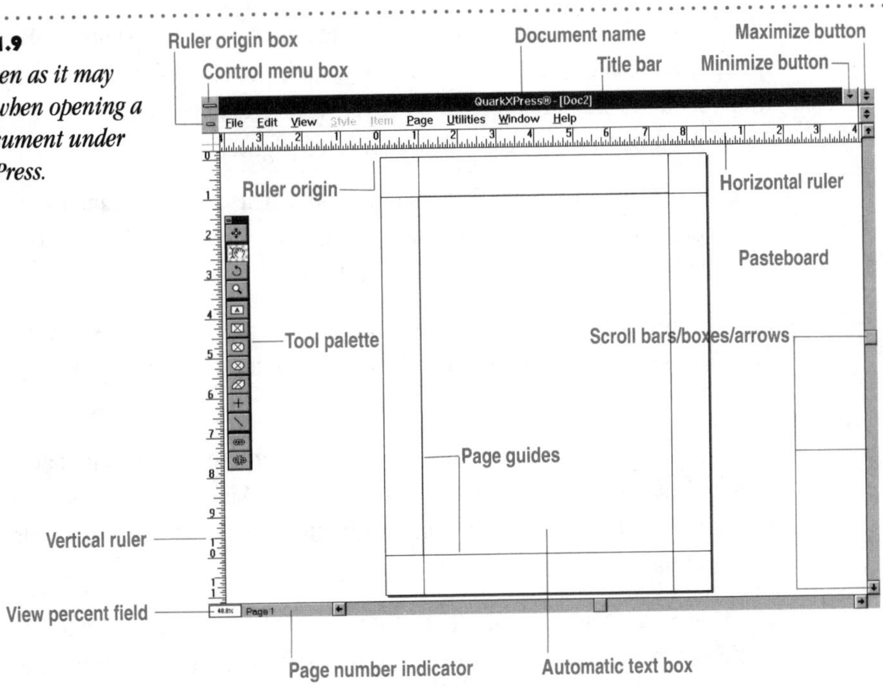

Ruler origin box

Control menu box

Document name

Title bar

Maximize button

Minimize button

QuarkXPress® - [Doc2]

File   Edit   View   Style   Item   Page   Utilities   Window   Help

Ruler origin

Horizontal ruler

Pasteboard

Tool palette

Scroll bars/boxes/arrows

Page guides

Vertical ruler

View percent field

Page number indicator

Automatic text box

NOTE

Not all users have their Windows and QuarkXPress software configured exactly alike. Certain parts of the work area may show on some people's applications and hide in others. Why? Because QuarkXPress gives you a lot of flexibility about showing certain elements like the rulers, guide lines, tools, etc.

Depending on your configuration, certain parts of the work area may or may not be visible. The following list tells which items must be showing on your first Quark-XPress document, along with the settings you should use.

▸ The document work area is distinguished by the scroll bars on the right and bottom (see Figure 1.9). If you don't see this, go back and repeat the first step of this section. If you still don't see the document work area, check to be sure you are still active in QuarkXPress. Then select View ➤ Actual Size. The document may have been opened in a smaller size if your defaults have been reconfigured to a reduced size.

- You should be at Page 1, not Master or any other page (see Figure 1.9). To jump from Master page to Document page use the menu Page ➤ Display option. Set it to Document. Use the vertical scroll bar to position yourself on the top left corner of Page 1, as shown in the figure.

- You should be viewing the document at 100%. This represents the page size as it appears on the screen; double-click on this number and key in **100** to replace it, if it does not already read 100%.

- You should show the horizontal and vertical rulers. You can do so by choosing View ➤ Show Rulers. In most cases the default will show rulers (see Figure 1.9).

- The Tools palette should be showing (you encountered this palette back in Figure 1.6). To show this floating palette, choose View ➤ Show Tools. You can move floating palettes anywhere using the usual click-and-drag technique in the active title bar area.

- A text box was automatically created if you checked the Automatic text box option in the New dialog box (see Figure 1.10). If you do not have an automatic text box, it probably easiest to abandon your document and repeat the first step of this section. Create another new document, this time making sure to check the Automatic text box. To view the entire text box, select View ➤ Fit in Window (see Figure 1.10). Then change it back to 100% for your work!

STEP 3: CLICKING IN THE TEXT BOX AREA

Now that everything is set on the document work area you can key in the text. QuarkXPress works on the idea of text in text boxes; graphic elements such as pictures and drawings go in graphic boxes (or picture boxes). Lines need no special box configurations. You can draw lines anywhere. This system will quickly become second nature, even if you're more comfortable with other layout program styles.

QuarkXPress is not a drawing program, but you can simulate basic geometric shapes through proper use of the tools. To create an outline geometric, you must create a text or picture box. You can frame the box to get an outline by selecting Item ➤ Frame. To fill a box, use the Shade option in the Modify dialog box (Item

FIGURE 1.10
The text box (created automatically) sits inside the original margins of the page. This reduced view of the page shows the text box area inside the margins.

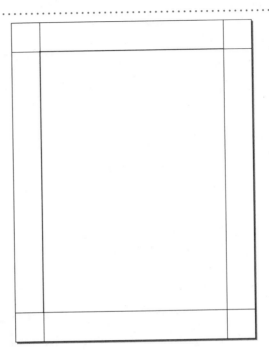

➤ Modify). For more complex graphic drawings, use the appropriate software application and import your picture into QuarkXPress.

NOTE

You can place text in an active text box only. If a text box is not active, you will not be able to key text into it.

To key in text, you must make the text box active. Place your cursor in the middle of the work area and click the mouse button. This activates the text box. When you click on the text box area, there should be a change in the box's outline. It will change to a solid line with the familiar grab handles (the little black squares—see Figure 1.11). This means that you have correctly highlighted (or made active) the text box. You can now place characters in the text box area.

FIGURE 1.11

Click on the text box and the mouse cursor changes to the text editing tool. Note the word processing style cursor at the first keystroke position within the text box.

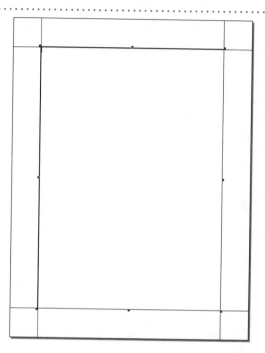

At this point, your Tools palette should have either the Item tool (the top tool in the collection) or the Edit tool (the second tool down) highlighted. The Edit tool is also called the Content tool. You want the Edit tool highlighted. Click it if necessary (see Figure 1.12).

When used in a text box, the Edit tool appears as a flashing cursor, similar to those in other word processors. The flashing cursor indicates that you can begin typing in the text box. QuarkXPress more closely resembles a true typesetting program than most other desktop-publishing programs. For this reason, when you click on the text area, the cursor will always go to the last keystroke position in the box. If it is a new box with no text, your cursor will take the first position in the box. You can edit and format type in the box using leading, alignment, and other kinds of typographic commands.

FIGURE 1.12

Select the Edit tool to create or edit text within a text box. The same tool is used in picture boxes to edit their contents.

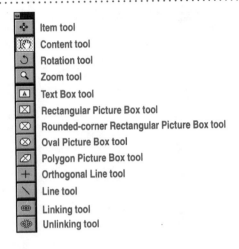

Item tool
Content tool
Rotation tool
Zoom tool
Text Box tool
Rectangular Picture Box tool
Rounded-corner Rectangular Picture Box tool
Oval Picture Box tool
Polygon Picture Box tool
Orthogonal Line tool
Line tool
Linking tool
Unlinking tool

In the text box you have just clicked on, key in the following text, placing a return at the end of each line:

Eddie Merrik Spring Specials
NovaPed PR-12 Clipless Pedals
$149.95
Velloce Gel Saddles
$29.95
Scede MB3 Rims
$28.95
Sunlite Gamma Headsets
$39.95
Fujitaho Dura XK Brake Levers
$59.95

Your screen should resemble the example (see Figure 1.13). This information is the basis for a sales flyer, your first QuarkXPress document. Later in the book you will build on this and create other documents relating to corporate communications.

STEP 4: CHANGING THE FONT

QuarkXPress allows you to change font information at any time. You are going to take advantage of this ability now. Change the text just keyed in to the font Times

FIGURE 1.13

Key into the text box the text for your first Quark-XPress document.

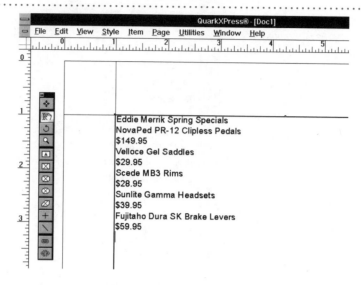

(or whatever typeface in your system that closely resembles the example) by highlighting all the text you have just keyed in. Click and drag over the text or just press Ctrl+A, for Select All. Your highlighted text should look somewhat like the example (see Figure 1.14). Remember, not all systems are set up alike, so you may have font discrepancies between examples depicted in this book and your own system.

NOTE

Menu commands with right-pointing deltas, such as the Font, Size, Type Style, and Color options on the Style menu, indicate that the command leads to another menu (a submenu).

Next, select Style ➤ Font and choose Times (see Figure 1.15). Your highlighted text should change to Times. If you don't have Times, use a typeface similar in look and style to the Times shown in this example.

FIGURE 1.14

In QuarkXPress, you must highlight text before you format it. Here all the text is highlighted so that type style characteristics can be changed.

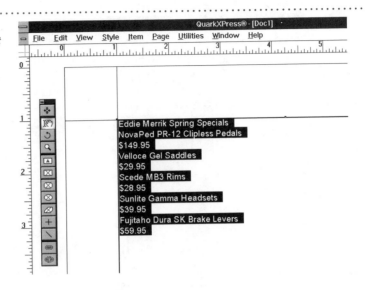

FIGURE 1.15

Choose Style ➤ Font, after highlighting the text, to change its type font.

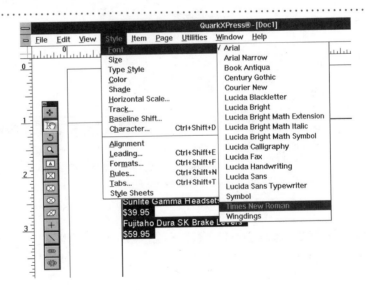

STEP 5: CHANGING THE TYPE SIZE

Highlight the text again. Then, choose Style ➤ Size and select 36 point. Your highlighted text should change to 36 point size (see Figure 1.16).

FIGURE 1.16

*Your document will look
something like this after
you have changed the size
of the type.*

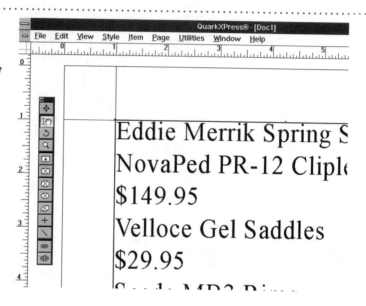

STEP 6: CHANGING THE LEADING FOR THE COPY

Highlight all the text again and choose the Style ➤ Leading option. The setting is probably Auto; this is the default. Change leading to 30, representing 30 points of leading. Then click on **OK** (see Figure 1.17). You may want to change to the View to Fit option within the View menu selections to see the entire page on your screen.

STEP 7: CHANGING THE SIZE OF THE PRICE TYPE

This time you will have to highlight each price individually, since there is no way to highlight every other line. First, click and drag over the $149.95 (see Figure 1.18). Then, choose Style ➤ Size and select 24 point as the type size. Repeat this for each of the other prices until they are all each 24 point in size. Your document should look like the example shown in Figure 1.19.

FIGURE 1.17

In the Leading dialog box, key in the leading you want in points.

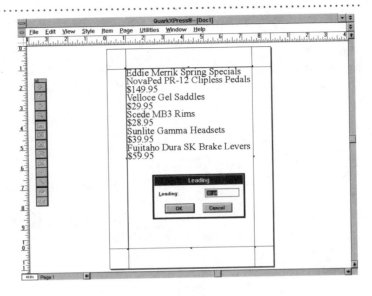

FIGURE 1.18

Highlight individual characters or lines to change only those features.

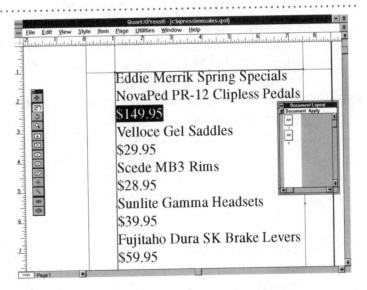

FIGURE 1.19

Once you change the size of the type for the prices, your document will have two different type sizes.

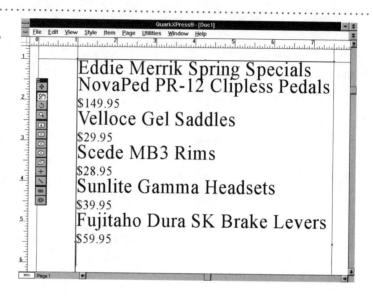

STEP 8: ADJUSTING THE LINE SPACING

An underrated design tool in desktop publishing is the Enter key. Let's use it now to create extra leading between lines. We will place an additional 30 points in key locations of the text for better aesthetics using the Enter key. Position the cursor before the *E* in Eddie, then click the mouse button to anchor the cursor at that spot. Press the Enter key once. This adds one line of space (30 points of line space). Next, place the cursor before the *N* in NovaPed; then click the mouse button. Press the Enter key three times (equals 90 points of additional line space). Then put the cursor after each price. Click the mouse button again to anchor the cursor; press Enter once after each price. Don't put an extra return after the last price ($59.95). Your page layout is shaping up; it should now look like Figure 1.20.

STEP 9: CENTERING THE TEXT IN THE TEXT BOX

To improve the look of this page, you should center the text. Highlight all text elements in the box. Use the Select All (Ctrl+A) or simply click and drag to highlight all the text. Then, from the menu, choose Style ➤ Alignment ➤ Centered.

FIGURE 1.20
Additional line space is added to help the layout.

Eddie Merrik Spring Specials

NovaPed PR-12 Clipless Pedals
$149.95

Velloce Gel Saddles
$29.95

Scede MB3 Rims
$28.95

Sunlite Gamma Headsets
$39.95

Fujitaho Dura SK Brake Levers
$59.95

STEP 10: SAVING THE DOCUMENT TO YOUR HARD DISK DRIVE

Choose File ➤ Save. Since you haven't saved this document yet, the Save As dialog box appears (see Figure 1.21). This dialog box gives you the option of where to save the document and what name to give it. Once the document is saved, this dialog box will not show unless you explicitly choose the Save As option.

TIP

The general rule about saving is "Save Early, Save Often." That means that practically before the first line of text, save the document. Then about every 15 to 30 minutes, press Ctrl+S to save document changes.

Choose File ➤ Save to
save your document to
the hard disk. The Save As
dialog box will appear,
since you've not yet saved
this file to disk.

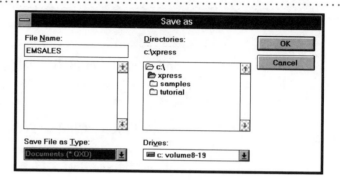

TIP

Since it is an excellent idea to save frequently, you might consider
purchasing an automatic save utility program. This kind of
program will automatically save your work every few minutes,
without your having to remember. A utility like this could be a
good investment in a production environment. Nothing is quite as
frustrating as working on a new document for four hours and
have a system glitch take it all away!

Save this document in the existing directory (which should be the QuarkXPress
directory) under the name **EMSALES**, as shown in Figure 1.21. Click on the **OK**
button to accept. Your document is now saved under the name EMSALES, in the
QuarkXPress directory, on the hard disk. Your document's new name will now
appear in its title bar.

STEP 11: PRINTING THE FLYER ON YOUR LASER PRINTER

This step assumes that your PC is connected to an output device of fairly high quality, such as a laser printer. If not, just follow along. You really do need such a
printer to proof QuarkXPress documents properly.

TIP

To really take advantage of all of the remarkable power and versatility of QuarkXPress, you will need a high-quality printer, such as a laser printer, or at least access to one.

Select the laser printer through the menu File ➤ Printer Setup option. The Printer Setup dialog box will appear (see Figure 1.22). This dialog box has many important options, which we will explore in more detail later in the book. For now, just click on printer type connected to your system. If your machine is not listed here, you may have to go back to the Windows Control Panel and add a printer to your Print Manager. See your Windows manual for help.

You are now ready to print a copy of your first QuarkXPress document. Select File ➤ Print. Again, a dialog box pops up with options. Ignore them for now; just click on **OK** to print.

Congratulations! You've printed your first QuarkXPress document. Welcome to the club! If you choose to quit QuarkXPress at this time, you can close the QuarkXPress window. Documents changed since the last save will be noted and a dialog box will ask you if you would like to save changes. After you are satisfied, the

FIGURE 1.22

In the Printer Setup dialog box, set the Printer Type to match your equipment.

Printer Setup

Printer
- ● Default Printer
  (currently HP LaserJet IIID on LPT1:)
- ○ Specific Printer:
  HP LaserJet IIID on LPT1:

OK
Cancel
Options...

Orientation
- ● Portrait
- ○ Landscape

Paper
Size: Letter 8 1/2 x 11 in
Source: Upper Tray

Image
- ☐ Flip Horizontal
- ☐ Flip Vertical
- ☐ Invert

Halftone Frequency: 60 (lpi)
Printer Resolution: (dpi)
Material: ○ Paper ○ Film

Paper Width:
Paper Offset:
Page Gap:

☐ Use PDF Screen Values

dialog box closes, open documents close, and the window (and application) of QuarkXPress closes.

SUMMARY

To create your first QuarkXPress document (The EMSALES flyer) you followed these steps:

1. Launch QuarkXPress.

2. Create a new document.

3. Click in the text box.

4. Change the font.

5. Change the size.

6. Change the leading.

7. Adjust the line spacing.

8. Center the text.

9. Save the document.

10. Print the document.

In general, to create, store, and print any new QuarkXPress document, you follow these procedures:

1. Launch QuarkXPress.

2. Select File ➤ New, adjusting the settings as needed.

3. Save under a new document name.

4. Input text (and graphics).

5. Save.

6. Edit text and graphics.

7. Save.

8. Print.

9. Quit.

ANATOMY OF QUARKXPRESS

To work in QuarkXPress   32

you must know the Work Area's properties and capabilities. This is where your document activities occur. It includes the document window with scroll bars, rulers, grid lines, page number indicator, page size indicator, pasteboard, and any text, line, or graphic elements you may create.

To work with up to seven documents simultaneously   32

you simply open or create as many as you need, up to the seven maximum. Resize and relocate the documents as necessary on your screen, using Windows 3.1 protocol.

To view different sized representations of the document   35

resize it in one of two ways. You can select the View menu and an appropriate resize option, or highlight the size percentage number at the bottom left corner of the window, then overstrike with your new view.

To add more guide lines to your document layout   36

first make sure the Guides option in the General Preferences (Edit ➤ Preferences ➤ General) are set to In Front. Then, click on a horizontal or vertical ruler (your choice), and drag to the document area where you want the new guide. Repeat as necessary.

TRACKS

To hide rulers or guides 37

in the document, select the appropriate menu selection. Choose View ➤ Hide Guides to temporarily hide (not display) the guide lines, including margin guides. To show again, use View ➤ Show Guides. To hide or show rulers, select View ➤ Hide Rulers or View ➤ Show Rulers, respectively.

To show or hide any of the seven floating palettes 40

select the Show/Hide options from the View menu. Floating palettes include the Tool, Measurements, Document Layout, Colors, Style Sheets, Trap Information, and the Library palettes. Palettes are always displayed in front of document windows.

To find on-line help and useful information from the menu area 56

select the Window Menu and Help Menu options. These follow Windows 3.1 format and are extremely useful. To select one of these menu options, use the mouse, keyboard equivalents, or Windows Alt+keys.

Q uarkXPress, as it appears on the screen, consists of three main components, the work area, the floating palettes, and the menu bar. This chapter dissects the three main areas of QuarkXPress.

THE WORK AREA

The work area includes the document window with its scroll bars, rulers, grid lines, page number indicator, page size indicator, pasteboard, and any text or graphic elements of the document page, as you saw in *Chapter 1*.

The work area shows only if a document is open, so when you launch Quark-XPress, no work area will show. If you launch QuarkXPress by opening an associated QuarkXPress document, though, you will immediately start with the document's work area. Check your Windows manual on instructions for setting the Associate function.

BASIC COMPONENTS OF THE DOCUMENT WINDOW

Once you start a new document, or open an existing document, a full size (100%) work area window shows. It has scroll bars, a title bar, and every other component of a typical Windows working window (see Figure 2.1). You can manipulate the size and location of this window like any other Windows window.

You can open up to seven document windows at a time. The active window will have a highlighted (active) title bar. This is the way Windows works with most other multiple window situations to indicate which is the active window (see Figure 2.2). You can make changes only in the active window. Multiple document windows can be displayed in typical Windows fashion, i.e., tile, cascade, or icon views.

The QuarkXPress document window has two additional items that enhance its functionality. They are the page size indicator (the percentage of full size) and the page identification indicator (see Figure 2.1). You can change the page size on the

FIGURE 2.1

The QuarkXPress document window

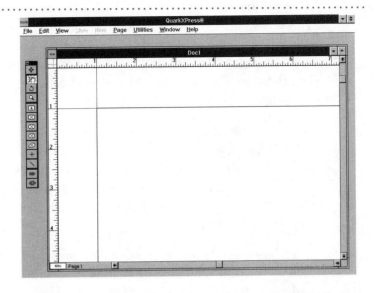

FIGURE 2.2

Seven documents can be open simultaneously with only one active at a time. These documents are displayed in a "cascade" Windows format.

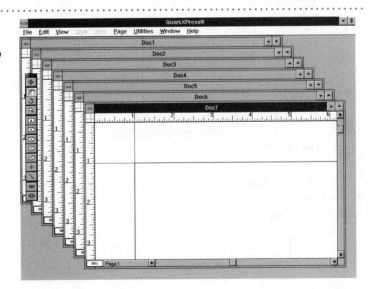

screen by changing this percentage. Highlight the existing percentage and over-strike with the new display size desired. Press Enter to activate the change. Later in the book, we will discuss using the Zoom (magnifying) tool and the View menu options to change the size of the page. Page sizes may range from 10 percent to 400 percent. A size called "Thumbnail" is also available through the View menu. Thumbnails do not show a percentage.

The page identification represents the page number, as displayed at the top of your screen. In the event that part of two or more pages are shown, the top page is indicated. If parts of two or more pages show, the page number identifies the first page in that sequence. If pages are facing (side-by-side), the page number lists the left or first in the sequence. The Master Page option is an exception. When chosen, the page identifier reads *Master.*

You can move the displayed page within the window by a variety of methods. The scroll bars move or jump the document from page to page. Most enhanced keyboards have Page Up, Page Down, Home, and End keys that are very helpful for moving around the document. The Page ➤ Go To option allows you to jump directly to the page of your choice.

Another quick method of jumping from page to page is through the Document Layout palette. Show this palette by selecting it from the View menu. To change from page to page, double-click on the page icon of your choice (see Figure 2.3).

FIGURE 2.3

The Document Layout palette allows you to move from page to page by double-clicking on the page icon you want.

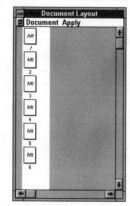

NOTE

The Library palette is available from the Utilities menu. It is considered a "floating palette" because you can move it around the work area.

There are other parts of the QuarkXPress document window that may not appear immediately because they are options you can choose to display or hide by choosing Show or Hide from the View menu (see Figure 2.4). They are guides, the baseline grid, the rulers and invisibles. Also included under the View menu are the floating palettes.

FIGURE 2.4

The View menu with its numerous Show and Hide options

View	
Fit in Window	Ctrl+0
50%	
75%	
√ Actual Size	Ctrl+1
200%	
Thumbnails	
Hide Guides	
Show Baseline Grid	
Snap to Guides	
Hide Rulers	Ctrl+R
Show Invisibles	Ctrl+I
Hide Tools	
Show Measurements	
Show Document Layout	
Show Style Sheets	
Show Colors	
Show Trap Information	

RULERS AND GUIDES

TIP

To create and see the guides properly, first make sure the Edit ➤ Preferences ➤ General menu setting is set to Guides: In Front; also, choose View ➤ Show Guides if the guides are not showing.

Most QuarkXPress users leave the rulers showing. It's convenient, first, because it tells where you are in the page layout, and second, because you can use the rulers to create additional guides. Guides may also be called *page guides*. They are the nonprinting lines added to help position items on the page. Guides function as an artist's non-photo blue guide lines on a mechanical layout. In QuarkXPress, guides appear colored (dotted on monochrome monitors). Margin guides and ruler guides are examples of page guides. To make a vertical guide, click in the vertical ruler and drag to the right. Once the guide is in place, release the mouse button. You bring horizontal guides down analogously from the horizontal ruler.

TIP

To eliminate all vertical guides in the document, press the Alt key and then click on the vertical ruler. To eliminate all horizontal guides, press Alt and click on the horizontal ruler. You cannot eliminate both the horizontal and vertical guides at the same time.

To relocate a guide, click and drag it (you must grab it outside a text or picture box area) to a new location (see Figure 2.5). To remove a single guideline, simply drag it back to the ruler. To eliminate all vertical or all horizontal guides, move the cursor to the appropriate ruler, hold down the Alt key, and click the mouse button.

FIGURE 2.5

To relocate a guide, just click and drag. To eliminate a single guide, click and drag it back to the ruler. To eliminate all guides, hold down the Alt key while clicking on the ruler.

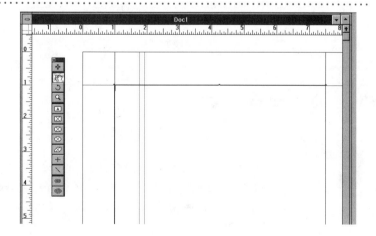

Horizontal and vertical guides cannot be removed at the same time by this method. To hide all guides, choose View ➤ Hide Guides. This does not actually delete the guides, it just hides them from view.

The Show/Hide Guides menu option also affects the original guides of your document page, the margin guides (see Figure 2.6).

THE BASELINE GRID

Another group of lines that may show on the work area is the baseline grid. Select View ➤ Show Baseline Grid to see it. It consists of a gridwork of horizontal lines, their positions based on the settings in the Typographic Preferences area—choose Edit ➤ Preferences (see Figure 2.7). This is helpful in graphic design for aligning text or graphic elements. The problem with the baseline grid option is that you might expect the linework to follow the text baselines, as the name implies, but it doesn't. Instead, it

FIGURE 2.6

This is a reduced page layout, showing the margin guides. These can be shown or hidden from the View menu along with all the other guides.

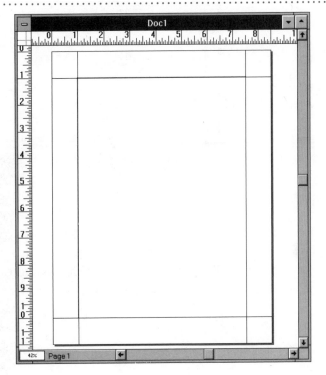

is a predetermined numerical value. If the text changes in size or leading, it may not conform to the baseline grid any longer. The baseline grid value is changed only when you change the Typographic Preferences option yourself.

FIGURE 2.7
The baseline grid lines as they appear when you choose Show Baseline Grid. These are only guides; they will not print.

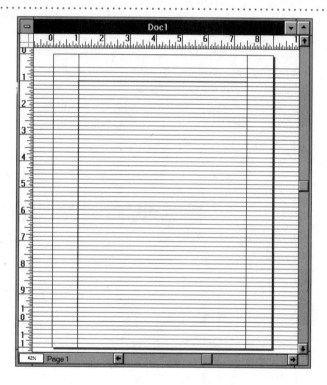

You can have the rulers show a variety of measurement systems. Choose Edit ➤ Preferences ➤ General. The horizontal and vertical rulers can even act independently. The available units of measure are inches, inches decimal, picas, points, millimeters, centimeters, and ciceros (see Figure 2.8).

Regardless of the measurement system chosen, the top left corner of the document page always defaults to the 0,0 position on the ruler. This 0,0 position can be repositioned by clicking and dragging the ruler corner box (see Figure 2.9).

Select the unit of measurement to use from a variety of options. You may choose a horizontal measurement independent of the vertical.

General Preferences for Doc1

Horizontal Measure:	Inches	Points/Inch:	72	
Vertical Measure:	Inches	Ciceros/cm:	2.1967	
Auto Page Insertion:	End of Section	Snap Distance:	6	
		☐ Vector Above:	72 pt	
Framing:	Inside	☒ Greek Below:	7 pt	
Guides:	In Front	☐ Greek Pictures		
Item Coordinates:	Page	☐ Accurate Blends		
Auto Picture Import:	Off	☐ Auto Constrain		
Master Page Items:	Keep Changes	OK	Cancel	

FIGURE 2.9

Click and drag the top left corner from its original 0,0 position to relocate the 0,0 indicator. To revert to the default, double-click on the original 0,0 box.

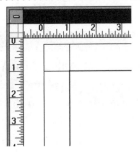

Another useful option under the View menu is Show Invisibles. Invisibles are those characters or keystrokes that are not normally seen, such as spaces, returns, and tabs. Showing invisibles can be handy for complex projects to keep track of your progress within the document. It doesn't take a very complex layout before you wonder where these keystrokes are (see Figure 2.10).

FIGURE 2.10

You can show or hide invisibles from the View menu. Invisibles show keystrokes such as spaces, tabs, and returns.

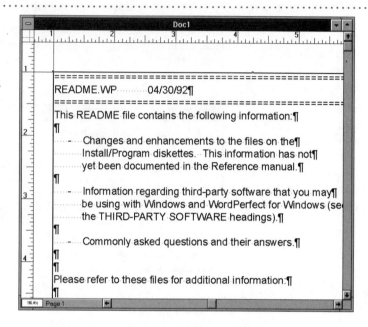

THE FLOATING PALETTES

There are separate windows of information within QuarkXPress called floating palettes (see Figure 2.11). You can show, move, and often resize these to fit your needs. Rarely would you want to have all palettes showing at once; but if you had multiple monitors, you could use one just for floating palettes and the other for documents. With just one standard monitor, though, they needlessly waste screen space. For instance, you don't need Trap Information when working on a document that you intend to print in black-and-white. Trap Information is useful when you are working on a full-color job you intend to separate on an imagesetter. You will soon learn to be selective of the vast array of options within QuarkXPress!

FIGURE 2.11

You can show as many of the floating palettes as you like, but it is best to use them judiciously to save screen space.

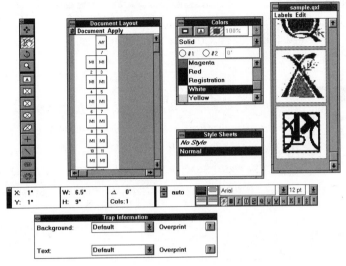

NOTE

At QUI 92 (Quark User International conference 1992) the attendees were informally polled as to their use of large monitors when working on QuarkXPress. Nearly 90 percent of the attendees indicated that they use large monitors. This is ideal for placing floating palettes on the screen while working on the document. Naturally, the larger the monitor the better, but cost is a major factor here.

We will discuss the floating palettes—which are called Tools, Measurements, Document Layout, Style Sheets, Colors, and Trap Information—later in the book as applicable.

THE MENUS

A third major area in the anatomy of QuarkXPress is the menu bar. In Windows 3.1 it consists of the File, Edit, View, Style, Item, Page, Utilities, Window, and Help menus.

NOTE

If QuarkXPress for Windows follows the path of QuarkXPress for the Macintosh, there will eventually be dozens of third-party add-on programs called XTensions. Several of these XTensions may actually create new or augment existing menu items. These programs add functionality to the main program.

THE FILE MENU

The File pull-down menu has five separate areas of operation (see Figure 2.12). The first section, which you used in *Chapter 1*, deals with opening or creating a new document.

Next, there are commands for saving and closing documents. Also, if there is a mistake, the Revert to Saved option retrieves the last saved copy of the document. The Revert to Saved option is your friend! Anytime you make a mistake, consider using this option.

FIGURE 2.12

The File menu options in QuarkXPress

File	
New...	Ctrl+N
Open...	Ctrl+O
Close	
Save	Ctrl+S
Save as...	
Revert to Saved	
Get Text/Picture...	Ctrl+E
Save Text...	
Save Page as EPS...	
Document Setup...	
Printer Setup...	
Print...	Ctrl+P
Exit	Ctrl+Q

NOTE

EPS stands for Encapsulated PostScript. This is one of the highest quality images you can work with, because a PostScript file can be resized without loss of quality when imported or exported to other PostScript-compatible programs. In addition, EPS files will print equally well at almost any size.

The Get Text (or Picture), Save Text, and Save Page as EPS options allow you to import or save document elements. Get Text (in a text box) allows you to import text from a word processed file directly into a text box. In a graphic box, the option reads Get Picture, allowing you to import a photograph or graphic element. The Save Text option exports text to a separate ASCII file format. The Save Page as EPS option takes a "snapshot" of the page and saves it as a separate Encapsulated PostScript (EPS) file for future use in QuarkXPress or other applications.

The next section under the File menu consists of Document Setup, Printer Setup, and Print. Each option brings up its own dialog box, allowing you to fine-tune certain options. Document Setup lets you change the page size or specify facing pages (see Figure 2.13). The Printer Setup option determines various configurations for the output printer (see Figure 2.14). The Print option brings a dialog box that determines number of copies, specific pages, and other printing variables (see Figure 2.15).

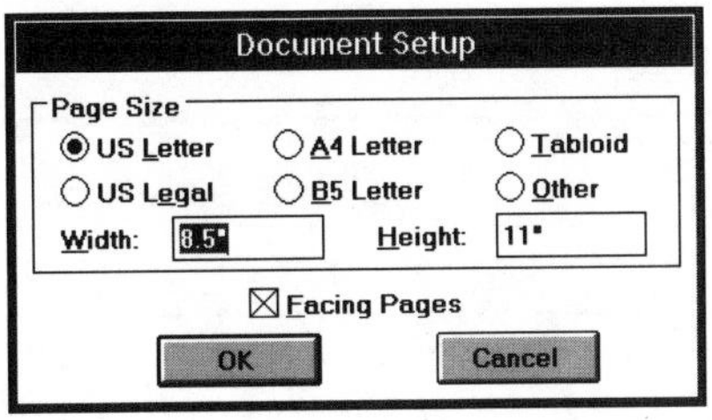

FIGURE 2.13

The Document Setup dialog box allows modification after the document has been created.

Document Setup

Page Size
- ● US Letter
- ○ US Legal
- ○ A4 Letter
- ○ B5 Letter
- ○ Tabloid
- ○ Other

Width: 8.5"   Height: 11"

☒ Facing Pages

[OK]   [Cancel]

FIGURE 2.14

The Printer Setup option allows you to preset output specifications for your printer.

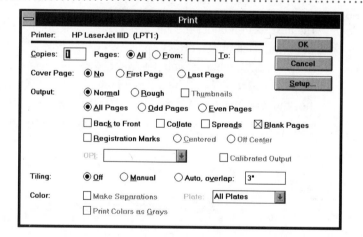

FIGURE 2.15

The Print dialog box contains options for QuarkXPress specific to imagesetter and color output.

TIP

The Exit option is only for applications. If you want to close an active document, use the Close command dictated by Windows 3.1 or the keyboard equivalent Ctrl+F4.

As customary in most Windows 3.1 applications, the File menu option also contains the Exit command. It allows you to end and close the application. Any open documents not recently saved with changes will yield a dialog box, asking if you want to save before closing. This and other commands can be selected by keyboard equivalents, in this case, Alt+F4. These shortcuts are listed on the menu.

THE EDIT MENU

The Edit Menu in QuarkXPress 3.1 includes commands for editing text, pictures, and other items, for changing QuarkXPress default specifications and for controlling text formatting features. Under the Edit pull-down menu are five separate categories for changing the document. The first area is your "safety net." It is the Undo option. Every QuarkXPress user relies heavily on the undo command! It will undo the last edit or command; this can be a change of type style, deletion of text, or any other single action. As long as the error is noticed before another action, it can be reversed with the Undo command.

The next group, under Edit, enables you to edit text, pictures, or other items depending on the tool used (i.e., Content tool or Item tool). These include the Cut, Copy, Paste, Paste Special, Paste Link, Delete, and Select All options. These work the same in QuarkXPress as they do in most other Windows applications. However, use caution when cutting and pasting across software applications. Sometimes, QuarkXPress items like text and graphic boxes may not cross over to other applications. This is because of the wide variety of file formats available in the DOS/Windows environment. You can, of course, cut, copy, paste, and drag various elements from one QuarkXPress document to another (see Figure 2.16).

NOTE

For those QuarkXPress users who are multiplatformed, that is, using QuarkXPress on both the Mac and Windows environments, the Link and Paste Link commands of Edit are unique to QuarkXPress for Windows. Link refers to Object Linking and Embedding (OLE), similar to Mac's Subscribe To capability. The difference here is that this is worth using in QuarkXPress for Windows!

FIGURE 2.16

*The Edit menu in
QuarkXPress*

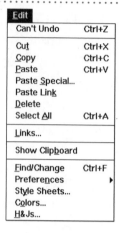

Two commands that may be new to some QuarkXPress users, especially if they
were trained on the Macintosh version of QuarkXPress, are the Paste Special and
Paste Link capabilities. The Paste Special function lets you make a decision about
the format of an object that you simply paste, paste and embed, or paste and link
into your QuarkXPress document. The Paste Special function works if three conditions are met. These include selection of the Content Tool, an active picture box,
and the Clipboard must contain a picture copied from an OLE (Object Linking and
Embedding) server application. OLE is a function of Windows 3.1. Choose Paste
Special to display the Paste Special dialog box (see Figure 2.17).

FIGURE 2.17

*The Paste Special
dialog box*

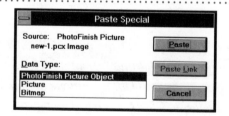

This dialog box consists of the following:

▶ Data Type: To choose a format for the object you want to paste in the active picture box, select a format from the Data Type scroll list. The Data Type scroll list displays all the formats that QuarkXPress can use to paste the object copied to the Clipboard. Many server applications provide a variety of formats for an object copied to the Clipboard. For example, a picture on the Clipboard might be displayed in the Data Type scroll list as a bitmap, a metafile, or an OLE object. Choose a bitmap or metafile format if you want to simply paste the object. Choose a format with a name that contains the word *object* if you want to paste and embed or paste and link it.

▶ Paste: To simply paste an object copied to the Clipboard (without linking or embedding it), click Paste when a bitmap or metafile format is selected in the Data Type scroll list. (An object copied to the Clipboard as a metafile will be listed as *Picture*.) To paste and embed an object copied to the Clipboard, click Paste when a format with a name that contains the word *object* (for example, *Excel Worksheet Object*) is selected in the Data Type scroll list.

▶ Paste Link: To paste a representation of an object copied to the Clipboard and link that representation to the object in the server application, click Paste Link. (Note: Paste Link does not paste the object itself. QuarkXPress will display a representation of the object for placement.) Paste Link is available when a format with a name that contains the word *object* is selected in the Data Type scroll list.

Paste Link enables you to paste a representation of an object copied to the Clipboard and link that representation to the object in the server application. Paste Link does not paste the object itself, rather it displays a representation of the object for placement. To work properly, there are three conditions that must be met. The Content tool must be selected, a picture box must be active, and the object copied to the Clipboard must be in a format that QuarkXPress can link. Choosing Paste Link from the Edit menu has the same effect as clicking the Paste Link button in the Paste Special dialog box.

NOTE

*Some of the new linking functions are capabilities of Windows 3.1.
Please check your Windows manuals for more details in DDL and
OLE capabilities.*

The Links command is a uniquely Windows capability. It allows you to link data
from any application that supports DDE (Dynamic Data Exchange) into the active
QuarkXPress document. You can automatically update the copied data in the document when the original data changes in the source file. Links enables you to control the way in which objects in a QuarkXPress document are linked to their server
applications. The Links command is available when the active QuarkXPress document contains linked objects. Choosing Links displays the Links dialog box. Options in the Links dialog box enable you to update, cancel, or change a link.

You might wonder why would anyone use this option if you can already import text
and picture material. There are probably several reasons, but unless you are in a
business that really needs this function it seems like a wasted feature. Consider the
situation where a linked spreadsheet is somewhere in the network. If you are
working on the company's annual report in a QuarkXPress document and part of
the information you are using comes from the linked spreadsheet, you could have
up-to-the-minute data as your document hits publication. Simultaneous production can take place and give "current" information in linked DDE documents.

The Show/Hide Clipboard option gives a window that has the last item saved there
with the Cut or Copy commands. It can hold only one "item" at a time. For a library of stored items or images, use the QuarkXPress Library feature or some
third party software, such as Mosaic in CorelDRAW.

The last area under Edit combines several seemingly unrelated features. First, the
Find/Change option allows the user to search and replace a particular word or
phrase. One beautiful feature of Find/Change is the ability to Find/Change type attributes. You can use Find/Change for type attributes for a specific *range* of text if
it is highlighted (see Figure 2.18). In this event, the Find/Change dialog box resembles much of the Font Usage dialog box (Utilities ➤ Font Usage). The two options
differ in that Find/Change must find a character or range of characters to alter type

FIGURE 2.18

The Find/Change dialog box with options

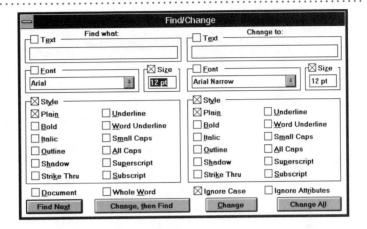

attributes. The Font Usage dialog box does not require searching for any text; you can search for attributes only and change according to your needs.

An extremely important command on the Edit menu that may alter all your documents created in QuarkXPress is Preferences. It has four subcategories: Application, General, Typographic, and Tools. The Preferences dialog boxes enable the user to establish certain criteria for the application or document, such as the color of guides, automatic leading, etc. In most of the preferences areas, changes to a dialog box affect the entire application, not just the document open at the time.

Style Sheets is an option that allows a predetermined type, look, and arrangement for a text area (see Figure 2.19). For example, create one style sheet for the paragraph text of a document. It contains information on the font, style, size, indentation, and any other pertinent material for that text block. Use that stored information in the style sheet again for other blocks of type that require those specifications. You can also assign a "hot key" to the style sheet. This means you can just highlight paragraph text and press a predefined style sheet key, like F5; perhaps F6 is the style sheet key for subheads and F7 is the key for headings. This feature is a real time-saver in document processing!

FIGURE 2.19

The Style Sheets dialog box

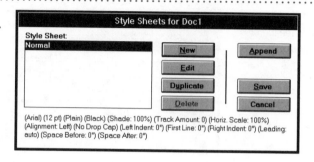

NOTE

Several options lead to other sub options or submenus in dialog boxes.

The Colors option allows you to determine which colors will be available from the color palette at any one time. QuarkXPress has a wide range of color options, including six color models: Pantone, Focoltone, Trumatch, HSB (Hue, Saturation, Brightness), RGB (Red, Green, Blue), and CMYK (Cyan, Magenta, Yellow, Black). It would be impossible to position all colors on one color palette, so QuarkXPress shows a limited number of colors at one time.

H&Js is the last option on the Edit menu. It enables you to determine the scope of hyphenation and justification use in the document. Selection of this option brings up a new dialog box for the H&J area.

NOTE

If you are a multiplatform QuarkXPress user, you must be careful not to confuse the menu selections. Although all menu options are available in the Menu bar in both Mac and Windows versions, the Microsoft Windows protocol dictates a certain arrangement of menu items. Quark has indicated that a software patch will be available if you find this annoying. The patch will mimic the menu items placement as given by the original QuarkXPress program, the Macintosh version. Contact Quark for further information on availability if this is of interest.

THE VIEW MENU

This option has three main components, starting with a resize option for the display of the page (see Figure 2.20). Specifically the options for resizing include Fit in Window, 50%, 75%, Actual Size, 200%, and Thumbnails size layouts. Fit in Window and Actual Size have the keyboard shortcuts Ctrl+0 and Ctrl+1.

FIGURE 2.20

The View menu with its many Show/Hide options

View	
Fit in Window	Ctrl+0
50%	
75%	
√ Actual Size	Ctrl+1
200%	
Thumbnails	
Hide Guides	
Show Baseline Grid	
Snap to Guides	
Hide Rulers	Ctrl+R
Show Invisibles	Ctrl+I
Hide Tools	
Show Measurements	
Show Document Layout	
Show Style Sheets	
Show Colors	
Show Trap Information	

As described earlier, this is one method of resizing the page as it appears on the monitor. Other methods include editing the Size Percentage box in the document window and using the Zoom tool from the Tools palette.

The remaining two sections under the View menu include the Show/Hide options. The first area includes functions to hide or display various document parts, including guides, invisible keystrokes, grid lines, and rulers. These are all available to help you in the layout of the page elements. They are not mandatory for function of QuarkXPress and certain options are often hidden.

The Show/Hide options for the floating palettes are in the next group. They allow you to display any of the floating palettes, including Tools, Measurements, Document Layout, Style Sheets, Colors, and Trap Information.

THE STYLE MENU

The Style Menu has two areas that control the typographical look of the document (see Figure 2.21). First, options are available for selecting the proper font, size, style, etc., plus color and kerning. These change the individual type character's look. Then the bottom section of this pull-down menu contains selections for how the entire line or group of lines will look. It includes selections for leading, alignment, tabulations, etc.

FIGURE 2.21

The Style menu in QuarkXPress

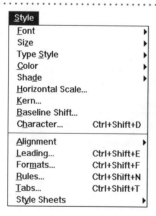

THE ITEM MENU

This menu controls "items" defined as text boxes or picture boxes (and their enclosed elements) or lines. There are five areas of interest on the Item menu (see Figure 2.22). The first area includes Modify, Frame, and Runaround. These areas bring up dialog boxes that control certain capabilities of the text and graphic boxes. They control such capabilities as placement, size, layers, and frames of the box areas. Once an item is selected as a text box, picture box, or line element, you can manipulate it using one or more of these dialog boxes.

The second group of options also works with selected items. The Duplicate, Step and Repeat, and Delete options reproduce or delete items.

The options of Group, Ungroup, Constrain, and Lock control several groups of elements for movement control. Group combines several elements into one for movement or duplication; Ungroup reverses the Group command; Constrain combines one or more elements to be constrained in the box; and Lock makes sure that you can pin down an item so it will not be repositioned (moved) on the page accidentally. You can Unlock locked items for future repositioning.

FIGURE 2.22

The Item menu in QuarkXPress

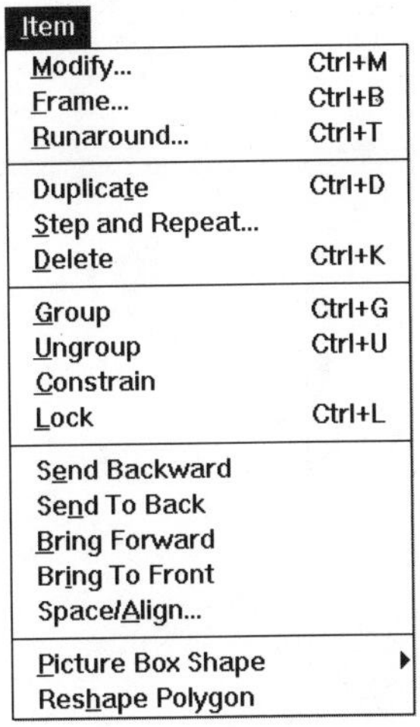

Item	
Modify...	Ctrl+M
Frame...	Ctrl+B
Runaround...	Ctrl+T
Duplicate	Ctrl+D
Step and Repeat...	
Delete	Ctrl+K
Group	Ctrl+G
Ungroup	Ctrl+U
Constrain	
Lock	Ctrl+L
Send Backward	
Send To Back	
Bring Forward	
Bring To Front	
Space/Align...	
Picture Box Shape	▶
Reshape Polygon	

The Send to Back and Bring to Front options give control to layering of elements. Each item sits on a separate layer controlled by these options. The Space/Align option aligns objects on the same plane (vertical and horizontal positioning, as opposed to layering).

Picture or graphic boxes can take on shapes other than simple rectangular dimensions. The last group of options— Picture Box Shape and Reshape Polygon—on the Item menu allow the user to control the graphic box shape.

THE PAGE MENU

TIP

Many features and options are available in QuarkXPress through different methods. Page options listed here are also available in the Document palette through manipulating page icons.

The Page menu encompasses all options for page manipulation (see Figure 2.23). It includes functions to add, delete, and move pages, as well as to group and display pages. It also has menu options for maneuvering through the document from page to page. This menu group gives the user the ability to jump from document pages to master pages.

FIGURE 2.23

Page menu options in QuarkXPress

THE UTILITIES MENU

The last QuarkXPress menu is Utilities (see Figure 2.24). As the name suggests, this menu contains additional tools intended to make your job a little easier and to give you a great deal of quality control. There are five areas under the Utilities menu.

The first section comprises the dictionary and spell-checker. It allows spell checking from a listed dictionary or from supplemental dictionaries you create.

Next, a dialog box involving hyphenation control is available through Suggested Hyphenation and Hyphenation Exceptions options. The Library option follows, giving you control over archive directories of graphic materials.

The Font Usage and Picture Usage options are in the next group. Font Usage is similar to the earlier Find/Change option under the Edit menu. It does everything the Find/Change option does, but in font information only; this option does not search for character or word information. It is invaluable for changing font options throughout a document. For example, you can key in copy using a font that is easy to read on the screen, then change it later for high print quality. The Picture Usage option allows you to scroll through a visual representation of all pictures within the document.

FIGURE 2.24

The Utilities menu has, among other things, the Library floating palette.

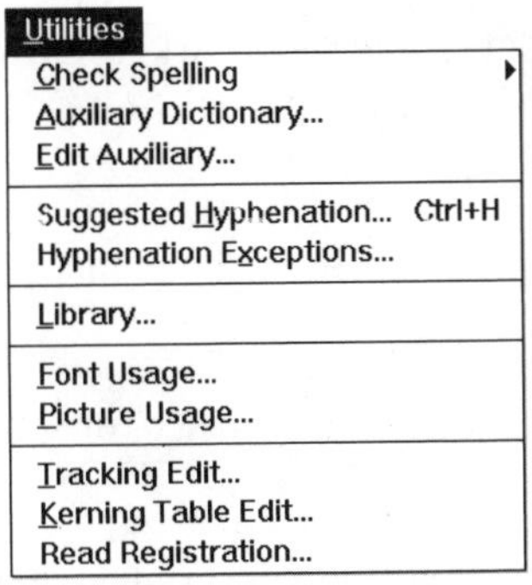

Utilities
Check Spelling ▶
Auxiliary Dictionary...
Edit Auxiliary...
Suggested Hyphenation...   Ctrl+H
Hyphenation Exceptions...
Library...
Font Usage...
Picture Usage...
Tracking Edit...
Kerning Table Edit...
Read Registration...

WARNING
If you get involved with QuarkXPress XTensions, they may alter the appearance or contents of the menu bar. Be aware that the menu items may vary from one machine to another depending on the XTensions loaded in that version of QuarkXPress.

The last options under the Utilities menu include controls for editing tracking and kerning tables by typeface. Selective editing of the kerning and tracking tables for a font will allow those changes to take place for that font in each combination of letters changed.

THE WINDOW MENU AND HELP MENU

The last two items on the Menu bar are generic to Windows 3.1. They include the Windows group and the Help group. These include commands standard to all Windows applications and can be very useful, especially in a multi-application, multi-document environment such as electronic publishing. One unique feature to note under the Help menu is that of the "About QuarkXPress" option. If you simply click on this option to open, you get the standard QuarkXPress logo screen. If, however, you hold the Ctrl key down while clicking on the "About QuarkXPress" option, you get a great information window called the "QuarkXPress for Windows Environment" (see Figure 2.25).

This gives some interesting data about your working environment that may be helpful in fine tuning your system. The QuarkXPress for Windows Environment includes the following:

▸ QuarkXPress Version: represents the version number of the QuarkXPress application.

▸ Patch Level: represents the revision level patch, or software correction given to the main application.

▸ Serial Number: the software application's serial number is different with each copy you purchase, networks prevent multiple copies of the same serial number from being open at the same time.

FIGURE 2.25

The Environment information box under the Help menu

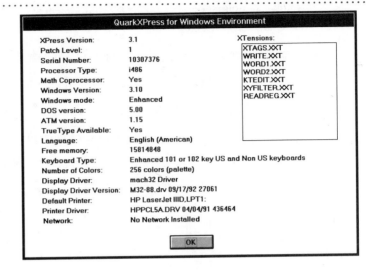

- Processor Type: your PC microchip designation.

- Math Coprocessor: installation information; note that some microchips have the math coprocessor built into their design.

- Windows Version: version number of the Microsoft Windows application.

- Windows mode: indication of the mode you are currently running the Windows application.

- DOS version: your currently installed version number of DOS.

- ATM version: your currently installed version of Adobe Type Manager.

- TrueType Available: an indication that you have and are using TrueType fonts.

- Language: what language you have set in your applications.

- Free Memory: free RAM in your system.

- Keyboard Type: keyboard arrangement.

- Number of Colors: colors capable on your system according to your hardware and software setup.

- Display Driver: what display driver software you have currently installed.

- Display Driver Version: the version number of the Display Driver software.

- Default Printer: indication of what printer you have set as the default printer.

- Printer Driver: the name of the printer driver currently active.

- Network: indication of the network type, if connected to a network.

- XTensions: the names of all installed XTension programs.

3

Document Construction

FAST

TRACKS FAST TRACKS FAST TRACKS FAST TRACKS FAST

To specify page size alternatives   62

you can select one of the predetermined page sizes when creating a new document. This gives you the choice of several sizes, including US Letter, US Legal, A4 Letter, B5 Letter, Tabloid, and Other. The Other option allows you to specify custom width and height measurements. QuarkXPress allows documents from 1 inch square to as large as 48 inches square.

To create multiple page spreads   66

check the Facing Pages option box in the New dialog box when creating a new document. This allows you to work with spreads allowing for such layout considerations as trim, fold, and binding. Margin guides can be adjusted to compensate for these production situations.

To see a document's baseline grid   68

(hidden by default) select View ➤ Show Baseline Grid. The grid is specified in the preferences dialog box and can be changed to any alternative that suits your needs. To access the dialog box and make changes select Edit ➤ Preferences ➤ Typographic.

To see and alter elements on the Master Page   68

you can select Page ➤ Display ➤ Master. This enables you to display the master page in the work area. Don't forget to change back to document!

60

To drag or copy items from one document to another 69

open both documents, the one containing the element to copy, and the one to target. Resize and relocate so they are both seen on the screen (you can use Windows Tile feature). Maneuver the windows so that both the item and its recipient area are shown. Click on the item and drag it from its present location, across the border to the recipient document, then drop (release the mouse button).

To insert page(s) at specific locations in the document 70

use Page ➤ Insert. This gives a dialog box enabling you to select the number of pages and their insert locations. Location choices include before current page, after current page, or at the end of the document.

To save a document page as an EPS (Encapsulated PostScript) file 72

you can select File ➤ Save Page as EPS. This saves the entire document page and its contents as an EPS file, which can be later imported into an appropriate manipulation application or output directly to a PostScript printer.

uarkXPress has several fantastic features that make it the leader in its software category, desktop publishing. In fact, desktop publishing, as the phrase was originally coined, is perhaps an inaccurate description of the function of Quark-XPress today. A better moniker today is *electronic publishing*.

Electronic publishing may be a more appropriate description for QuarkXPress as it is used in the printing industry. Software in this area is designed to be an appendage of the printing process. Unlike desktop publishing software, which was originally designed to print on the desktop laser printer, electronic publishing software is best utilized on a professional laser imagesetter. This product is then converted to film and used for the printing plate image.

To differentiate a desktop document maker from a true professional publishing package we must examine certain aspects of the software. Let's first consider document construction.

QUARKXPRESS PAGE SIZE CAPABILITIES

QuarkXPress has five predetermined page sizes available when you create a new document. This is a quick way to enter data on a default page size rather than specifying the dimensions of each page (see Figure 3.1). You can also specify custom dimensions for a page that may not be listed among the five standard page sizes.

FIGURE 3.1
Choosing File ➤ New brings up the New dialog box.

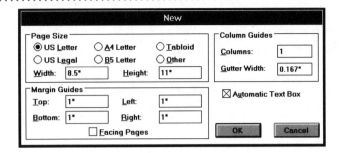

TIP

QuarkXPress has the capability of changing the measurement system and adapting to your needs. For example if the measurement system were placed in inches in Edit ➤ Preferences ➤ General, but you needed to make a new document in pica measurements, just place the pica measurement in the page size fields. Be sure to include the units (such as pt for points), though! QuarkXPress will convert it to inch measurements for you. This applies to all measurement systems in QuarkXPress.

The letter (8½″×11″), legal (8½″×14″), and tabloid (11″×17″) sizes are most commonly used in the United States, while the A4 and B5 letter sizes are predominant in European paper sizes. The A4 dimension works out to 8.268″ wide by 11.693″ high, which is equivalent to 210 mm × 297 mm (see Figure 3.2). The B5 size is 176 mm × 250 mm (6.929″×9.843″).

If you want to change the page size after a document is created, choose File ➤ Document Setup. Adjustments in this dialog box change the document size even in the middle of document construction (see Figure 3.3). As before, the option to

FIGURE 3.2

*Here are two examples of
Page Size options, the A4
Letter and the B5 Letter.
Both of these options are
most commonly used in
Europe.*

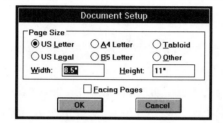

FIGURE 3.3

*The Document Setup
dialog box.*

create a custom page size in QuarkXPress allows document sizes from 1″×1″ to as
large as 48″×48″. If you change the page size after starting the document, you
may affect items on that page. Usually, a warning will appear in QuarkXPress indicating that you may have problems if you change the page size.

TIP

*To tile a large document means to print it in pieces, which you
must then assemble. You will probably have to do this any time
your document is larger than your printer is capable of producing.*

Larger documents often must be printed by tiling them—at least until a 48″ imagesetter is developed. Tiling is an operation in which a document larger than the size
of the printer paper is broken up into smaller pieces and printed. The smaller
pages resemble a puzzle of sorts, which you must piece together to form one large
mural. To enable tiling, check the Tiling option in the Print dialog box (see Figure 3.4).

FIGURE 3.4

The Tiling option in the Print dialog box enables you to print larger documents than the printer can accommodate. This is done by breaking them down into pieces in a puzzle-like manner.

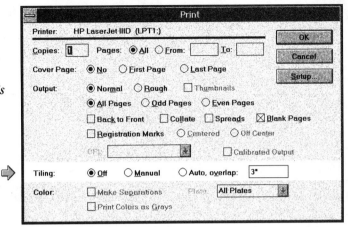

MAXIMUM DOCUMENT LENGTH

A feature which must be annoying to the "page-making" desktop publishing software companies is that QuarkXPress can create documents up to 2,000 pages long or 2 gigabytes in file size (whichever comes first). Document length was one of the first areas to differentiate page-making software from software that could be used in a publishing environment. Publishing implies the process of creating a document of some length, such as a newspaper, magazine, or book. Software that purports to be designed for publishing must therefore be able to create hundreds, if not thousands, of pages to compete in the publishing market today (see Figure 3.5). It seems that most traditional publishing houses of fine magazines and books are moving toward or have already converted to the desktop publishing environment. Many well-known publishing houses were represented at the 1992 Quark User International conference in New York City, including Gannett, Inc., Readers Digest, Time, Hearst, Prentice Hall, Standard Publishing, Life Magazine, and Simon & Schuster. These companies are all incorporating QuarkXPress in their publishing plans.

FIGURE 3.5

*You may insert from 1 to
100 pages at one time, before or after a specific
page number.*

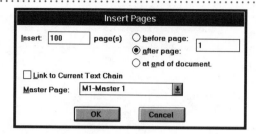

MULTIPLE PAGE SPREADS

QuarkXPress allows the creation of multiple page spreads so the user can see
from page to page how the document will appear in print (see Figure 3.6). By use
of the Document Layout palette, you can arrange up to five standard size pages
side by side. A large monitor is best when working on a double-page layout because it allows you to work on both pages simultaneously. Remember, QuarkX-
Press is a production tool; if production can be created faster with higher quality,
it is a more profitable environment. A large, high-resolution monitor is almost a
must for a high-volume, quality-conscious QuarkXPress environment. The Document Layout palette lets the QuarkXPress user arrange document pages regardless
of the predetermined single or facing page document (see Figure 3.7).

FIGURE 3.6

*QuarkXPress allows
you to work on multiple
page spreads.*

FIGURE 3.7

The Document Layout palette lets you arrange multiple page spreads for your convenience while working.

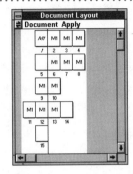

USING TEMPLATES

Templates are available in QuarkXPress so you can create and reuse a base form or layout. That base layout can be used to create other documents without altering the original template layout. When you first save a new document, you have the opportunity to choose whether the layout will be saved as a template or document. Documents can be called up and altered. Templates cannot be altered after they are saved, although you can alter a template and save it under a new file name. This takes more time, but prevents accidental changes to the file (see Figure 3.8).

FIGURE 3.8

You have the option of saving a new document as a document or a template.

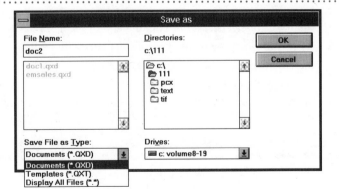

GRIDS, GUIDES, AND SNAPPING DISTANCES

When you create a new document, a default grid system will be in place. This can be shown or hidden with View ➤ Show/Hide Baseline Grid. It displays horizontal lines (baselines) as specified in the Typographic Preferences dialog box (Edit ➤ Preferences ➤ Typographic). The Baseline Grid system can be changed; the increments for baseline grid can be anywhere from 1 to 144 points. The baseline grid is hidden by default.

If the Snap to Guides option in the View menu is enabled, the edges of items you move or resize will snap to the grid, similar to the way they snap to other page guides. To specify the distance at which objects snap, enter a value in the Snap Distance field. This is located in the General Preferences dialog box. You may specify a Snap Distance value from 0 to 216 pixels. The default value is 6 pixels. Keep in mind that pixels on one machine may be closer or farther apart than pixels on other machines. This depends on the resolution quality of the monitor and graphic card of your computer.

WARNING

Use the Item tool to select and move a guide line; using the Content tool will select the text box, picture box, or line beneath the guide.

Guides can be generated by clicking and dragging in the ruler. As noted in *Chapter 2,* you can move them by selecting them with the Item tool (the topmost tool in the Tool palette; it resembles a compass). New for version 3.1 is the ability to drag a ruler guide even when the pointer is over an item. In previous versions of Quark-XPress, you had to click on the guide somewhere other than over the item.

MASTER PAGES

QuarkXPress allows the creation of master pages (maximum of 254) for a document. The master page contains items that are to be shown on all subsequent document pages. For example, a line running across the head of each document page should be created once on the master page. This displays the line on each page, even though it was drawn only once. Page numbers are also frequently placed on the master page.

NOTE

Only pages originating from a master will take on the changes of that master. Pages originated from some other master will take on changes only from the "parent" master page.

Even after the master page and subsequent document pages are created, you can still go back to the master and make changes as needed. Your changes will be reflected in all document pages that originated from that master. Individual items from the master page can be edited on the document page as well. Those changes will be reflected on the master page, as well as all subsequent document pages. For example, if you place a heading on the master page, it will appear on all subsequent document pages. If you then noticed the line needed a greater thickness, this could be edited on the existing document page. The changes would appear on the master and thus on all document pages. There is more information and examples on master pages in *Part II*.

DRAGGING PAGES BETWEEN DOCUMENTS

A unique feature in QuarkXPress is its facility for dragging a page layout and its contents from one document to another, providing multiple documents are open. To do this, follow these steps:

1. Change the view to Thumbnails.

2. Open a second document and change the view to Thumbnails here, too.

3. Click to highlight a page of the first document and drag it across to the second document (see Figure 3.9).

This might take a bit of practice to get the page where you want it. There are several advantages to this feature, such as the ability to drag and create multiple master pages. If you drag a page from one document to another and they have different master page specifications, the new document will have both styles, a Master "A" and a Master "B". The feature is also good for quickly duplicating a

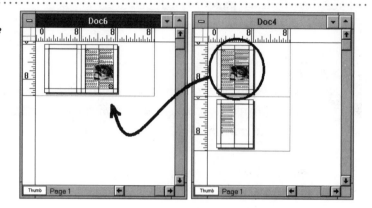

page layout or multiple elements of a page, such as the text and graphic boxes. In
a work-group publishing environment you can combine several documents into
one using this QuarkXPress feature.

MULTIPLE PAGE MANIPULATION

QuarkXPress has the ability to insert, delete, and move multiple pages (see Figure 3.10). You can choose from three automatic page insertion options or insert
pages manually. These are time-saving options. Trying to do these operations with
other desktop publishing packages can get frustrating, because you must constantly be aware of adding more pages as the document length increases. Quark-
XPress gives the option of adding pages automatically, linking sequential text, or
manually placing pages in anywhere in the document. These page manipulations
are part of the Page menu options, or you can use the Document Layout palette.

Frequently, you will have no idea how many pages a document will have prior to inputting its contents. The options in QuarkXPress that allow you complete control
over the addition or subtraction of pages at any time are extremely helpful.

FIGURE 3.10

You can manipulate pages using the options on the Page menu or by using the Document Layout palette (shown in Figure 3.6).

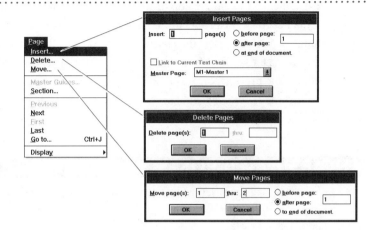

SECTIONS

Each document can be subdivided into sections. Sections can have their own page numbering sequence, even though they are still a part of the original, larger document. For example, in this book, the pages near the front are numbered with a i, ii, iii sequence (Roman numerals), while the text is numbered in a 1, 2, 3 fashion (Arabic). Thus, this book as a document would contain at least two sections. These settings are controlled by using the Page ➤ Section command (see Figure 3.11).

FIGURE 3.11

You have several choices for numbering style in the Section dialog box.

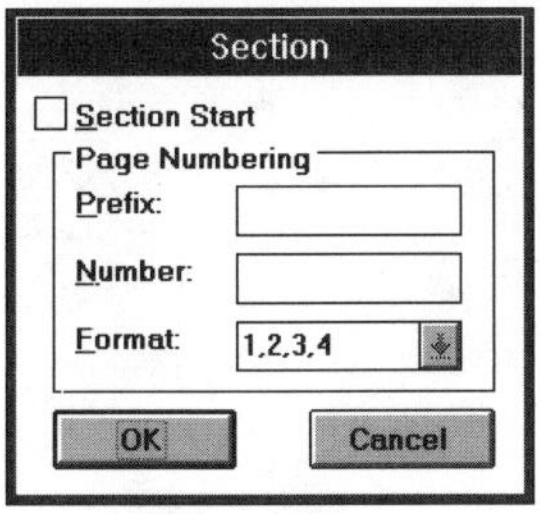

Page numbers in any section or in the entire document can be placed in automatic sequence, or you can specify an automatic Continued on and Continued from page number. You can insert the character for Previous Box Page Number (Ctrl+2) or the character for Next Box Page Number (Ctrl+4). These refer to the page numbers of the previous or next linked boxes. They can be used after phrases such as *continued from page* and *continued on page*. The correct page number will appear automatically.

ENCAPSULATED POSTSCRIPT PAGES

Each page can be saved as Encapsulated PostScript (EPS) file. This allows you to import it into other software applications, such as illustration programs for further enhancement (the command is File ➤ Save Page as EPS). It can also be imported back into a QuarkXPress document picture box. Saving anything as a PostScript file allows you to manipulate and resize it in other documents that take PostScript format. For example, you may want to save a page as the EPS format to later be retouched by a photo retouching program. This would allow you to import the EPS file directly into the retouching program and edit as needed.

PAGE LAYOUT

To create a text box item in the document page 76

you should first have the Tool palette showing. Then select the Text Box creation tool (the one with the letter in it). Start anywhere on the document page; click and drag to the opposite corner, creating a "rectangle" suitable for keying in text. Use the Content tool to input text in your new text box.

To create a picture box item on the document page 77

select one of the picture box tools from the Tool palette. These are represented by graphic shapes with an *X* in them. After the tool is selected, move the mouse cursor to the document area, click and drag to the opposite corner just as if you were creating a new text box item.

To create a line item 77

simply select one of the line drawing tools from the Tool palette. Line drawing tools include the Orthagonal Line tool (looks like a plus sign), and the standard Line tool (looks like a backslash). Once selected, you can draw lines anywhere, as no initial item box is necessary with line items.

To group two or more items together as one item 78

simply use the Item tool to select an item, then hold the shift key and select additional items to add to the group. Once all items are selected, choose Item ➤ Group. Once grouped, they can be manipulated as one product. To ungroup, select the grouped item and choose Item ➤ Ungroup.

To rotate an item   78

select the item by clicking on it with the Item tool, then rotate through
one of three techniques: specify the rotation angle on the Measurements
palette; use the Rotation Tool from the Tool palette; or manipulate the
Modify dialog box (Edit ➤ Modify). Items can be rotated in increments
as small as 0.001°.

To run text around or behind other items   85

you should select the appropriate runaround option. To do this, first click
on the text box or graphic box to change runaround features. Use the
Item tool to identify the item. Then select Item ➤ Runaround. Several options are available. Certain options are available only for text items, others only for picture items. These work together in harmony and should
be experienced in several arrangements to get the full impact of
runaround capabilities.

To frame a text or picture box item   91

select the item with the Item or Content tool, then choose Item ➤ Frame.
This dialog box gives several options, including frame shape, thickness,
color, and shade.

QuarkXPress has a great many options for manipulating items in your document. You may find many of these invaluable if you are doing a lot of prepress work. In this chapter, we'll explore those features, options, and tools that allow you to manipulate or edit items on the document layout page.

ITEMS IN QUARKXPRESS

QuarkXPress works through the manipulation of what it calls *items*. An item can be any of four different elements: text box, picture box, line, or grouped element. Throughout the book, emphasis is placed on the text box, picture box, and line as items. The grouped item is manipulated in much the same manner as the three other kinds.

THE TEXT BOX AS AN ITEM

The text box is considered an item on the page and may be created either automatically or manually. To create a text box automatically, you must check the Automatic Text Box option in the New dialog box (File ➤ New). This places a text box on your first page and sets up automatic linking of text boxes. For example, with Automatic Text Box checked, you can import a five-hundred page document into a text box on page 1. Once the box fills with text, other pages with text boxes will be added to accommodate all imported text.

NOTE

Both the Item and Content tools can be used to resize box items. To relocate an item, use the Item tool or the Modify dialog box (Item ➤ Modify). The Content tool is typically used to relocate an item.

The other way to create a text box item is to generate it manually using the Text Box tool (see Figure 1.6). You select the tool, then click and drag to form a new rectangle on the page. This rectangle will be your text box. You can place text in it using the Content tool. Once drawn, the text box can be resized by manipulating the grab boxes of the item. Click and drag them as you would resize other items in a standard Windows fashion. When resized, the text fills the box according to its new size.

THE PICTURE BOX AS AN ITEM

The Picture Box has many of the same attributes as the Text Box. That is, you can create it manually with a selected tool from the tool palette. Once created, you can manipulate the image in the picture box by importing files (File ➤ Get Picture) and through the Content tool. A picture box can be resized and relocated using the Item tool. You can also frame it and apply specific runaround features.

You can use any of the following tools to create a picture box:

- The Rectangular Picture Box tool

- The Rounded-corner Rectangle Picture Box tool

- The Oval Picture Box tool

- The Polygon Picture Box tool

NOTE

Any item style, text box, picture box, line, or grouped item can be rotated using the rotation tool. Text and Picture boxes can also be rotated with the rotation option in the Measurements palette.

The characteristics of each are the same, only the shape differs. You can resize or reshape a picture box with the Item tool or Content tool and the grab boxes (once the item is selected). The Item tool can also be used to reposition the picture box item.

THE LINE AS AN ITEM

The line element is an item in a QuarkXPress document because it has several of the same manipulation characteristics as the picture or text box items just described. That is, you can manipulate it (style, color, endcaps, width, and shade). The line item can have runaround features, like the box items. It can also be manipulated through the Item and Content tools.

GROUPED ITEMS

NOTE

You can also rotate grouped items. Use either the Rotation tool or the rotation field in the Measurement palette to manipulate the grouped item. After rotation, you still can ungroup as necessary.

Any combination of items can be *grouped* together as a single item. Grouping allows you to move entire element clusters together as one. Once moved they can be ungrouped.

You can perform many of the same functions on grouped items that you would to any single item. They may be cut and pasted, moved, rotated, and so on.

ROTATING LINES, TEXT BOXES, AND PICTURE BOXES

QuarkXPress is the leading desktop publishing program in the area of item rotation. As explained above, the main elements of any QuarkXPress page are the text box, picture box, group, and line. Any item can be rotated in increments of as little as 0.001°. Rotation is accomplished by one of two techniques.

The first technique is to do the rotation manually. Follow these steps:

1. Highlight the item by clicking on it. (The grab boxes indicate that an item has been properly highlighted.)

2. Click on the rotation tool (see Figure 4.1). The cursor changes to a register mark icon.

3. Use this new cursor to click and drag on a grab bar of the item to rotate. The movement of your drag will dictate the angle of rotation.

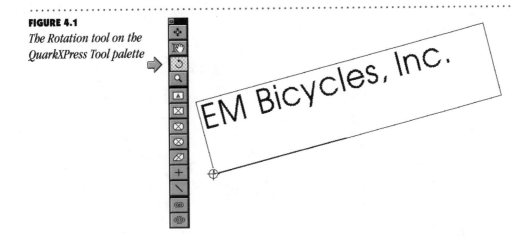

FIGURE 4.1
The Rotation tool on the QuarkXPress Tool palette

The finished product may not appear as crisp on your screen as it did before rotation, but it will print fine using the PostScript language. Text, especially when in a small type size, is next to impossible to read after rotation on a standard screen, so it is a good idea to do any editing before you rotate it (see Figure 4.2). However, QuarkXPress does allow complete text editing after rotation.

The disadvantage of rotating by eyeballing is that you may want to be more accurate, which is difficult to do in a manual rotation. A better method for accurate rotations is to use the Measurement palette, which is perhaps more simple. Follow these steps:

1. First, make sure the measurement palette is showing (see Figure 4.3).

2. Then, as before, click on the item to see the grab handles.

NOTE

Text box items can be edited while in their rotated form. You do not necessarily have to unrotate a text item to edit it, as long as you can read the copy.

FIGURE 4.2

Text blocks can be edited after rotation, but they are more difficult to read (on the screen).

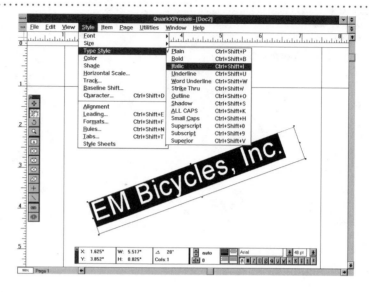

FIGURE 4.3

Use the Measurement palette for accuracy to 0.001° in rotation.

3. Next, highlight the number next to the rotation icon in the Measurement palette.

4. Edit the number to suit your rotation angle. When you're done, press Enter. The item is rotated precisely as specified!

EXTENDING AND BLEEDING ITEMS

Page layouts have often been a problem in the electronic environment, because items could be placed on the page only and could not extend beyond its boundaries. The technique of extending items to bleed off the page or to spread across multiple pages is taken care of handily in QuarkXPress 3.1. It is so simple it hardly warrants discussion.

To make an item bleed off the page, simply enlarge the item box and, if necessary, the item itself. Move the item beyond the boundary of the page (see Figure 4.4). When you print, include trim marks and your bleed should also print. Some software programs assume that these overextended items are to be carried to the next page of the document. QuarkXPress, however, understands a bleed as a bleed.

WARNING

Use caution in selecting spreads, though, because, in a signature (printer's layout of the press sheet), the design spread pages may not be exactly across from each other, as they appear in the QuarkXPress document layout! A solution to help here would be an appropriate XTension if available. The Mac QuarkXPress environment has two such XTensions. They convert the page layout spread in QuarkXPress to the appropriate configuration for the printer's spread on the signature. Hopefully, these will soon be rewritten and offered to the Windows market and help alleviate page spread confusion.

FIGURE 4.4

The sprocket area is to bleed off the page in this example. It extends beyond the page boundaries.

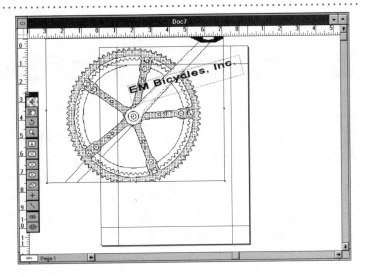

To move items across multiple pages of a spread, just design them to occur on your document layout. In Figure 4.5, the sprocket is intended to range across the spread. Select the Spreads option of in the Print dialog box (File ➤ Print). QuarkXPress will break the item where necessary.

FIGURE 4.5

The item containing the sprocket is stretched across a two page spread.

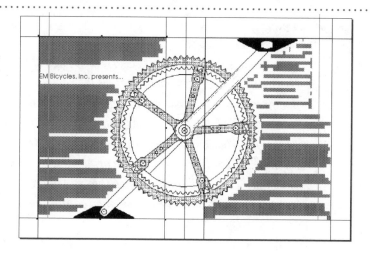

WORKING WITH MULTIPLE ITEMS

TIP

You can save a great deal of time if you group certain items and "store" them on your pasteboard area. For example, when working on a form, you may want to draw a ruled line, repeat it as many times as possible, then group them all as one item. This item can then be placed off to the side (on the pasteboard) for future use. When you need it, just click and drag it into position.

Multiple items on a page or spread can be selected simultaneously by one of two methods. One method is the tried and true Windows-lasso approach, in which the Item tool encircles a selection of items until their grab bars all show at the same time. The second method is to select one item at a time while holding down the Shift key. The Shift key enables you to keep accumulating items that have grab bars. Once multiple items are selected, they can be grouped together as one item by choosing the Item ➤ Group option. The advantage in grouping items comes in moving or duplicating the new grouped item (see Figure 4.6). If desired, the items can later be ungrouped. Once the Item ➤ Ungrouped option is used, each element in the larger grouped item becomes independent once again.

You can cut, copy, paste, duplicate, drag, or rotate single or grouped items (see Figure 4.7). Single or grouped items can also be dragged between documents.

Multiple duplicates can be created automatically and positioned using the Item ➤ Step and Repeat command. This command saves a tremendous amount of time in production of the layout. It allows automatic control of alignment and space when items are duplicated multiple times. The Step and Repeat dialog box allows you to duplicate single or multiple items in the horizontal or vertical dimension of your choice.

FIGURE 4.6

You can group multiple items of different types together. In this example, a text box and a picture box are lassoed with the item tool and grouped together (Item ➤ Group). They can now be manipulated as if they were one item.

EM Bicycles, Inc.

FIGURE 4.7

*Grouped items can be
manipulated for rotation
as well as step and repeat.
This example shows the
grouped elements of a
text and picture box
grouped, then rotated. Finally, the group was
duplicated with the step
and repeat option (Item
➤ Step and Repeat).*

LOCKING AND UNLOCKING ITEMS ON THE PAGE

TIP

*Locking and unlocking items becomes extremely helpful as you
prepare more sophisticated layouts with QuarkXPress. With dozens
of elements in close proximity, you will invariably select the
wrong element and move it, just by accident. Even slight
movement may be enough to damage your layout. Avoid
accidental selection and movement by locking items in place. You
can unlock them later if they need manipulation. Text can be
edited within a locked text box.*

When you're working on a page layout, creating elements, and positioning them
on the page, accuracy becomes very important. Occasionally, situations arise when
a simple mouse click can cause an item to highlight and somehow move. To avoid

any accidental movement of elements on the page QuarkXPress allows you to lock items in position. Once locked, the item cannot be repositioned until unlocked. This helps avoid the time-wasting mistakes that may occur in electronic layout. The Lock and Unlock options are under the Item menu.

NUDGING

A problem working with the mouse or roller ball is they sometimes are not very accurate. There seems to be that last-minute slip as the button is lifted. To help solve this dilemma, the good people at Quark have included an option that allows nudging of items. You simply click on the desired item to highlight it, then use the arrow keys (up, down, left, right) to reposition the item as desired.

The increment of nudge is one full point for each arrow press. If the Alt key is held down and then the arrow is pressed, the nudge is in $1/10$-point increments. This can be a very useful feature.

VIEWING ITEM CONTENTS WHILE DRAGGING OR ROTATING

This capability, like so many others in the software, saves a great deal of designer agony. With some programs, moving an item by dragging removes it from view on the screen while the move takes place. After the move is complete, the item reappears. This makes for too much trial-and-error layout. QuarkXPress allows the item and its contents to be viewed during the move, at your option. The same feature is available for rotations.

RUNNING TEXT AROUND OR BEHIND ITEMS

Any desktop-publishing program worth its salt should allow you to integrate text and graphic items in any way you desire. You should be able to place text on top of the graphic, and vice versa. You should also be able to place text so it runs around graphics, and be able to control *runaround* specifics. The term runaround refers to the manner and details in which text runs around graphics.

QuarkXPress gives you the several options in runarounds. It allows you to form a runaround where the text goes around the contour of the graphic item (see Figure 4.8).

Item ➤ Runaround allows you to control the distance separating the graphic from text. You decide how close the text gets on each side of the graphic. By selecting Item from the Runaround Specifications dialog box you can specifically choose the runaround distances. Other options include None, Auto Image, and Manual Image modes (see Figure 4.9).

FIGURE 4.8

*This is an example
of Auto Mode.*

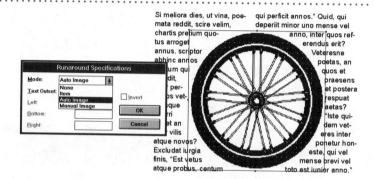

FIGURE 4.9

*Select the mode of
choice to runaround
the targeted item.*

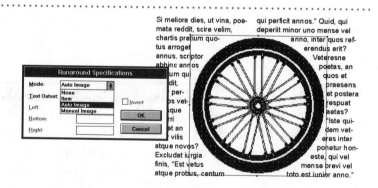

NOTE

Picture-style graphics in the TIF format may have trouble with some forms of runaround because the background and foreground of the picture in a TIF item are considered all as one.

If the item is an irregularly shaped picture, you may wish to conform the runaround more to the shape of the item than the picture box containing it. The Runaround dialog box enables you to choose a Manual Image runaround or an Auto Image runaround (see Figure 4.10). In the manual option, QuarkXPress creates a polygon around the item and you control the distance and flow by moving the polygon's handles. If you move the box containing the picture, the runaround polygon moves as well.

FIGURE 4.10

The Manual Mode of runaround allows you to change the shape of the polygon surrounding the item. This enables you to customize the runaround for a better look!

To change the shape manually, follow these steps:

1. Click on one of the *grab handles* of the odd shaped polygon (see Figure 4.11).

2. Drag it and the polygon reshapes.

3. To create a new grab handle, click on the polygon outline where you want the new handle while holding the Ctrl key down. This forms a new grab handle in that location, which can be used to reshape.

FIGURE 4.11

A close up of the "grab handles" used to reshape the runaround for manual mode. To create additional grab handles, place the cursor over the location you want the new handle, press Ctrl, and click on the runaround line.

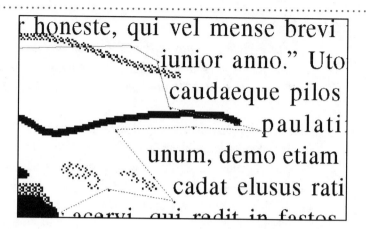

The results of the manual and automatic methods are essentially the same, although you have more control with the manual option.

Finally, there is the option for None. This enables you to remove the runaround and give the text the right-of-way to flow over or through the graphic item. This may be used in situations where you would want to have an overprint effect.

FLOWING TEXT INSIDE A PICTURE SHAPE

A QuarkXPress capability similar to a runaround is that of flowing text inside a picture shape. This can be used in certain design situations when you want that extra bit of something in the layout (see Figure 4.12). This feature is a bit goofy in that you really have to play around with it to master its full potential. At first it appears to be rather cute, then as you work with it, it is one of those features you hope you never need!

WARNING

Although placing text inside an irregularly shaped area is unique, it is a trick that can easily be misused. Remember, bad design is still bad design, regardless of the tool.

NOTE

On this and other examples, as given throughout the book, you may wish to use the sample graphics and text provided in your QuarkXPress tutorial disk set.

Here is a basic example of how to create text inside an irregularly shaped object. You should play around with it to get the full benefit. To flow text inside an irregular shape, you need to perform the following steps:

1. For this example, create a new document with two columns. Select two columns from the option in the New dialog box. Size and margin information is not too important in this example.

2. Click on **OK** to accept information in the box.

3. A new document page appears with the text box divided into two columns. Key in text, any text, to fill the two columns. Remember, this is to show that text will flow in an area, so you don't have to read the text to demonstrate that! You might want to type a paragraph, then copy and paste it until the page is filled.

4. Using the Select All command (Ctrl+A), highlight all the text and justify it (Style ➤ Alignment ➤ Justified). This makes the text in your example fill the shape better.

5. Create a circular picture box anywhere on the document page. Create this with the appropriate picture box tool (the Oval Picture Box tool). Hold down Shift while drawing the picture box to create a circle. To draw the box, click in the work area and drag diagonally. The same technique is used to create all other picture or text boxes. For the sake of this example, make a circle that is approximately 3–4″ in diameter. You may want to change the View to Fit in Window so you can see the whole document page.

6. Using the Item tool, click on the picture box to select it.

7. Move it to the approximate center of your two column text area if it isn't already there.

8. Select Manual Image mode from in the Runaround Specifications dialog box (Item ➤ Runaround). Then select Invert. Click on **OK** to accept the settings.

9. Presto! Your text follows the oval shape. You might have straggler lines that have to be attended to; some fine-tuning is usually necessary. (See Figure 4.12)

As stated earlier, using the inverting technique takes a bit of practice. You can invert and fill text to a picture box shape, or if your feeling brave, fill text in a picture shape within the picture box. Remember, practice makes perfect. Good luck!

WARNING

Often inverted text doesn't exactly fill the area as you had planned. Some modification is usually necessary after the automatic inversion process fills text in the shaped area. Justified text fills an area better than other alignments.

When Invert is used to place text inside the polygon, the text box itself is largely unaffected. Text that can fit in the polygon will flow there, other text will continue to flow throughout the text box, as usual.

FIGURE 4.12

An example of INVERT, text flowing within the shape of a polygon.

Si meliora dies, ut vina, poemata reddit, scire velim, chartis pretium quotus arroget annus. scriptor abhinc annos centum qui decidit, inter perfectos veteresque referri debet an inter vilis atque novos? Excludat iurgia finis, "Est vetus atque probus, centum qui perficit annos." Quid, qui deperiit minor uno mense vel anno, inter quos referendus erit? Veteresne poetas, an quos et praesens et postera respuat aetas? "Iste quidem veteres inter ponetur honeste, qui vel mense brevi vel toto est iunior anno." Utor permisso, caudaeque pilos ut equinae paulatim vello unum, demo etiam unum, dum cadat elusus ratione ruentis acervi, qui redit in fastos et virtutem aestimat annis miraturque nihil nisi quod Libitina sacravit.

Ennius et sapines et fortis et alter Homerus, ut critici dicunt, leviter curare videtur, quo promissa cadant et somnia Pythagorea. Naevius in manibus non est et mentibus haeret paene recens? Adeo sanctum est vetus omne poema. ambigitur quotiens, uter utro sit prior, aufert Pacuvius docti famam senis Accius alti, dicitur Afrani toga convenisse Menandro, Plautus ad exemplar Siculi properare Epicharmi, vincere Caecilius gravitate,

FRAMING TEXT AND PICTURE BOXES

In QuarkXPress, you can frame both text and picture boxes by using Item ➤ Frame. You must first have a text or picture box selected. You may use either the Item or Content tool to select the item. When you select Item ➤ Frame, a dialog box appears giving you options for the frame's style, width, color, and shade (see Figure 4.13). You may select from a variety of frame styles in the library.

FIGURE 4.13

After a box is selected, go to the Frame Specifications dialog box (Item ➤ Frame). Here you can select style, width, color, and shade for the intended box frame.

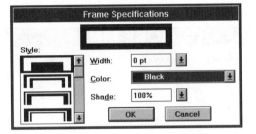

NOTE

Text boxes, picture boxes and grouped text/picture boxes can have frames. Lines and/or grouped items containing line items cannot have a frame in QuarkXPress 3.1.

ANCHORING ITEMS TO TEXT

Earlier versions of QuarkXPress had a system of "nesting" items on the page. It would enable any item created within a larger item to become the "child" item of its parent. If the parent were moved, the child was moved along with it. Apparently, this was a radical departure from other competitors and many users were uncomfortable with the operation. Since version 3.0, QuarkXPress has enabled people to use the conventional "non-nested" style of page layout. But for the old timers who have become accustomed to this and use nesting as a manipulation tool, QuarkXPress has it as a selectable option. Choose Auto Constrain option under the

General Preferences dialog box (Edit ➤ Preferences ➤ General). This is an all-encompassing function; you cannot nest certain items and not others.

TIP

To use the parent/child relationship of older versions of QuarkXPress, as introduced on the Macintosh platform, select the Auto Constrain option in the General Preferences dialog box.

LINES, LINES, AND MORE LINES

The last in the trio of items in QuarkXPress is lines. The simple line has many options in QuarkXPress; it takes on a character of its own. You can draw lines in perpendicular fashion using the Orthogonal Line tool from the Tool palette. Or, if you would rather, the regular Line tool allows you to draw lines at any angle on the page. Both tools use the click and drag technique.

Lines can be manipulated in a variety of ways. First, you may want to draw a line and highlight it. Then go to the Style menu. The Style menu options change specifically for lines. You may also wish to manipulate line information directly from the Modify dialog box (Item ➤ Modify). In this dialog box, you can change several specification options at once.

Finally, you can use the Measurement palette. When a line is highlighted, the information on that line appears in the Measurement window. You can change any of this information directly in the Measurement palette. Once you've made your changes, press Enter, and the changes are reflected in your line.

ROTATING LINES

Line rotation in QuarkXPress is differs slightly from that of other items through use of the Measurements palette. Yes, you can still use the Rotation tool, just as you do with other items. Select the item; select the tool; move a grab bar. It is relatively straightforward.

For finer control, use the Measurements palette. First select the line. Then in the Measurements palette, click the option showing Endpoints, Midpoint, Left Point,

Right Point (see Figure 4.14). Select an option other than Endpoints, and the Rotation field will appear, as shown. To replace the rotation angle, highlight the angle degree value and replace it with your own value. Activate by pressing Enter.

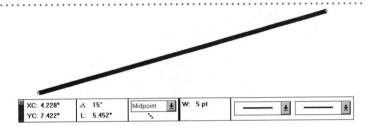

FIGURE 4.14

Rotate lines, from the Measurements palette, by first selecting Midpoint, Left Point, or Right Point. Then change the rotation angle and press Enter.

MANIPULATING MARGIN GUIDES

WARNING

Changing the Document Setup option after a document has already been created may have an effect on elements you have placed on the page. Be careful if you choose to make document size changes on existing documents.

You have already seen how QuarkXPress gives a complete set of margin guides to help locate the main text area of the page. This is established as you create a new document, in the Margin Guides area of the New dialog box. This information sets the text box size and the Margin Guides.

To change the Margin Guides after a document has been started, you must first select the menu option—Page ➤ Display ➤ M1-Master. At that point you will be in what is called the Master Page. Next, select Page ➤ Master Guides. Change the dialog box according to your needs. Don't forget to change back to the document page (from the master). Change back to the document page by selecting Page ➤ Display ➤ Document.

OTHER GUIDES

Just like the layout artist who needs the help of a non-repro blue line for placement of items on the page, QuarkXPress helps by allowing you to place guides as needed on the layout. These guides are obtained by dragging them from the rulers. Just click and drag from the ruler, horizontal or vertical. You can place as many guides on the page as you want. You can manipulate or move these guides by clicking and dragging them (outside a box area).

To change the colors of any guides, choose Edit ➤ Preferences ➤ Application. Click on the guide you wish to change and a color wheel appears. It gives you options for selecting the color of that guide (see Figure 4.15). Regardless of the colors selected, the guides will not print out when you send your product to the laser printer or imagesetter.

FIGURE 4.15

A color wheel is available for you to customize the guides in the color of your choice.

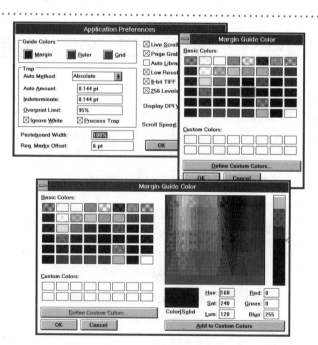

SNAP TO GUIDES

Another of the myriad of options available to you is the ability to dictate the Snap to Guides distance. This is the distance at which an item—text, line, or picture—will jump to the next guide when repositioned. Choose Edit ➤ Preferences ➤ General and adjust the Snap Distance option (in pixels). A setting of 6 indicates that anywhere within six pixels of the guide, an item will jump to that guide. This capability helps alleviate problems of inaccuracy that layout artists have in manual format.

P A R T

II

Assembling Multiple Page Documents

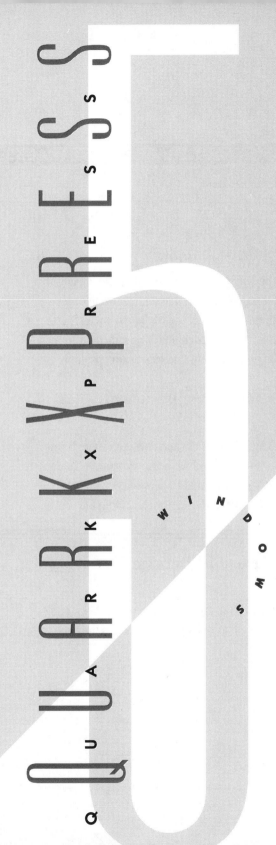

CREATING A MASTER PAGE

To have an item on all subsequent pages   102

place it on the master page. Henceforth, all subsequent document pages that are created based on that master page will have that item showing on the document page. For example, to place a line at the top of each page, go to the master page and draw the line. All new document pages made from that master page image will have that line drawn in that exact same position.

To create a new master page in the Document Layout palette   107

select the Document Layout palette. If not showing, show the palette through View ➤ Show Document Layout. Use the palettes menu and choose Document ➤ Show Master Pages. At that point, to add a new master, choose Master ➤ Insert and select the style of master you want to add from the submenu choices.

To delete a master page from the Document Layout palette   108

go to the master pages portion of the Document Layout palette again. Click once on the master page icon you wish to delete. This identifies the page. Then select Masters ➤ Delete.

To delete a document page from the Document Layout palette 108

go to the Document Layout palette. Select the document layout, as opposed to showing the master pages (click on the icon to the left of the menu item Document or Master and you can toggle to Document layout or master layout). Double-click on the document page you wish to delete to identify it. Then select Document ➤ Delete from the menu.

To rename a master page in the Document Layout palette 108

toggle to the master page layout in the Document Layout palette. Click once on the master page name you wish to change. Overstrike the existing or default name with your new name.

To copy a master page layout from one document to another 111

bring two documents up in QuarkXPress. Reduce each to Thumbnail size and Tile the windows so that both images are seen. Click on one document page thumbnail and drag it across the boundary to the next document window. Drop it in position on the second document. Not only will the page layout, if any, carry over, but the master page it was constructed upon comes over too! Check the second document for its new master page added to the inventory.

master page is a non-printing page used as a template or format for other pages in your document. As you add new pages to the document, they automatically follow the format of the master page. Master pages can contain elements that print on the document pages (such as page numbers or headers) even though the master page itself does not print.

When you launch QuarkXPress, you often want to create a new document (File ➤ New). This brings a New (document) dialog box. Changes in this New dialog box affect the document pages and master pages. The box includes options for page format, guides, facing or non-facing pages, automatic text boxes, and columns.

NOTE

Page size ranges in QuarkXPress from 1" by 1" to 48" by 48" for non-facing pages, with a maximum of 24" wide by 48" tall for facing pages. Columns, as set up in the New dialog box, can range from 3 to 288 points (4"). You may set the number of columns anywhere from 1 to 30.

Not only are you establishing the look of your document page in this New dialog box, but you are also establishing the look of the first master page. Your master pages will follow the format in page size, guides, columns, and automatic text box in the default master page, Master 1.

MASTER PAGES OF FACING AND NON-FACING PAGES

NOTE

After a new document is created, show the Document Layout palette (View ➤ Show Document Layout) to see icon representations of document and master pages.

As you create a document (File ➤ New), QuarkXPress immediately gives two or three master pages, depending on the type of document. If the option for facing pages is unchecked on the New dialog box, you will have non-facing pages. Facing pages and non-facing pages help in your layout for imposition and bindery planning. Facing pages spread open to each other, while non-facing pages are independent single pages. Your Document Layout palette (View ➤ Document Layout) will represent these facing and non-facing pages (see Figure 5.1).

TIP

Blank master pages have multiple uses. One involves creating a new document page based on the blank for a place-holder in your document. This can hold the position for a photograph or advertisement. All editorial material will link or run around this blank page. Page numbers will also continue to work in sequence, taking into account the placeholder page.

Non-facing pages have two initial master pages (plus an original document page). The two master pages consist of one blank master page, and one Master 1 page designed with the guides and text box information from the New dialog box. The blank master page can create other master pages or blank document pages. Unlike a Master 1 page, blank pages have no items or guides.

Check the Facing Pages option in the New document dialog box and you get page layouts in spreads. That is, page one is a single right hand page, two is a left hand page of a two-page spread, facing page three, and so on. See the Document Layout palette for an icon inventory of master and document pages. Figure 5.1 represents the Document Layout palette with multiple pages, as facing pages.

FIGURE 5.1

*The Document Layout
palette will represent
facing and non-facing
pages.*

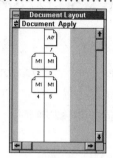

Facing pages have three master pages at the start. One master page is the blank
page, just like that given to the non-facing document. Another master page is Master 1. Again, the Master 1 page follows guides and text box information outlined in
the New dialog box, as you created the document. The third master page, unique
to the facing pages layout contains another type of blank master page. It is a blank
facing-page master page. Use this to create other facing-page document pages or
other facing-page master pages. The facing-page master page also includes information detailed in the New dialog box.

THE DOCUMENT SETUP DIALOG BOX

You have created a document in the New dialog box, giving size, guides, etc. As
you work on the document, however, there may be changes necessary. You can
make some changes in document layout through the Document Setup dialog box
(File ➤ Document Setup) shown in Figure 5.2.

FIGURE 5.2

*The Document Setup dialog box allows you to
change dimensions after
the document is set up.*

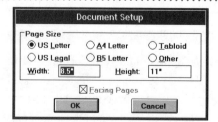

The Document Setup dialog box allows changes to page size or guide values for the current document. You must be careful here, as changes may affect existing document items. Figure 5.3 shows a message box warning about existing page items.

FIGURE 5.3

Improper field input will result in a message box informing you of your limits.

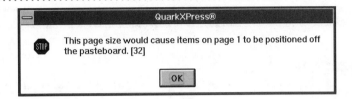

REPEATING ELEMENTS

Master pages can contain all elements you wish to repeat on each page of your document. This may include page numbers, any header and footer information, or graphic elements. Certain items, such as page numbers will reflect numerical changes in their accompanying document pages, as you will see in *Chapter 6*. You may also place boxes, lines, or grouped items on a master page.

You can modify any of the elements contained within the master page at any time. You can make changes right on the master itself or on the document page related to it. The changes will be reflected in all document pages related to that master page.

When you apply a new master page to an existing document page (from another master page) you can specify to Keep Changes or Delete Changes. You access these choices in the General Preferences dialog box (Ctrl-Y). In this dialog box, the Master Page Items option gives these choices through a pop-up menu. Click and hold on the field to see the two options. Then choose and release the mouse button.

Typically, when you apply the new master page to a document page, any unmodified master items are deleted on the document page. The default setting is Keep Changes. This enables old modified master page items on the document page to remain as you apply a new master page design to that document page. If you choose Delete Changes, both modified and unmodified master page items on document pages will be deleted.

Use this feature when modifying master pages of a document, such as updating a newsletter or magazine. If you want the changes for the document pages, apply Keep Changes. If you want changes to only apply to existing document pages, select Delete Changes in the General Preferences dialog box.

MASTER PAGES IN THE DOCUMENT LAYOUT PALETTE

TIP

To help your performance in QuarkXPress, get a large monitor or a second monitor (and graphics card). The second monitor can even be monochrome, because all you really need to use it for is to house your floating palettes.

You can manipulate master pages with the Document Layout palette (View ➤ Show Document Layout). You can resize and move this palette around like other QuarkXPress palettes. The Document Layout palette is probably one of the floating palettes you will want to have on your screen always. Unfortunately, it takes up so much space, that leaving it showing is impractical on a 13″ monitor.

NOTE

All Master Pages and Document pages appear as icons within the Document Layout palette. Use this palette to create new pages based on the master pages.

Master pages are also helpful in the creation of new document pages. Again, use the Document Layout palette. Select the palette options Document ➤ Insert ➤ M1-Master1 (see Figure 5.4). A new icon appears suggesting the placement of your new page. Move the icon to the location you want the new page (in the Document Layout palette page icons) and click to position. The palette can be scrolled, or the palette window resized to see more of the document pages.

FIGURE 5.4

One way to create a new document page is insert the page from the Document Layout palette options.

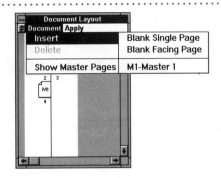

NEW MASTER PAGES IN THE DOCUMENT LAYOUT PALETTE

The full size Master Page in the working area will have no guides initially, except for the margin guides, established in the New dialog box. There may be times when you want another master page layout, differing from your original M1-Master 1. The easiest way to solve this problem is to add other master pages based on the original design. You can use the original M1-Master 1 as a guide or you can make masters from blank pages. To add a master page based on the original, it would be efficient just to copy the M1-Master 1 layout, complete with existing margin guides, etc. You can make other master pages by selecting the Master Guides option in the Document Layout (choose Document ➤ Show Master Guides). This will change from the document page view in the Document Layout palette to that of the Master Page view. Note, another method is to simply click on the icon just left of the Document Layout menu's Document item. This toggles the view from document pages to master pages. Once in the Master Pages view of the Document Layout palette, select the palette menu options Master ➤ Insert ➤ M1-Master 1 (see Figure 5.5). This will add another master page based on the initial attributes and margins in master page M1-Master 1.

FIGURE 5.5

*Create a new master page
by selecting the Docu-
ment Layout palette
menu options of Docu-
ment ➤ Show Master
Pages ➤ Insert ➤ M1-
Master 1.*

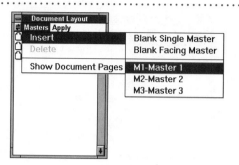

If you prefer, insert a new master based on one of the other options, i.e., single
blank page or facing blank page. Either way, once your "mold" for the master
page has been selected, click in the Document Layout palette layout where you
want to place the new page. After you click in that location, the new page icon appears, representing a successfully added new master page.

WARNING

*When you are moving the mouse, just before positioning the new
page, make sure you know where to place the new page icon. You
can easily misplace the new page icon and throw your sequence
out of whack!*

To create a master page with no guides, based on no previous master, select the
option of blank single or facing page when inserting a new master. These will resemble blank pages when enlarged on the work area, but can be altered as any
master can.

RENAMING THE MASTER PAGE(S)

Once you have created the master page or pages of choice, you may benefit from
naming them something notable. Typically, it helps to name them something related to
their use. For example, you may want to name a Master Page with general Text work,
as **TEXT**, a cover page may be **COVER**, an open page for the advertisement may be

ADVER-1, and so on. The names and specific designations are up to you and your work style. To rename a master page, show the master pages in the Document Layout palette. Then click on and overstrike the default names after the master page icons (see Figure 5.6).

ADDING NEW DOCUMENT PAGES IN THE DOCUMENT LAYOUT PALETTE

Adding a new document page or pages in the Document Layout palette is done exactly like adding a new master page. In the layout palette, you select the Document pages view (as opposed to Show Master Pages), and choose the menu options Document ➤ Insert ➤ Master. Substitute Master for whatever you want as a master page to be based the new page upon, it could be an established master page or one of the blank pages (see Figure 5.7).

FIGURE 5.6

To rename the master page, overstrike its original or default name in the Document Layout palette.

FIGURE 5.7

Adding a new document page in the Document Layout Palette is similar to adding a new master page.

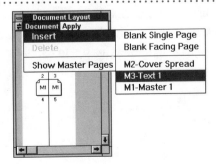

*As you add new pages in the Document Layout palette, there will
be an icon representing your new page to insert. Be very careful
where you "drop" this new page icon. Placing it in the wrong
position will renumber all your pages and possible play havoc with
any text linking that may be available.*

EDITING MASTER PAGES

You have two options to view and modify a master page. One option is to choose
the master page you want to view from the Display submenu (Page ➤ Display). Select the page you want and it will display in your work area (see Figure 5.8). You
can edit as you would any document page. If you select Document from the submenu options, QuarkXPress takes to a full view of the last document page viewed.

NOTE
*To modify only the master page guides, choose Page ➤ Master
Guides. Select this when you are viewing a specific master page,
as not all master pages will have the same guides. Reposition the
margin guides by changing the appropriate values in the dialog
box. The master page you are viewing will change according to the
new values entered.*

The second method to view and modify a master page is through the Document
Layout palette. This useful window enables you to select a particular page icon,
master or document. Just scroll to find the icon of choice and double-click on that
page. Your selection opens in full view for you to modify as necessary.

FIGURE 5.8

This menu option shows you the inventory of document and master pages.

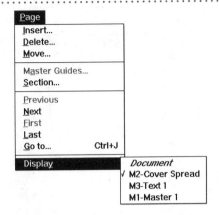

COPYING MASTER PAGES

Another method for incorporating multiple master pages within a document is by copying a master from another document. When you copy a page from one document to another, its master layout follows, becoming an additional master page. To see how this works, follow these steps:

1. Open two different documents (preferably with two different page layouts).

2. Resize the work area so that the two documents can rest side-by-side on the screen.

3. Change both documents to Thumbnails view by choosing View ➤ Thumbnails (see Figure 5.9).

TIP

If you want to copy just the layout of a document page and not its text, you should make a new document page based on a master, copy that new page (which will still have master-page related material), and then delete that new page from one or both documents. The master page will stay no matter what.

FIGURE 5.9

*Copying pages from
one document to another
also copies their master
pages. Document 1 on the
right will inherit the master page of the document
page copied from
Document 2.*

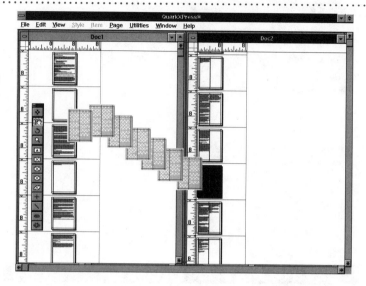

4. Now you can copy a selected page. Click and drag a page of one document
to the other document. Position it where desired and release the mouse button. Since QuarkXPress allows you to open as many as seven documents simultaneously, you can use this technique of copying page layouts (and
master pages) for up to seven documents at a time. After duplication, the
Document Layout palette will indicate an additional master page as well.

Multiple master pages will not automatically follow page number sequence from
one page to another. That is, if the first few pages of the document were formed after M1-Master 1 and the next few pages were in M2-Master 2, page numbering
from Master 1 will not automatically follow to the Master 2 pages. You must start
page numbering sequences anew on each master. See *Page Numbering* and *Sections* in *Chapter 6*.

6

Applying a Master Page to a Document

QUARKXPRESS

QUARKXPRESS WINDOWS

To delete pages and master pages   116

from the Document Layout palette, click on the page to delete in the palette, then select the appropriate menu option (Document for a document page, or Master for a master page) then choose delete, i.e. Document ➤ Delete.

To view pages from the Document Layout palette   117

simply double click on the page icon you wish to view. This page or master will become full size and fill the work area. You can scroll and edit as you normally would in this work area.

To make modifications to a master page from the Document Layout palette   118

select the master page in the palette layout you wish to edit. Double click to open to full size and make any edits or modifications as necessary. Don't forget to go back to Document view. This can be accomplished either from the Document Layout palette or from the main menu option Page ➤ Display ➤ Document.

When you have a job that requires only a few pages, the master page capability of QuarkXPress seems overbearing. If, however, you are like so many QuarkXPress users who routinely produce documents dozens or hundreds of pages in length, master page is a boon! This chapter shows you how to apply master pages to your documents and to get the most of them.

You spent some time in the last chapter learning how to get a master page for your document and how to duplicate them as necessary. But what is the functional side of a master page? What can you do with them to increase productivity? What are some tricks that help you create master pages quicker? What kind of hints will enable you to be more efficient in the master page applications? You will find these answers here, in this chapter.

DELETING PAGES AND MASTERS

TIP

When you see a dialog "button" with a dark frame around it, (for example the OK button), you can select it by pressing the Enter key. These only work when the button has the thick frame around it. Also, because Windows was developed for the non-mouse user, you also have keyboard equivalents for most other movement actions, such as the Tab key to go to the next field. Speed is a critical issue in the competitive environment of electronic publishing and you should learn as many shortcuts as possible.

To delete a document or master page using the Document Layout palette, click on the page icon to identify the page you wish to delete; then select the Document ➤ Delete option (or Master ➤ Delete for masters). You can select multiple pages by holding down the Shift key while identifying pages to ax; then after they are all highlighted, select Delete (see Figure 6.1).

FIGURE 6.1

The sequence to remove pages in the Document Layout palette is to first identify the pages (through their icons), then select Delete from the Document menu.

WARNING
You cannot Undo the deleting function after you have deleted pages. The only way to get your pages back is through the revert to last saved version (File ➤ Revert to Saved).

Another way to delete a page is through the Page ➤ Delete option, which brings up a dialog box. Key in the page number(s) to delete, then press **OK**. Pages cannot be undeleted, but again, you may choose File ➤ Revert to Saved.

VIEWING PAGES

There are two ways for you to view the master pages in your document. First, you can use the Document Layout palette to view document and master pages. To do this, open the Document Layout palette, then double-click on the page (document or master) you wish to view. Remember, to get the Master Pages in the Document Layout palette you must click on the master pages icon within the palette (see Figure 6.2). This page shows in full size in the work area. Use this technique to close the page and view another if you wish. In each case where you view a page in the work area, the appropriate icon will highlight in the Document Layout palette.

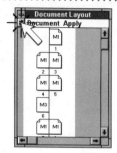

FIGURE 6.2

*To toggle between the
master page icon(s) and
document page icon(s)
in the Document Layout
palette, click on the icon
as indicated.*

Also, the document window indicates the page number identification at the lower-left corner of the work area. Using the Document Layout palette allows you to select any particular page to view.

NOTE

*The Document Layout palette is a versatile feature that enables
you to see or scroll through all page icons of the document. It can
be resized and relocated with the standard Windows convention.
Horizontal or vertical scrolling is accomplished through use of the
scroll bars.*

Another method of viewing the document or master page is using the Page ➤ Display submenu. You can choose between the document view and a master page view in the work area. This is not quite as selective as using the Document Layout palette, because it doesn't let you go to a specific document page.

MODIFYING THE MASTER PAGES

You can modify master page items on the master itself or on one of the pages related to it. Relating to a master page means the document was originated from a particular master page. When you create the document page, it includes master items. The document page becomes a clone of the original master page. You can create a document page based on a particular master in one of two ways, either through the

Document Layout palette or by using the Page ➤ Insert menu options. Both of these techniques were introduced in the last chapter. You may want to review them before the example in this chapter, as it asks you to set up master pages for a newsletter. The example does not cover making document pages from masters.

Your document may have several master pages within the construction of the product. Each document page is molded from one of the master pages. The problem of having multiple masters for the new QuarkXPress user is that of possible confusion. In QuarkXPress, masters contain certain key items that do not carry over from one master (and document page) to another. Sequential page numbering, for example, does not follow from one master to another.

PAGE NUMBERING AND SECTIONING TECHNIQUES

TIP

To use the page box number codes, often it is best to use them on the Master Pages of the document. This will prevent the redundancy of placing them on each document page. Also, if you use the Previous Box Page Number and Next Box Page Number codes, place them in their own text box, but position the box on the Master Page inside the master text box (automatic text box). They will not work if placed outside the text box area.

It is best to place the sequential page number commands on the master page so that all document pages are numbered in the font, size, and style you choose. The command to place these sequential page numbers is Ctrl+3 (see Figure 6.3).

QuarkXPress also includes commands in reference to other document pages as well. This gives you a great tool for document processing. It "tags" various story parts so that even if the page numbers change due to editing, the *continued on* and *continued from* page numbers are accurate. These may be placed either on the master page or directly on the document page, as needed. The Previous Box Page Number (Ctrl+2) and the Next Box Page Number (Ctrl+4) are handy for creating automatic page number lines such as *Continued from page...* and *Continued on...* page. Page numbers

FIGURE 6.3

Use the Ctrl+3 keyboard shortcut on the master page to create sequential page numbers on the document pages. You can alter the font, size, and style of the command to match that of your page number.

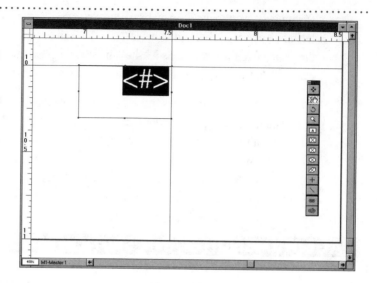

are displayed and updated automatically if you insert the proper Page Box Number code. Even as pages get repositioned in the document, the previous/next page codes reflect the changes.

TIP

Get the Section dialog box by choosing Page ➤ Section or from the Document Layout palette. In the Document Layout palette first click on the document page you want to begin the section, then click on the page name area of the Document Layout palette. The Section dialog box will appear.

Use these page box number codes with format in Section (see Figure 6.4).

The Section dialog box enables you to specify the starting page number of the section, number type, and preface the page number with a four character information

FIGURE 6.4
The Section dialog box

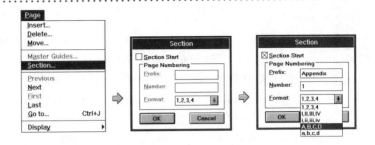

piece. This could be useful for example, in prefacing the appendix pages with App, to indicate the appendix in your document. Following is a list of the shortcuts.

COMMAND	SHORTCUT COMBINATION
Previous Box Page Number Character	Ctrl+2
Current Box Page Number Character	Ctrl+3
Next Box Page Number Character	Ctrl+4

USING AUTOMATIC PAGE NUMBERING IN SECTIONS

Another use for multiple master pages is creating sections within your larger document. Sections are small, isolated groups of pages, typically with special activity or emphasis in your publication (e.g., index, appendix, or glossary). You should treat these with automatic page numbers highlighting their uniqueness. For these areas, use the Section option. To specify a document page or group of pages as a section, go to the first page in that sequence. Look at the page number in your document to confirm the page you are on. Then select Page ➤ Section. The Section dialog box appears. Check on the Start Section option. Controls in the page numbering area become active (black not gray). At that point the current page becomes the first page of the new section.

In this dialog box, you have an option for placing a prefix for the page number. You may use up to four letters (e.g., App for Appendix).

NOTE

Page numbering and sections are detailed in this chapter of this book because you will often number pages from the master pages. Working from page to page is all right for smaller documents, but remember larger documents yield tighter deadlines. For some reason, it seems that the larger the project, the less time you have for it. Automatic page numbering and sectioning on the master pages saves a lot of agony if done right!

To specify a sequential page number for the current document page, place the starting page number in the page number field (see Figure 6.5). To specify the format of page numbering, click and select from the page number section (see Figure 6.6). When you are finished, click **OK**.

CUSTOMIZING PAGE NUMBERS

To make the page numbers look the way you want, including the font, style, size, etc., work from the master document. Make the automatic box page number a part of the master page. Start by creating a text box in approximately the position you want to have the page number. Then key in the automatic box page number (Ctrl+3). This will ensure that all future document pages from that master will have proper page numbers. Then customize the page number by highlighting the <#> characters of the automatic box page number. While highlighted, change the type characteristics as you would any normal type. Those type characteristics will reflect in the document page numbers.

FIGURE 6.5

You may use up to four characters in the prefix area of the Section dialog box. This prefix will go before page numbers in the Section.

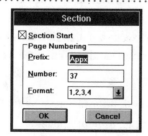

FIGURE 6.6

You can choose from a variety of page number formats within the Section dialog box.

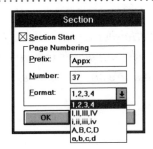

ABSOLUTE PAGE NUMBERS

Combining a series of automatic page numbers and section numbers can get quite confusing. To print out certain groups of pages, the print dialog box lists only From and To. This doesn't help much if you have three page 1s in the document. To get around this, QuarkXPress has Absolute Page Numbers. This means that if you want to print "physical" page 16 through "physical" (or absolute) page 21, you input the From and To fields as +16 and +21 respectively (see Figure 6.7). Regardless of the page sequence and section names, QuarkXPress calls the first absolute page +1, the second +2, and so on, throughout the document.

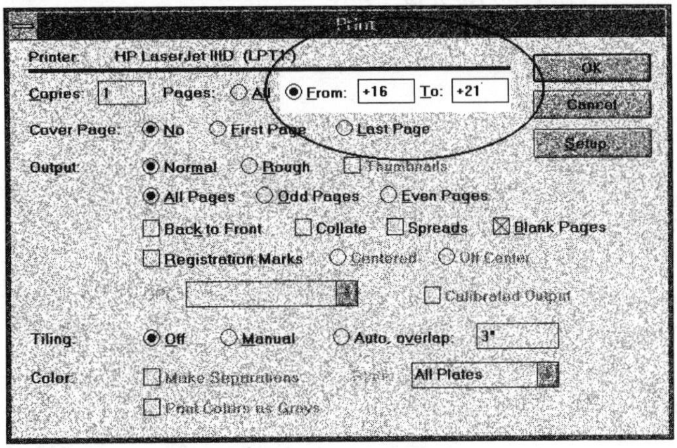

FIGURE 6.7

Use Absolute Page Numbers when printing a document with various sections. Section page numbers are not accurate for printing specific pages.

TIP

The Document Layout palette shows you both the page numbers and absolute numbers. Click on a page's icon and the page number will show in the title bar area of the palette; the absolute number is, of course, on the page's icon.

LINKED TEXT BOXES ON THE MASTER PAGE

You establish information for new documents in the New dialog box (File ➤ New). One of the options here is Automatic Text Box (see Figure 6.8). Checking this option creates an automatic text box in the master page (following established margin guides). It also automates the creation of similar new text boxes on all future pages (following that master page layout). These text boxes will link automatically. Linked text boxes allow type to flow from one text box to another. If you bring the master page up to the document area, you will notice a link icon at the top-left corner of the page.

TIP

It is often easiest to link and unlink graphically by reducing the view to a small percentage (Thumbnails won't work, though), selecting the Linking or Unlinking tool from the Tools palette, and clicking on a text box.

FIGURE 6.8

If you check Automatic Text Box in the New dialog box, a text box is created with linking capabilities.

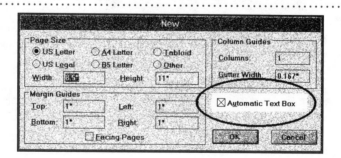

As detailed earlier, edited items on the master page reflect on all related document pages. The exception is that of the linked text box. QuarkXPress will not allow you to place text inside a linked text box on the master page. You must place any text on the master page in its own unlinked box. Select linking and unlinking through the appropriate tool in the Tool palette.

The automatic text link icon on the master page indicates that, as text flows into the text box, if the text is a greater quantity than will fit, it may need to go beyond that box. If so, QuarkXPress adds a new page to the end of your document with an automatic text box the same size, shape, and position as that of the preceding page. The remaining text flows on to the new page, and so on, until all text is taken care of and positioned.

If you have chosen multiple columns on the New dialog box, then text flows first in column one, then two, etc., for the entire page. More text will cause the addition of other pages and text will continue to flow in like manner on the new pages.

WARNING

Mixing manual linking with automatically linked text boxes can get confusing. Try to keep track of where your text is by keeping a saved copy in reserve.

You can also have manual control of text flow through use of the Linking and Unlinking tools on the Tools palette (see Figure 6.9). To link two text boxes so that the text will flow from one chosen text box to another, select the Linking tool. Click on the first text box. Then click immediately on the linked text box. An arrow will show indicating the direction of text flow from the original text box to the linked text box. To break a link (Unlink), select the Unlinking tool. Then click on a text box until the arrow appears, then click with the Unlink cursor on the end or "feather" part of the arrow. The link is now broken.

Linking frequently, but not exclusively, occurs through master pages. In small documents, as noted to earlier, you may not have the same need for master pages as perhaps in a larger document.

FIGURE 6.9

The Tool palette with tools identified that you will use throughout this chapter's exercise

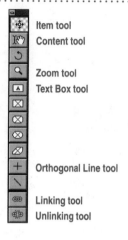

Item tool

Content tool

Zoom tool

Text Box tool

Orthogonal Line tool

Linking tool
Unlinking tool

ANCHORING ITEMS ON MASTER PAGES

Sometimes the feature that allows you to change Master Page items on related document pages is unwanted. This may be true primarily if you are working with a complex document page and accidentally click on a master page element. You may move it slightly or accidentally delete it. To avoid these problems, it is wise to "lock" certain items on the master pages. The procedure is simple. Click on the item and select Item ➤ Lock. This anchors the item, preventing it from accidental movement or deletion. You can edit on the master page or the related document page. Remember, QuarkXPress works through item boxes: text goes in text item boxes and graphics are placed in picture boxes. While anchored in position, the text or picture box cannot be moved, but its contents can be edited. Locking only anchors the box!

YOUR SECOND QUARKXPRESS DOCUMENT

Now you get an opportunity to place all this newfound knowledge of master pages to work in your second QuarkXPress document. You will be creating a master page document layout for a future EM Bicycles newsletter QuickRelease. It's rather simple, and you are only working on the master pages in this example. You can add more to it later if you wish to see how it prints. For now, the master pages are our primary focus.

Begin by creating a new document with the specifications shown in Figure 6.10. This will be a two column layout. Guides will be $^3\!/_4$ on all sides and the facing pages option will be checked. Once all fields are setup accordingly, click on **OK**.

FIGURE 6.10

Use the specifications shown in this illustration for your new document.

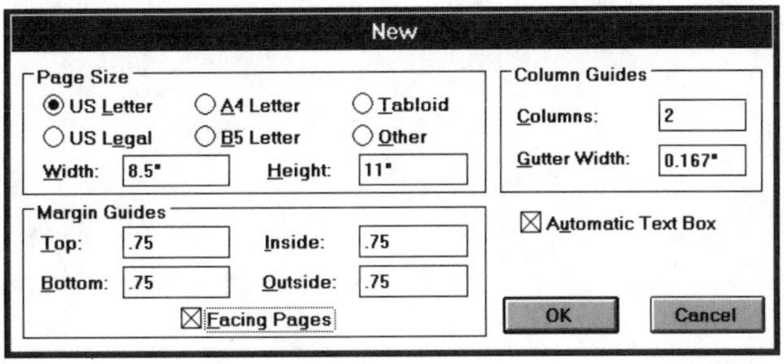

Your screen should show part of page 1 (100% size). If the size is not 100%, select View ➤ Actual Size. Another way to select 100% is to use the keyboard equivalent (Ctrl+1).

Now, make sure your Tools and Document Layout palettes are showing (see Figure 6.11). The Document Layout palette shows that you have one document page and three master pages. The master pages consist of one blank page, one left/right combination blank page, and one M1-Master 1 page.

You are going to set up a format for the newsletter to make it easier to produce month after month. To do this, you are going to establish most of the repeatable information in the master pages. You will have a total of three master pages.

▸ The first master will be for the cover page of QuickRelease.

▸ The next master will be for all inside material.

▸ The third master page will be set up for the back cover of the newsletter, with material such as mailing information.

FIGURE 6.11

*Make sure the Tools and
Document Layout pal-
ettes are showing. If they
aren't, choose the appro-
priate Show command(s)
from the View menu. Af-
ter they show you can
reposition them by drag-
ging their title bars.*

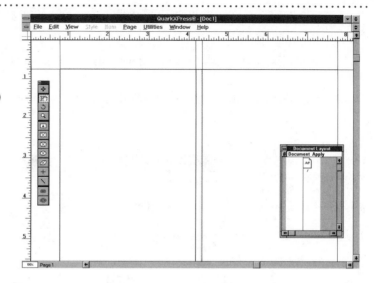

CREATING TWO NEW MASTER PAGES

First you should create two new master pages. Until you rename them, they will
be Master 2 and Master 3, respectively. Create the Master 2 page by toggling to the
master pages icons, then select Document ➤ Insert ➤ Master 1. Place the new
page icon after Master 1 on the Document Layout palette. Repeat the process for
a total of three master pages as shown in Figure 6.12.

NOTE

Check back in Chapter 5 *if you need to review techniques for
adding master pages.*

In order to have each master page the same as Master 1, each new page was copied from Master 1. You could have made masters from the blank or page layout,
but they would not have had the automatic text box, as indicated when you created
the document with the New document dialog box.

FIGURE 6.12

The Document Layout pal-
ette showing three master
pages for the document

Next, you should rename the master pages. Master 1, 2, and 3 are not informative enough for the document. Click on the Master 1 icon and its name will appear in the space to the right. Select the name and rename it by overstriking. Call it QR Cover (see Figure 6.13). Next, click the Master 2 icon, select the name, and rename it *QR Body*. Finally, rename Master 3 *QR End Mailer*. These names will be reflected in the Page ➤ Display submenu.

Remember, you can use this menu option to go to a particular page (document or master) instead of using the Document Layout palette (see Figure 6.14).

FIGURE 6.13

Highlight and replace the
generic names of the mas-
ter pages with a more
descriptive monikers.

FIGURE 6.14

*The Page ➤ Display
option will show the
names of your master
pages. You may select
one of the master
pages to edit from
this menu also.*

And of course, you can also scroll from page to page, including vertical and horizontal scrolls. This is a feature absent in some of the competing products.

EDITING THE MASTER PAGES

Now you are going to edit the master pages. That is, you are going to include text or graphic elements that will repeat on each issue of the newsletter in their respective pages. In the Document Layout palette, double-click on the QR Cover icon (formerly, Master 1). This opens up the master page QR Cover full size in the document work area.

Start by preparing a banner for the newsletter. To do this, first move or adjust the size of the automatic text box. You are going to lower the top of this text box so a new text box containing the banner will appear at the top of the page. You don't want the two text boxes to interfere with each other.

NOTE

It is important to click on the item that you want to modify so that it will be properly identified. Without the grab handles on the text, picture, or line item, you cannot make modifications.

Click on the automatic text box once with the Item or Content tool and you will see grab handles appear at the corners and mid-points of the text box outline. Next, key in Ctrl+M (equivalent to Item ➤ Modify) to bring up the Text Box Specifications dialog box. Change the Origin Down field to **2.75** and the Height field to **7.5** (see Figure 6.15). Click **OK**. These changes will give an additional 2 for the banner.

FIGURE 6.15
Match the specifications given here for your text box.

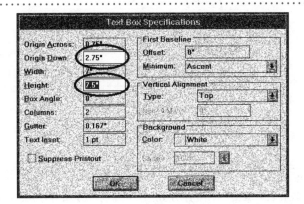

CREATING THE QUICKRELEASE BANNER

To create the banner, you are going to have to create a new text box at the top of this master page. First select the Text Box tool from the Tool palette. Next, at the point where your margin guides intersect at the top-left corner of the page, click and drag down and to the right to create the box. The actual size of the text box is unimportant, because you are going to modify it. After the new text box is drawn, use the Content tool and click on the new text box to show grab bars. Key Ctrl+M to get the Text Box Specifications dialog box for this text box. Change the size fields as shown in Figure 6.16. Click **OK**. This will give you two text boxes in the master page QR Cover.

FIGURE 6.16

The banner is set up through the Text Box Specifications dialog box.

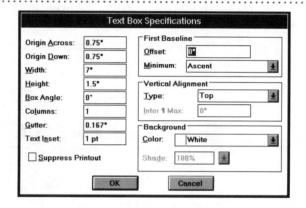

TIP

You can leap nimbly from field to field in a dialog box by using the Tab key.

Select the Content tool and click on your new text box. Key in the following: **QuickRelease** (see Figure 6.17). Then press Enter. On the next line, key in **Volume X, Number X**. Naturally, you will replace the X on each issue with the appropriate number.

Now change the type characteristics of the letters by highlighting the first line only (highlight QuickRelease). Select Style ➤ Character (or the keyboard equivalent, Ctrl+Shift+D). In the Character Attributes dialog box, make changes to reflect those in Figure 6.18.

Include not only the font, style, and size, but also the horizontal scale and tracking information. Click **OK** when the information is correct. Next highlight the second

FIGURE 6.17

Key in the text for your banner as shown here.

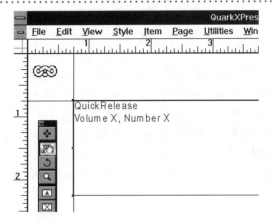

FIGURE 6.18

Key in specifications to match this illustration.

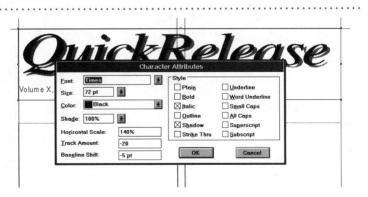

line of text, Volume X, Number X. Choose Style ➤ Character again, and change the settings as follows:

Font: Times Plain

Size: 12 pt

Horizontal Scale: 150%

Track Amount: 0

When you are finished, click **OK**.

NOTE

Your text may not look good on the screen if you lack the appropriate screen font sizes and styles installed. Adobe Type Manager may improve the screen quality. Use of TrueType fonts may even be better! Regardless of what your screen fonts look like, remember that screen quality is not what counts. Your product should print fine with the appropriate font and printer drivers.

Now you want to center both lines of text. To select both lines, simply use the short-cut Ctrl+A. Then choose Style ➤ Alignment ➤ Centered (or use its keyboard equivalent, Ctrl+Shift+C). The text should resemble that in Figure 6.19.

FIGURE 6.19
Once you've changed the typeface and size and centered the text, your document should look something like this.

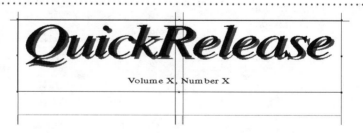

Finally, you will add a line to this master page that separates the banner from body copy. Use the Orthogonal Line tool. Click and drag to form a line. The length and location of your line are not critical at this point. You will position the line exactly, according to specifications.

NOTE

In this example, you are experiencing many new features of QuarkXPress. For this reason, you are asked to reposition items using Item ➤ Modify according to numerical specifications. Later in the book, you will have an opportunity to explore manual methods of item manipulation. For now, this is the quickest technique.

Use the Item tool and click on the new line to select it. Then choose Item ➤ Modify (Ctrl+M) and change the specifications as shown in Figure 6.20. Then press the Enter key to accept changes.

FIGURE 6.20
Modify the line according to specifications shown in this illustration.

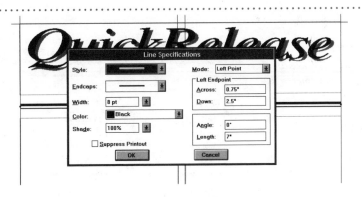

Ta da! You have created and edited your first master page.

EDITING THE QR BODY MASTER PAGE

Editing the Body Master Page will be much simpler. You have only to place a page number at the top center of the page. To begin, open the appropriate master page. There are two ways to accomplish this. You can choose Page ➤ Display ➤ QR Body option or double-click in the Document Layout palette on the QR Body (M2-Body) master page icon.

With the QR Body master page showing at Actual Size in the work area, click on the Text Box tool. Click and drag in the document work area to create a new text box. Highlight (click on) the box and choose Item ➤ Modify (Ctrl+M) to reach the Text Box Specifications dialog box. Change it according to the settings in Figure 6.21. Press the Enter key or click on **OK**.

Next, select the Content tool. Click on the new text box and note the flashing cursor. Key in an Automatic Box Page Number (Ctrl+3).

Now change the type characteristics by first highlighting the text in this new text box (click and drag over the text). Then go to Style ➤ Character. Change the text to Times, 8 point. Leave all other information in the default setting without changes. Click on **OK** to accept the changes.

FIGURE 6.21

*Modify the page number
text box to match these
Text Box Specifications.*

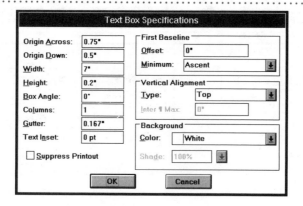

Finally, change alignment to centered. To do this, highlight the text (click and drag with the Content tool). Change alignment to Centered through the use of the keyboard shortcut Ctrl+Shift+C (or choose Style ➤ Alignment ➤ Centered). The second master page in your newsletter is now complete. The page number change on this master page should look like the example in Figure 6.22.

FIGURE 6.22

The automatic page number box, properly altered, on the body master page will allow all subsequent document pages made from this master to have sequential page numbers in the style and size prescribed.

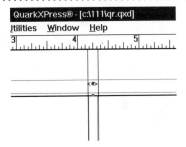

THE BACK PAGE OF YOUR NEWSLETTER

The back page of your newsletter also has its own master page. It will have a page number, identically placed and styled as in the body pages, but it will differ by including postal information. You have a few options when copying certain attributes from one master page to another. For example, you may want to just copy the specific text box from M2-Body to M3-End. This would involve opening each and doing a click, copy, and paste for each appropriate item. The way this example was started, this could be your best option. However, for the sake of creativity, here is another approach!

To begin, go back to the Document Layout palette where the master page icons are shown. Click on the M3-End master page icon to identify it. Now, select the Master ➤ Delete option (see Figure 6.23).

After deleting, you want to create a new master page M3-End through the Master ➤ Insert menu option. This time create your new M3 master page by using the M2-Body master page as your "mold" (see Figure 6.24).

FIGURE 6.23
*Delete the M3-End
master page.*

FIGURE 6.24
*Create a new M3-Master
page by using the M2-
Body master page as its
"mold." This allows all
characteristics of the M2-
Body to be on the new
M3-End Mailer.*

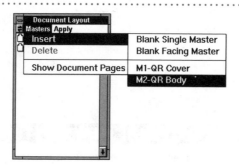

After you have successfully created the new master page, M3-Master Page, you
should rename it accordingly. Then double-click on its icon in the Document Layout palette. Showing at 100% size in the work area, you need to make a few modifications. Begin with modifying the large text box (for two column copy). Click on
the text box with the Content or Item Tool. Then, go to the Text Box Specifications
dialog box (Ctrl+M). Change the size and location of the box as follows:

 Origin Across: 0.75

 Origin Down: 0.75

 Width: 7; and Height: 4

Then click **OK**.

Select the Text Box tool from the Tool palette. Create a new text box and modify it according to Figure 6.25.

Change to the Content tool and click on the new text box. The cursor will show that you are ready to type. Key in the following address:

EM Bicycles, Inc.
1325 Pontiac Street
Detroit, MI 54236.

After each line, press Enter to go to the next line. Highlight all the text and choose Style ➤ Character. Change the font to Times, size 10 and leave other attributes alone. Click on **OK** to accept. Your copy should look like that in Figure 6.26.

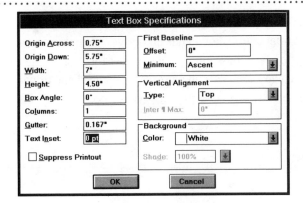

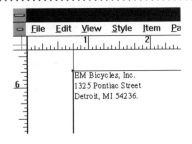

That's it! The master pages of this newsletter are complete. Of course you can't use them yet, because you have no document pages. Before you solve that problem, you should save. This is work you don't want to lose. Choose File ➤ Save and save it under the file name *QR_News* in the QuarkXPress directory. That way, it will reside in the same directory as your the document you created in *Chapter 1.*

PRINTING MASTER PAGES

NOTE

Although master pages do not normally print in the document, elements on master pages can print. You can print master page elements as displayed in the document window.

Master Pages normally do not print when you output the document; however, you can print information that is on a page. When the master page is displayed in the document window, most print controls are available through their appropriate dialog boxes. So as a final exercise, go ahead and print out your work if you wish, setting your particular printer specs as necessary.

P A R T

III

Word Processing

IMPORTING TEXT

To import text from a saved file 151

select the Content tool from the Tool palette, then click on a text box. Select File ➤ Import Text from the menu. Locate the file to import, then click on **OK** to accept.

To convert symbols and quotes while importing 153

check the Convert Quotes option in the dialog box. This changes such items as double hyphens (--) to the em dash (—), quotes from inch marks to curly typesetter's quotes, and so on.

To accept style sheets from imported text files 153

Use the option box called Include Style Sheets. Select File ➤ Get Text, check on the option box for Style Sheets. The appropriate style will import with the text, provided you have the proper XTension filter to allow it.

To use specific coding structures for type or document attributes 156

use XPress Tags. These are keyboard command codes that translate through ASCII text. You can use XPress tags in both imported text and exported text situations.

uarkXPress has an abundance of word processing capabilities. It allows you to import text from a wide variety of word processing software packages. If you choose, you can even use the built-in QuarkXPress word processor, obviating the need for an outside one. It has many of the functions you may be looking for in a dedicated word processor. Once you import or generate text, you can manipulate it with a wide array of features including kerning and tracking.

WORD PROCESSING IN QUARKXPRESS

Perhaps the easiest way to get text into QuarkXPress is to create it with a separate word processor and to import it. Importing and exporting word processed material is really almost transparent these days.

In a publishing environment, there is often a staff of quick-typing individuals who work at word processing stations. They may be working on WordPerfect or Microsoft Word or some equally efficient program. They may even be working on a different computer platform, such as a Macintosh- or Unix-based system. Today, it really doesn't matter. All you need to bring text in from a foreign application is a little cooperation and communication at the outset.

WHY OUTSIDE WORD PROCESSORS?

Why would anyone advocate using an outside word processor when the function is built into QuarkXPress? The answer is simple: Word processing should be left to the word processor! Although QuarkXPress has word processing features, it cannot compete in that arena with a full-fledged word processing program. Also, there are people highly skilled in those specialized programs. For highest productivity, the philosophy to follow is to leave specialty work to the specialists and let them use the tools they work with best.

NOTE

QuarkXPress has built-in translators for some word processors, while others can be purchased through outside vendors. All popular word processing packages are supported in some fashion, so you need not worry about migrating files into QuarkXPress.

HOW TO GET TEXT FROM OUTSIDE WORD PROCESSORS

One method of bringing text from an outside word processor starts with communicating your needs. Often, word processing applications today are on a Macintosh, DOS, or Windows platform. Most give you options on the formats you want to save in. For example, text for this book was written in a Windows-based word processor, WordPerfect 5.1. Available formats to save documents in the WordPerfect 5.1 menu include:

Ami Pro 1.2

Ami Pro 1.2a

Ami Pro 1.2b

ASCII Delimited Text (Windows)

ASCII Generic Word Processor (Windows)

ASCII Delimited Text (DOS)

ASCII Generic Word Processor (DOS)

ASCII Text (DOS)

Displaywrite 4.0

Displaywrite 4.2

Displaywrite 5.0

IBM DCA FFT

IBM DCA RFT

MS Word 4.0

MS Word 5.0

MS Word 5.5

MS Word for Windows 1.0

MS Word for Windows 1.1

MS Word for Windows 1.1a

MultiMate 3.3

MultiMate 3.6

MultiMate 4.0

MultiMate Advantage II (3.7)

OfficeWriter 6.0

OfficeWriter 6.1

OfficeWriter 6.11

OfficeWriter 6.2

RTF (Rich Text Format)

WordPerfect 4.2

WordPerfect 5.0

WordPerfect 5.1

WordStar 3.3

WordStar 3.31

WordStar 3.4

WordStar 4.0

WordStar 5.0

WordStar 5.5

WordStar 6.0

NOTE

ASCII is an acronym for American Standard Code for Information Interchange. It is an industry standard, text-only format. Quark XPress can import and save text in ASCII format.

NOTE

XTensions are prevalent in the Macintosh QuarkXPress environment. There are over 100 programs (XTensions) that you can add to QuarkXPress to gain further functionality. Many of these will be rewritten for the Windows QuarkXPress environment, in due time. At this writing, there are only a few, noted in Chapter 20.

Of course, all this means little if you can't import text, regardless of format, to the proper QuarkXPress document you want. Quark has its own set of translators that allow text to come in from certain word processors "transparent" to the user. That is, you do not have to manipulate or translate any coding from a word processing document to make the text usable in QuarkXPress. These filters in QuarkXPress are special add-on files called *XTensions.* These are generally loaded in when you install QuarkXPress; however, as the field of XTensions grows and more filters become available, you should be able to install them at any time. See Figure 7.1 for the initial list of QuarkXPress filters available at publication time.

CONNECTING TO THE MACINTOSH AND OTHER PLATFORMS

Although DOS translation software is serviceable, sometimes information is lost (or added) when converting to QuarkXPress. For those individuals who work daily in a multi-platform environment, the new version of Apple File Exchange for the Macintosh helps convert the file to an appropriate DOS format.

FIGURE 7.1

The QuarkXPress Environment information box lists all filters you have installed to translate from specific word processors. To get this, hold the Ctrl key while selecting About QuarkXPress from the Help menu.

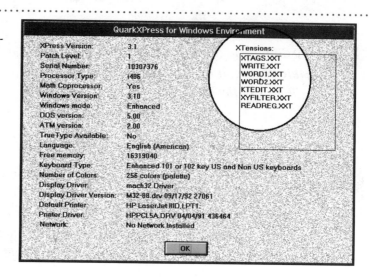

WARNING

One of the problems between moving information from one machine format to another is that of the physical connectivity. There are numerous solutions on the market for Mac/PC connectivity. The solution that may be easiest to work with is a combination of software application and sneaker net *(also known as* Shank's mare, *it means walking the file from one machine to another). To make this happen between platforms, you must first have the Mac read and write to a DOS format. The Apple File Exchange program (free with the operating system software) has the capacity for this, but you should check the manual for full instructions. The PC Does not yet have the capacity to read and write both DOS and Macintosh formats, so be careful how you connect your PC files with Mac files.*

Apple File Exchange is a translation utility that will take PC files and turn them into Mac files (and vice versa). It's fairly intuitive to use, and supports several common formats. For details on the Apple File Exchange, see your Macintosh documentation.

HOW TO IMPORT TEXT

If you can physically connect outside data to the Windows environment (e.g., network CD-ROM, SCSI drive, etc.), QuarkXPress can usually import any ASCII (text) files you want to use. This is the basic procedure.

1. Create a text box in your QuarkXPress document.

2. Select the Content tool from the Tool palette. (Hint: it's the second tool down; it resembles the I-beam/Hand combination.) It is important to select this tool, because you can import text only with the Content tool.

3. Click on the text box to select, or identify it. Remember, QuarkXPress has no idea where to place the text if you don't first identify the proper text box!

4. Choose File ➤ Get Text (see Figure 7.2). The Get Text option is available only when the Content tool is in use and a text box is active. If you identify a picture box with this tool, the option says Get Picture instead of Get Text. *Chapter 14* shows you how to deal with importing picture material.

NOTE

If you have enabled the automatic text box option when creating a new QuarkXPress document, a text box will show on the master page (within the margins). A text box of like size will also be on the first document page. In a text import situation, M1-master page has a linked text box. If the imported text takes up more room than there is in the text box, other pages will be added, and the text will automatically flow from one page to another. If the text box on the Master Page is not linked, you must do all this work manually. Thus, it may be best, until you gain more experience, to check the automatic text box option for importing text.

FIGURE 7.2

Use File ➤ Get Text to import a text file.

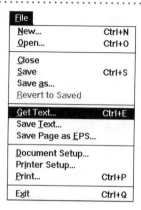

File	
New...	Ctrl+N
Open...	Ctrl+O
Close	
Save	Ctrl+S
Save as...	
Revert to Saved	
Get Text...	Ctrl+E
Save Text...	
Save Page as EPS...	
Document Setup...	
Printer Setup...	
Print...	Ctrl+P
Exit	Ctrl+Q

5. Once you select Get Text, a dialog box appears (see Figure 7.3). The Get Text dialog box should be familiar to experienced Windows users. It resembles the "open file" style of dialog box. You can look anywhere on any connected floppy disk, hard drive, or network drive that you have access to.

FIGURE 7.3

The Get Text dialog box enables you to search from among several drives or network connections to find the file you wish to import. Note also, the various file formats you can select to import!

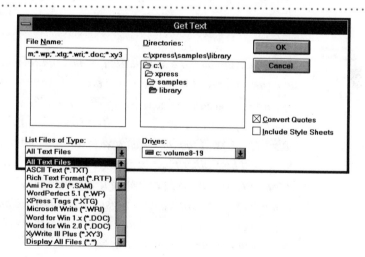

6. Once you have found the proper file to import, click on **OK** and the file imports in your designated text box.

NOTE

Some graphic representations in this book have been altered in an attempt to enhance various concepts and may not look as originally presented in QuarkXPress.

CONVERTING SYMBOLS AND QUOTES IN QUARKXPRESS

QuarkXPress gives you the option of using traditional word processing quotes ("") or the more stylized typesetting quotes (""). Typesetting quotes are different (they look like a *66* and a *99*), while word processing quotes look the same on both ends (they look like hash marks). Conversion also works on double hyphens and single quotation symbols.

To import text and automatically convert double hyphens (--) to the typographer's equivalent, the em dash (—), as well as converting foot (') and inch (") marks to apostrophes (') and typesetter's quotes (") , check the Convert Quotes option. If you do not want to convert these symbols, leave the option box unchecked.

STYLE SHEETS OF IMPORTED TEXT

In the Get Text dialog box (File ➤ Get Text or Ctrl+E), there is an option box called Include Style Sheets. This specifically works at this time only with Microsoft Word, but will no doubt include other file formats, as needed. To include the imported document's style sheet, check the Include Style Sheets option prior to import.

OTHER INFORMATION IN THE GET TEXT DIALOG BOX

Once you begin the process of import, you may find a new dialog screen appear (see Figure 7.4). QuarkXPress analyzes the file coming in to match all pertinent attributes and tells you if there is incongruence. In most cases, this is not a problem, you simply must make further alterations once the text is imported to your QuarkXPress text box.

WARNING

Be aware of the file size when importing. Although you can have up to 2000 document pages in QuarkXPress, it may be easier to work in smaller chunks. Consider breaking large word processing files down into manageable sized chunks, and then import them as necessary. That is, unless you have taken steps to install a gigabyte of RAM memory! As a Windows user, you know how frustrating it is to suddenly run out of memory. Working with enormous documents is likely to cause this problem and therefore is not advised.

TIP

To format imported ASCII text, specify attributes and paragraph formats at the text insertion point before you bring in the text. Otherwise, establish these in style sheets to apply later.

When you import a file, the original file remains untouched. Only a copy of the text imports from the original file. Once the copy imports, there is no need for the original text file disk or network connection. This is not a tagged file, but rather it is an actual duplication of each character of the primary text file.

FIGURE 7.4

A dialog box may appear upon importing a file if it contains certain attributes you have not established in your main QuarkXPress document.

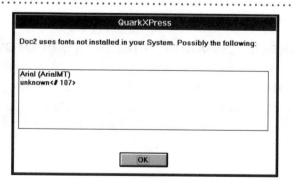

WARNING

If you use a data compression program, particularly one that renames the file, QuarkXPress may not recognize it as a text file, in which case it will not import it. You should first decompress the file and store it where accessible.

Once the Get Text dialog box is acceptable, click **Open**. After a pause, the text will stream from the host file into your text box. More pages and text boxes will form as needed if you have the automatic linking capability on. If you are importing text to a non-linked text box the text will flow to fill the box. Only text that will fit in the text box will show. The remaining text will not show until you extend the text box. A symbol representing *more text* will show at the bottom-right corner of the text box if more text is available than is currently showing.

WARNING

Often, in the process of creating a new document and importing text, it is common to omit a crucial step. You must save the document. This is a time-saving step, particularly if you work with large text blocks.

After the text imports, you can make changes in the QuarkXPress document. *Chapter 8* explores text formatting and other manipulation techniques.

WHAT IF YOUR WORD PROCESSED TEXT IS NOT PLAIN TEXT?

If the word processed document is not ASCII text, there are alternatives. As noted earlier, QuarkXPress comes with filters for certain popular word processors (see Figure 7.1.). Some of these file filters you may never need, others only occasionally. Strictly from a performance/economy point of view, you are recommended to place these filters in a separate subdirectory, outside of the QuarkXPress directory, if not needed. This will improve the performance of your QuarkXPress application if it doesn't waste time on files and filters unnecessarily.

As QuarkXPress 3.1 for Windows receives wider distribution in the months to come, the XTension developers will write add-on programs, including filters for the application. You may find there are more XTensions than you need at any given time. Consider getting an XTension controller program. This is an XTension that helps control the activity of other XTensions. Proper care of these auxiliary programs will enable you to fly through QuarkXPress without unnecessary system crashes. One of the main reasons for a system crash has to do with placing too much stress on the RAM (rapid access memory). When you load QuarkXPress and all its associated filters, files, etc. in the system, you place an unnecessary burden here. To be efficient, the capability of turning on or off an XTension load can be quite helpful. For example, if you are currently working with QuarkXPress and not importing any MS Word files, why take up RAM with the MS Word XTension for file translation? If you had an XTension manager, you could simply toggle this not to load. Without it, the best thing to do is go to your QuarkXPress directory and move all unnecessary files to an outside directory so that they will not take up memory when QuarkXPress launches. By the way, if you have recurring crashes, you probably are running Windows 3.0 or a using a CPU less than the 486DX! Upgrading will also help correct your problems.

XPRESS TAGS

XPress Tags are keyboard command codes for certain operations that transfer through ASCII text. You can use XPress Tags in imported text as well as in text you intend to export from QuarkXPress. XPress Tags' codes may come from an outside word processing system or text to import to QuarkXPress (see Figure 7.5).

NOTE

WYSIWYG *is an acronym for* what you see is what you get. *It more appropriately should be* WYSIWYHF: what you see is what you hope for!

FIGURE 7.5

An example of XPress tags as given in the tutorial disk, file c:\xpress\samples\text\xprstags.xtg

```
<v3.10><e1>
@DropCapParagraphStyle=[S]<*L*h"Standard"*kn0*kt0*ra0*rb0*d(1,3)*p(0,0,0,0,0,
0,g,"")*t(0,0," "):
Ps100t0h100z12k0b0c"Black"f"Times">
@BodyCopyStyle=[S]<*L*h"Standard"*kn0*kt0*ra0*rb0*d0*p(0,12,0,0,0,0,g,"")*t(0
,0," "):
Ps100t0h100z12k0b0c"Black"f"Times">
@FloatingSubStyle=[S]<*L*h"Standard"*kn0*kt0*ra(24,0,"Blue",100,T0,0,-
4.97)*rb0*d0*p(0,0,0,0,12,0,g,"")*t(12,0," ",93,0," ",0,0," "):
PBs50t0h100z18k0b0c"Yellow"f"Times">
@DropCapParagraphStyle:Si meliora dies, ut vina, poemata reddit, scire velim,
chartis pretium quotus arroget annus. scriptor abhinc annos centum qui decid-
it, inter perfectos veteresque referri debet an inter vilis atque novos?
Excludat iurgia finis, "Est vetus atque probus, centum qui perficit annos."
Quid, qui deperiit minor uno mense vel anno, inter quos referendus erit?
Veteresne poetas, an quos et praesens et postera respuat aetas?
@BodyCopyStyle:"Iste quidem veteres inter ponetur honeste, qui vel mense
brevi vel toto est iunior anno." Utor permisso, caudaeque pilos ut equinae
paulatim vello unum, demo etiam unum, dum cadat elusus ratione ruentis
acervi, qui redit in fastos et virtutem aestimat annis miraturque nihil nisi
quod Libitina sacravit.
Ennius et sapines et fortis et alter Homerus, ut critici dicunt, leviter
curare videtur, quo promissa cadant et somnia Pythagorea. Naevius in manibus
non est et mentibus haeret paene recens? Adeo sanctum est vetus omne poema.
ambigitur quotiens, uter utro sit prior, aufert Pacuvius docti famam senis
Accius alti, dicitur Afrani toga convenisse Menandro, Plautus ad exemplar
Siculi properare Epicharmi, vincere Caecilius gravitate, Terentius arte.
@FloatingSubStyle:        Subhead
@BodyCopyStyle:Hos ediscit et hos arto stipata theatro spectat Roma potens;
```

These tagged coding structures are probably not for the beginner or intermediate user of QuarkXPress, due to their structure. In essence, they are a throw-back to earlier days of computing when we had to insert command codes in text for such items as font, type size, style, alignment, etc.

If you are a nostalgic person, or work for a company that changes at the speed of most glaciers, XPress Tags may be for you. For the rest of the Desktop Publishing revolution, WYSIWYG is what we strive for!

CONVERTING XPRESS TAGS

To convert XPress Tag codes, check Include Style Sheets in the Get Text dialog box (Ctrl+E). If unchecked, tags do not convert; they display in the imported text. This can make a big difference in bringing in outside keystrokes. For example, if you were to use style sheets in MS Word, they would include information such as font, style, size, etc., all pertinent material for the publication. If you do not import this, all these details will have to be restructured once the text is imported in QuarkX-Press. Also, you may have additional coding structures to delete after import.

NOTE

The Get Text dialog box lists only ASCII files and files from word processing programs for which an import/export filter is available. QuarkXPress filters must be stored in the QuarkXPress directory or the system directory. If you need a particular text format filter, store it properly before you launch QuarkXPress.

XPRESS TAGS IN EXPORTING TEXT

If you wish to use the XPress Tags capability in exporting text from QuarkXPress, insert specific codes in your text structures. These codes are similar to what some word processors call style sheets. To export selected text, include the .XTG format (see Figure 7.6). Quark has taken a proprietary naming of them in the QuarkX-Press program: XPress Tags. Perhaps this is due to their already using the *style sheets* nameplate in another area, (Edit ➤ Style Sheets).

TIP

To Export all the text contained in a text box or a chain of linked text boxes, activate the text box by clicking on it. Then select File ➤ Save Text. To save and export a selected range of text, highlight that range of text only, then export. Although the export feature is available in QuarkXPress, it is not known to be applied widely throughout the QuarkXPress user community. This is due to the growing number of XTension programs available from third-party developers. In most cases, you can perform every manipulative function to text either before it is imported to QuarkXPress or through XTensions. See Chapter 20 for more information on XTensions.

FIGURE 7.6
Use the .XTG format option, when saving, to use XPress Tags.

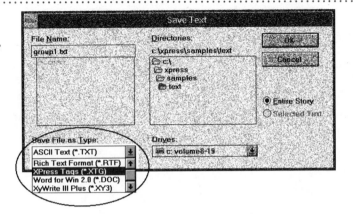

You can automatically insert specific style codes when you save text with Quark-XPress. Save the text as XPress Tags and the ASCII file you create will contain all embedded style tag codes. You can also exchange XPress tagged text with any program that supports this format.

Text Formatting

To change the font of selected (highlighted) text   165

choose from any of three basic techniques. You can use the font selection option in the Measurements palette, select the font choice from Style ➤ Font, or from the Style ➤ Character dialog box.

To change the size of selected (highlighted) text   165

choose from any of three basic techniques. You can use the size selection option in the Measurements palette, select the size choice from Style ➤ Size or from the Style ➤ Character dialog box. You may select a size not listed by keying in your own size in the appropriate location.

To adjust the type style of a section of text   168

highlight it with the Content tool. Then select Style ➤ Type Style.

To color highlighted text   169

select the Style ➤ Color option. This allows you to choose from a color palette of current colors available in the system. To add colors, select the menu options Edit ➤ Colors to edit or add a color on the system palette.

To alter the character's horizontal scale   170

select the text in the usual manner (click and drag over the wanted characters). After the text is selected for alteration, choose Style ➤ Horizontal Scale from the menu. This will give you a dialog box in which you key in your desired percentage of text stretch or condense. You may also use the horizontal scale feature on the Measurements palette.

To alter tracking for a particular group of characters in your text   171

highlight the characters to track. Select the menu option Style ➤ Tracking. A dialog box appears enabling you to select the value desired. Use either a positive or negative value, for more or less space, as suitable. You may also use the tracking scale feature on the Measurements palette.

To alter several attributes of text in one dialog box   175

first, highlight the characters for change, then go to the Character Attributes dialog box (Style ➤ Characters).

An essential part of word processing today is the ability to assign your text a proper font, size, style, etc. This chapter introduces you to the QuarkXPress feature directly dealing with these type attributes, the Style menu.

TEXT FORMATTING AND THE STYLE MENU

The Style Menu has three different appearances. It looks one way when using it for text boxes, another when adjusting style for the picture boxes, and yet another when editing style for a line item (see Figure 8.1). The focus in this chapter is to see how the Style menu works for text boxes.

TIP

As you read along, you will note a recurring theme. Whenever you want to change text, you must use the Content tool to highlight it. Only then can you alter it.

FIGURE 8.1

The Style menu changes, depending upon what kind of item you've selected. Here are the Style menu listings for the three item groups: text boxes, picture boxes, and lines.

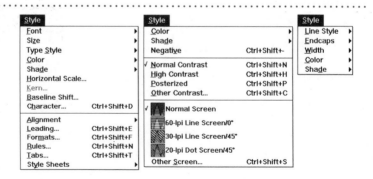

NOTE

Several of the options listed under the Style menu are also accessible through the Measurement palette and keyboard equivalents. If frequent changes are necessary, it may be a good idea to keep the Measurement palette in the document work area all the time. To change Measurement palette data, highlight and overstrike. Overstriking replaces the old measurement or name with the new one. When finished with your changes, press Enter. Specific keyboard shortcuts are listed in this chapter as well as on the inside front cover of this book.

The Style menu is accessible only if you are using the Content or Item tool. Also, you can use Style only if you have highlighted an item. Remember, you can tell an item is highlighted by the familiar black grab boxes.

THE FONT OPTION

The Font option allows you to select from a variety of typefaces. You must have each typeface resident in your system directory to select it. If you don't have a particular font in your system directory, you will not find it on the Font submenu.

To change the font of an entire section of text, click and drag to highlight the text you want to change (it can be a letter, word, phrase, or even the entire document), then select a new typeface from the Style ➤ Font menu. Once you have selected the typeface with the cursor, release the mouse button. The highlighted text changes to the new typeface.

THE SIZE OPTION

The size option allows you to select from a list of type sizes. You must identify the text to be resized through highlighting. Then select Style ➤ Size. The size menu consists of several type sizes, measured numerically in points (a printer's measurement system based on the days of hot lead typesetting—a point is $\frac{1}{72}''$). The point sizes listed represent the minimum number of sizes from which to quickly choose. Actually, in most cases, you have a much larger assortment of sizes to deal with, especially if you are using the PostScript fonts with Adobe's Type Manager, or TrueType fonts. At times you may have a specific bitmap font (BMP) loaded for use in your system. These BMP fonts were designed to print on the dot matrix printers, while performing an adequate job of rendition on the screen. Today, most of these have been overshadowed by the higher quality fonts for laser output. Windows affords you a wide variety of fonts to deal with, including PCL, PostScript, and TrueType fonts. You will have to deal with the proper font system to use in your Windows environment, based on your hardware configuration.

As for QuarkXPress, a few basic strategies to follow will keep you out of trouble and into quality page layout. First, if you are going to use any of Adobe's PostScript fonts (or their clones from the competition), it is probably best to install a copy of Adobe Type Manager (ATM). This is a separate software application, not affiliated with QuarkXPress (see Figure 8.2). Its function is to make the bitmap version of the PostScript font looking better on the screen, while improving quality for the raster image type character when it gets printed. Keep up to date with this, also, as new software is not always compatible with older versions of ATM.

Another alternative is to use TrueType fonts. Unlike PostScript fonts that have a separate font for the screen and another accompanying font for the printer, TrueType is a one-stop source for high quality typography. TrueType is a new type format developed

FIGURE 8.2

Use of ATM is almost a necessity for those Post-Script fonts you want high quality from in the document.

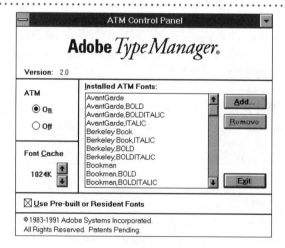

by Apple and licensed to Microsoft for use in Windows 3.1. If you have Windows 3.0, you probably will not be able to take advantage of TrueType. It's time to upgrade anyway!

WARNING

At the time of this writing, TrueType fonts are not interchangeable from Mac to DOS/Windows formats without the use of some third-party conversion. Since many of you may be in a cross-platform environment, this knowledge could save you a little time and agony.

The concept behind TrueType is that you have one font (file) for a specific type, including all sizes, styles, and variations of the font. To install, you just install the one font, under the Fonts Control Panel option in Windows. No ATM, no conversion, nothing else required! It is clean and simple. This enables you to place and view any appropriate size and variation of that font to work well on the screen and print well on your laser printer.

NOTE

For efficiency and speed of operation, try to avoid duplicating fonts in multiple formats. For example, if you use Courier frequently, as we all do, it may be a waste of resources to have it loaded in both the PostScript and the TrueType formats for QuarkXPress.

From the point of view of a Windows user, you should consider stocking up on TrueType fonts. It is the cleanest solution to the font problem yet. Don't throw away those bitmap and PostScript fonts, though, because some programs still are a bit cantankerous when it comes to TrueType. A few of the word processing programs in particular have trouble with TrueType. Regardless of how it looks on the screen, the printed version of the font probably looks better than that on the monitor. This is an adjustment that several of the typeface manufacturers are working on.

NOTE

TrueType fonts work well with QuarkXPress 3.1 and you may want to consider a total changeover, depending on your current library of PostScript fonts. So that other font formats won't be wasted, font editing programs such as FontMonger may help you convert existing fonts to TrueType fonts.

USING OTHER SIZES

If you want a size not listed, select the option Other (Ctrl+Shift+\). Selecting Other allows you to key the size you need, exactly! QuarkXPress allows you to select sizes ranging from 2 to 720 points. Not only that, you can select type sizes in increments as small as 0.001 of any measurement unit. That is, you can use points, inches, metric, and so on; any measurement system you have chosen in QuarkXPress can also apply to type sizes. Remember, odd sizes may not look good on the screen, but they should look fine when printed.

CHANGING FONT SIZES WITH THE KEYBOARD

It was noted earlier that you can change type sizes with the menu as well as through the Measurement palette. One additional technique you should be aware of is keyboard shortcuts. To increase the type size through a range of preset sizes (from 7 to 192 points), press Ctrl+Shift+>. To decrease the size through this same fixed range, press Ctrl+Shift+<.

To increase size in one point increments from 2 to 720 points (the total range), press Ctrl+Shift+Alt+>. To decrease in one point increments, press Ctrl+Shift+Alt+<.

THE TYPE STYLE OPTION

Again, if you are somewhat familiar with other Windows 3.1 programs you will understand the notion of changing the style or "look" of type. The Type Style option (Style ➤ Type Style) determines if the type will look outlined or plain, underlined, or strikethrough, etc.

NOTE

You can combine several options from the Type Style menu (e.g., Helvetica Bold Outline type).

To adjust the type style of a section of text, highlight it with the Content tool. Then select Style ➤ Type Style. There are several ways you can change the highlighted text. Slide the mouse cursor down to highlight a choice or use the keyboard short-cut (the shortcuts are listed on the menu to the right of each format). If you choose to use the keyboard equivalent, simply highlight the text and key in the appropriate key combinations for the change you want to make. For example to change the highlighted text to italics, press Ctrl+Shift+I. Figure 8.3 shows the Type Style submenu with all the keyboard shortcuts.

THE COLOR OPTION

To color the text of your choice, again select the Content tool. Highlight the text to apply color to. Then select the Style ➤ Color option. This allows you to choose from a color palette. To add or augment colors see *Chapter 17*.

THE SHADE OPTION

In addition to the other stylistic options, you can shade type. This means you are adding some kind of backscreen to the text box. To shade text, select the Content

FIGURE 8.3

All styles on the Type Style submenu have handy keyboard equivalents.

Style		
Font	▶	
Size	▶	
Type Style	√ Plain	Ctrl+Shift+P
Color	Bold	Ctrl+Shift+B
Shade	Italic	Ctrl+Shift+I
Horizontal Scale...	Underline	Ctrl+Shift+U
Kern...	Word Underline	Ctrl+Shift+W
Baseline Shift...	Strike Thru	Ctrl+Shift+/
Character... Ctrl+Shift+D	Outline	Ctrl+Shift+O
	Shadow	Ctrl+Shift+S
Alignment	ALL CAPS	Ctrl+Shift+K
Leading... Ctrl+Shift+E	Small Caps	Ctrl+Shift+H
Formats... Ctrl+Shift+F	Superscript	Ctrl+Shift+0
Rules... Ctrl+Shift+N	Subscript	Ctrl+Shift+9
Tabs... Ctrl+Shift+T	Superior	Ctrl+Shift+V
Style Sheets		

tool, highlight the text to change, and select Style ➤ Shade. This option gives you percentages of color or shade. If your text is black, it gives you percentages of black in grayscale. The scale is 0–100 percent in ten-percent increments (see Figure 8.4). Like the Size submenu, there is an Other option. Selecting this allows you to key in the exact percentage of shade desired. You can select from 0 to 100 percent in 0.1 percent increments. Once you have keyed in the size you want, click on the **OK** button.

THE HORIZONTAL SCALE OPTION

This option allows you to expand or condense the width of type. The original width of the type is a default of 100 percent. To use the Horizontal Scale option you first get the Content tool and select the text. Then select Style ➤ Horizontal Scale and a dialog box appears. The number is already in percentage, so there is no need to key in the percent sign.

A number less than 100 compresses the width of the type. Some typographers call this the *set width*. A number greater than 100 expands the width of the type design. This does not alter type height and size. The increment may range from 25 to 400 percent, in increments as small as one percent (see Figure 8.5).

FIGURE 8.4

The Shade submenu

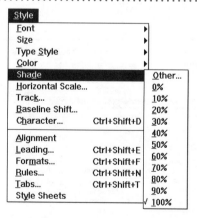

FIGURE 8.5

These examples show a line of type whose set width has been changed with Style ➤ Horizontal Scale to 100%, 200%, and 70%.

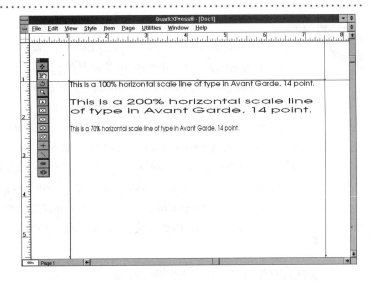

KERNING, LETTERSPACING, AND TRACKING

One of the capabilities that electronic publishing programs have, that few word processors provide, is the ability to *kern*. Kerning means adding or taking space from between two characters. This improves the appearance of type character combinations. When multiple characters or words are spaced, the proper name for it is tracking. This material is covered in greater detail in *Chapter 12*.

KERNING OPTIONS

To change the space between two characters, anchor the cursor between those two. With the cursor flashing, select Style ➤ Kern. A numerical dialog box appears allowing you to input a number from −500 to 500. The measurement unit for this manual kerning is 0.005, or $\frac{1}{200}$, em space. The default is zero. A negative value decreases the distance between two characters, while a positive number increases the distance.

NOTE

Normally, an em space (em) is a square the size of the point size. This is a relative term, meaning that if the point size is 10 points, its em would be a nonprinting space 10 points wide by 10 points tall. If the point size were 12, the em would be 12 by 12, and so on. (The em comes from hot lead type, where it was used as a nonprinting, spacing unit. Typesetters used it in combination with other nonprinting spacing units for alignment and indentation purposes). QuarkXPress adds a new definition to the em space. It defines the em as the width of two zeros in the current font. This sounds rather computer-programmer like, doesn't it?

KERNING WITH THE KEYBOARD

To use the keyboard for kerning purposes, anchor the cursor between the two characters of choice. To increase space in increments of 0.05 ems, press Ctrl+Shift+]. To increase letterspacing in increments of 0.005 ems, press Ctrl+Alt+Shift+]. To reduce space between characters, key Ctrl+Shift+[for increments of 0.05 ems or Ctrl+Alt+Shift+[for increments of 0.005 ems.

MAKING SPACE ADJUSTMENTS IN THE MEASUREMENT PALETTE

To adjust spacing with the measurement palette, press either of the kerning arrows in the palette (see Figure 8.6). This will increase or decrease space between two characters in increments of 0.05 ems. To adjust in increments of 0.005 ems, hold down the Alt key while clicking on the kerning arrows.

FIGURE 8.6
You can kern (or letter-space) directly from the Measurement palette by clicking on the kerning arrows (fourth box from left).

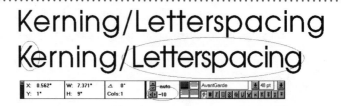

The Measurement palette method of kerning is wonderful because you can see the text as changes occur. Also, it is quicker for repetitive changes than bringing down a dialog box from the menu.

TRACKING

Tracking takes advantage of all the techniques outlined for kerning. The primary difference between kerning and tracking is that in tracking you must highlight the group of characters to change. In kerning, simply positioning the cursor between two characters is sufficient to identify the location.

NOTE

Kerning and tracking occupy the same slot in the Style menu, but when you highlight a group of characters or lines (as opposed to simply placing the cursor), the option changes from Kern to Track.

Highlight a group of characters using the Content tool and then select Style ➤ Track. If no groups of characters are highlighted, the Kern option shows (see Figure 8.7).

FIGURE 8.7

The Style menu option changes from Kern to Track depending on your needs.

Style	
Font	▶
Size	▶
Type Style	▶
Color	▶
Shade	▶
Horizontal Scale...	
Kern...	
Baseline Shift...	
Character...	Ctrl+Shift+D
Alignment	▶
Leading...	Ctrl+Shift+E
Formats...	Ctrl+Shift+F
Rules...	Ctrl+Shift+N
Tabs...	Ctrl+Shift+T
Style Sheets	▶

Style	
Font	▶
Size	▶
Type Style	▶
Color	▶
Shade	▶
Horizontal Scale...	
√ Track...	
Baseline Shift...	
Character...	Ctrl+Shift+D
Alignment	▶
Leading...	Ctrl+Shift+E
Formats...	Ctrl+Shift+F
Rules...	Ctrl+Shift+N
Tabs...	Ctrl+Shift+T
Style Sheets	▶

OTHER OPTIONS

Kerning and Tracking options go far beyond manual adjustments mentioned here. You have automatic adjustments, kerned pairs, etc. See *Chapter 12* for more details on customizing the kerning capability in QuarkXPress.

THE BASELINE SHIFT OPTION

The bottoms of most type characters rest upon an imaginary line known as the *baseline*. QuarkXPress has a feature that allows you to raise or lower type characters from their original baseline (see Figure 8.8).

FIGURE 8.8

*An example of a
baseline shift*

WARNING

Even when you use baseline shift on a line, the line still "remembers" its original baseline. This may cause confusion on your part if you must highlight the text again for another action. The text's new and old locations highlight together.

NOTE

Just a brief reminder: there are 72 points in one inch; 6 picas in one inch; 12 points in one pica.

To implement a baseline shift, highlight the character or group of characters you want to move from the baseline. Then select Style ➤ Baseline Shift. This will bring up the Character Attributes dialog box. Enter a number in the Baseline Shift field. A positive number represents the number of points you want the highlighted character(s) to rise above the baseline. A negative number moves the characters below the baseline.

EFFECTING A BASELINE SHIFT WITH THE KEYBOARD

From a production point of view, anything you can do from the keyboard without having to go to the menu is often faster. In the case of the Baseline Shift command, you can use a keyboard shortcut without using the menu options. To use the keyboard shortcuts, highlight the characters of choice again, then press Ctrl+Alt+Shift+plus (+) to move the text above the baseline in one point increments. Press Ctrl+Alt+Shift+hyphen to move the text below the baseline in one point increments.

THE CHARACTER OPTION

The Style ➤ Character selection opens a dialog box that contains a combination of most of the previously listed options (see Figure 8.9). You can directly access all the preceding list of Style options from this one dialog box (keyboard shortcut: Ctrl+Shift+D).

NOTE

You will probably find yourself using the Character Attribute option more than any other style option simply because it is like one-stop shopping. You can change everything in that one box and change multiple attributes simultaneously.

FIGURE 8.9

You can access most style commands from the Character Attributes dialog box.

Character Attributes	
Font: AvantGarde	Style
Size: 36 pt	☒ Plain ☐ Underline
Color: Black	☐ Bold ☐ Word Underline
Shade: 100%	☐ Italic ☐ Small Caps
Horizontal Scale: 100%	☐ Outline ☐ All Caps
Kern Amount: 0	☐ Shadow ☐ Superscript
Baseline Shift: 0 pt	☐ Strike Thru ☐ Subscript
	OK Cancel

MANIPULATING TYPE THROUGH THE STYLE MENU

Often, in processing words with a desktop publishing application, you have to make the decision how to align paragraph lines. This alignment takes the form of horizontal, left to right, and, today, you can even align vertically throughout the column. QuarkXPress has the ability to align in both horizontal and vertical directions.

ALIGNING TEXT WITHIN A TEXT BOX

Alignment refers to how the text sits within the text box. There are four options in alignment; Left (ragged right), Right (ragged left), Centered, and Justified (see Figure 8.10).

The default for alignment is flush left, at least in the United States version of QuarkXPress. To enforce a different alignment, activate the text box. Without further identification, the alignment change will affect all paragraphs in this indicated text box. If you want only an isolated paragraph to change, position the cursor within that paragraph. With the paragraph selected, choose Style ➤ Alignment and

FIGURE 8.10

You have four horizontal alignment options for text. Note, also, that you can change alignment through the Measurements palette icons.

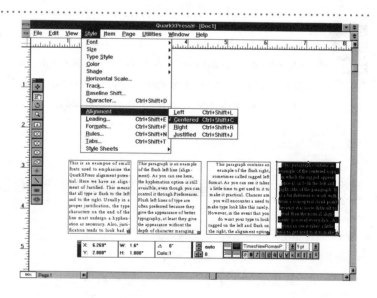

your selection, or use the keyboard equivalent. You can also make the change from the Measurement palette by selecting the appropriate icon.

Again, from a production standpoint, you will find yourself using the keyboard equivalent or measurement palette methods more often than the menu option. The keyboard shortcuts are listed next to the alignment options on the menu.

WHAT EXACTLY IS JUSTIFICATION?

Justification is a complex process whereby the computer decides how many characters will fit on a line. Of these words, perhaps the last word can hyphenate. Anyhow, a certain amount of extra (noncharacter space) remains. With justification, the extra space is distributed throughout the line, first between words, then between characters. If properly distributed, the text appears flush left and flush right (justified). If you choose Left (ragged right), all extra space is added at the end of the line, moving type left. In Flush Right, all extra space is added at the beginning of the line, moving the type to the right. With centered text, the space is evenly distributed on both sides of the line. Often the Left, Right, and Centered options have no hyphenated words. The Justified option requires hyphenation to work best. That is why hyphenation and justification together are known as H & J.

VERTICAL ALIGNMENT

QuarkXPress has an option that allows vertical alignment or justification of paragraphs. This is a handy option to use when placing text in constant columns such as in a magazine publication, book or newsletter. It seems that no matter how you try there are always that last remaining three or four points of space that have to be dealt with in some way. We used to take an X-ACTO knife to solve the problem. Now, with QuarkXPress 3.1, you can simply set up a vertical justification and the lines will spread as necessary to fill your allotted column depth. To use this capability, select the text box to align (click on the box with the Content tool). Next choose Item ➤ Modify. The Text Box Specifications dialog box appears (see Figure 8.11).

FIGURE 8.11

You can specify the vertical alignment of paragraphs in the Text Box Specifications dialog box.

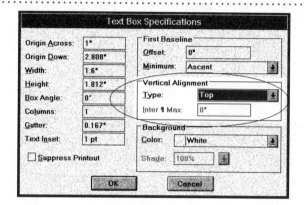

From the Vertical Alignment Type menu, select Top, Centered, Bottom, or Justified. If you select Justified, enter the maximum amount of space between paragraphs that you wish to allow in the Inter ¶ Max field. A number of zero distributes the space between lines and paragraphs evenly. The process is somewhat similar to that just described in Justification above. Only this time, a finite number of lines will fit within a specific text box height. The last fraction of a line distributes according to the setup.

Spelling and Dictionaries

FAST

To check the spelling of a single word   182

highlight the word or place the text insertion bar (I-beam cursor) within or immediately to the right of that word. Then select Utilities ➤ Check Spelling ➤ Word.

To replace a word   182

click on the desired replacement word and click on the Replace button. Another technique is to double-click on the replacement word.

To check the spelling of a story   183

activate the text box (click on it with the Content or Item tool). Then select Utilities ➤ Check Spelling ➤ Story.

TRACKS

ny desktop publishing program worth purchasing has a spell-checking diction-ary of some type built in. What differentiates QuarkXPress from other layout packages is the depth of its spell-check capabilities and the capacity of its diction-aries. Even though we suggested you use an outside word processor, QuarkXPress does a handy job internally, especially when it comes to making sure you spell right!

SPELLING OPTIONS

QuarkXPress allows you to check the spelling of a single word, of an active story, of the entire document, or of the text on master pages. A copy of the file Xpress Dictionary must be located either in the QuarkXPress directory or the System directory.

CHECKING THE SPELLING OF A SINGLE WORD

To check the spelling of a single word, highlight the word or place the text inser-tion bar (I-beam cursor) within or immediately to the right of that word. Select Utilities ➤ Check Spelling ➤ Word (see Figure 9.1). If the word is not in the Xpress Dictionary or other open auxiliary dictionaries, the Check Word dialog box appears (see Figure 9.2).

Here, you have the option of selecting a replacement word or of canceling the operation and returning to the document. To replace a word, click on the desired replacement word and click on the Replace button. Another technique is to double-click on the replacement word. Once you select the replacement, it takes the place of the misspelled word in your document and the dialog box closes. The spell-checking sequence is complete.

FIGURE 9.1

The Check Spelling menu options

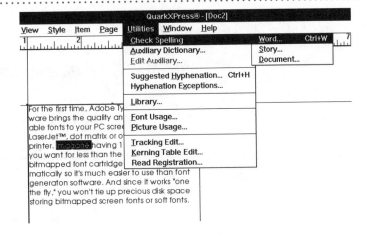

FIGURE 9.2

The Check Word dialog box first enables you to analyze the proper spelling of an individual word.

CHECKING A STORY

To check the spelling in a *story*, activate the text box (click on it with the Content or Item tool). Then select Utilities ➤ Check Spelling ➤ Story. First a Word Count dialog appears (see Figure 9.3). The Word Count dialog box displays three fields of information, Total, Unique, and Suspect.

NOTE

QuarkXPress understands a story *to be all text within a single text box or in a chain of linked text boxes.*

FIGURE 9.3

*The Word Count
dialog box*

For the first time, Adobe Type Manager software brings the quality and versitility of scalable fonts to your PC screen and your
LaserJet™, dot matrix or other non-PostScript®
printer. Imagane having 13 fonts in any size
you want for less than the cost
bitmapped font cartridge. ATM
matically so it's much easier to
generaton software. And since
the fly," you won't tie up precio
storing bitmapped screen font

Word Count

Total:	82
Unique:	61
Suspect:	5

OK

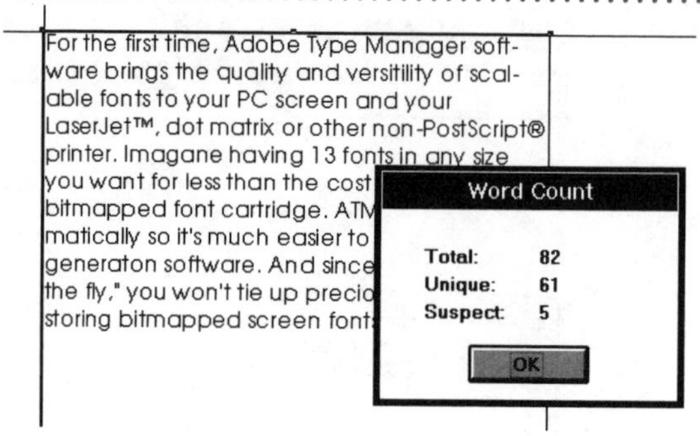

Total is the total number of words checked. Unique represents the number of unique words identified, as opposed to repetitions of words. Suspect represents the number of words not in the Xpress Dictionary or in any open auxiliary dictionary.

If no words are identified as possibly misspelled, displays in the Suspect Word field of the Word Count dialog box. Press Enter or click on **OK** to return to the document.

If anything other than 0 appears, when you click **OK** the Check Story dialog box displays. This acts very much like the Check Word dialog box in the way you select replacement words. The difference is that in the story there may be more than one word to check. If so, after each word, the checker goes to the next word in question. You then must decide its replacement, and so on. Eventually, after all suspect words of the story are replaced or passed, the process ends and you are taken back to the text.

The Check Story dialog box also includes a Replace With field. This enables you to key in a new word for replacement. It also includes three buttons called Lookup, Skip, and Keep (see Figure 9.4).

FIGURE 9.4

The Check Story or Check Document spell check option brings up a dialog box if any words are questionable.

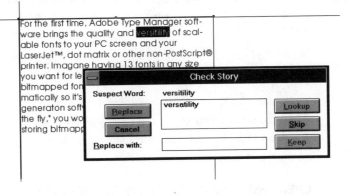

NOTE

You can add to Auxiliary Dictionaries; you may not, however, alter the Xpress Dictionary. There are 120,000 words contained in the Xpress Dictionary.

Skip allows you to overlook the word in question. After all, it may be correct even if it is not in the Xpress Dictionary. You can add the word to an auxiliary dictionary by clicking on the **Keep** button. Keep allows you to record a word identified as suspect into a currently opened auxiliary dictionary. **Lookup** displays similar dictionary words in the scroll lists.

CHECKING A DOCUMENT

Another option for spelling is that of Utilities ➤ Check Spelling ➤ Document. Use this the same way you would use Check Spelling ➤ Story. The difference is that Document option is global; it checks all stories within a document, not merely the current text box.

WORKING WITH AUXILIARY DICTIONARIES IN QUARKXPRESS

You may be working in an environment with specialized words not contained within the 120,000 in the Xpress Dictionary. This may call for an auxiliary dictionary to be created. *Auxiliary* dictionaries augment the Xpress Dictionary and make checking your words faster, because the checker flags fewer suspect words.

Open an auxiliary dictionary by choosing Utilities ➤ Auxiliary Dictionary. Auxiliary dictionaries have their own names and you can open and close an auxiliary dictionary at any time. You can create as many dictionaries as you want, but only one can be open at a time. Any number of documents can use the same auxiliary dictionary.

CREATING A NEW AUXILIARY DICTIONARY

To create a new auxiliary dictionary, select the Utilities ➤ Auxiliary Dictionary option. The Auxiliary Dictionary dialog box displays. Enter a name for the new dictionary in the New Auxiliary Dictionary field. If you create the new dictionary without a document open, it becomes the New Default Auxiliary Dictionary. Use the dialog box controls to select the location you wish to save the dictionary.

EDITING AN EXISTING AUXILIARY DICTIONARY

To make changes to one of the existing auxiliary dictionaries, you should select Utilities ➤ Edit Auxiliary. The Edit Auxiliary Dictionary dialog box appears, giving you the opportunity to **Add**, **Delete**, **Save**, and **Cancel**.

WARNING

The Auxiliary Dictionary augments the Xpress Dictionary. You cannot use an auxiliary dictionary if the Xpress Dictionary is not in the QuarkXPress directory or System directory.

CREATING STYLE SHEETS

To properly use Style Sheets in QuarkXPress   190

there are two steps to follow: first, you must have a Style Sheet defined and saved; second, you can use this recorded style sheet by calling it out appropriately as needed.

To create a new style sheet   191

select Edit ➤ Style Sheets. A dialog box appears giving you the option of editing the default style sheet (called Normal) or of creating a new style sheet.

To create a new style sheet for global use (not limited to one document)   192

follow the same procedure for creating a style sheet as noted above, but make sure you have no document open at the time. With no document open, any style sheet you create becomes global and is accessible by any future document you may create or open.

To create a style sheet for use only in a particular document   192

create a new or open an existing document first. Then follow the procedure(s) for creating a style sheet as noted above. Any style sheet that is created while a document is open will be associated only with that document.

To apply a style sheet in your document text   205

select one of three techniques for application. These include selecting the appropriate style sheet from the submenu in Style ➤ Style Sheets, using a keyboard equivalent that you programmed when creating or editing the style sheet, or picking the appropriate choice from the floating Style Sheets palette (View ➤ Style Sheets).

A very handy feature of the QuarkXPress word processor is the *style sheet*. Style sheets enable you to predetermine how a particular section of type will look. A style sheet is essentially a group of text-formatting commands all stored together in one place for the sake of convenience. You can use style sheets to change unformatted text into heads, subheads, captions, body copy, or whatever. You can access style sheets through a menu selection or, more conveniently, by using keyboard shortcuts.

The are two big advantages to style sheets:

▸ You will get a consistent look to your documents.

▸ It is easier to change attributes for a particular design element, because you can just change the style sheet applied to the element. This saves you from having to change each occurrence of the element individually.

ESTABLISHING STYLE SHEETS FOR YOUR DOCUMENT

New documents have one default style sheet (that applied to the general text). This may not suit your needs, however, so you should create your own. Using style sheets is essentially a two-part process:

1. You establish (program into memory) each style sheet attribute.

2. You *apply* a style sheet while editing a document. Applying a style sheet means associating text with it.

NOTE

Style Sheets consist of up to four main settings groups: character, format, rules, and tabs. These four are identical to the Character, Formats, Rules, and Tabs control available in the Style menu. Therefore, description of these features will only appear in detail only once here in this chapter. Other areas listed under the Style menu are detailed as they apply throughout the book.

NOTE

What may be considered a global style sheet is one not attached to a particular document. Instead, this style sheet may be placed in QuarkXPress, similar to the way you change preferences for the entire application. To create a global style sheet, use the same procedures as described for the document style sheet. However, create the style sheet and save it while there are no documents open. That is, either close all document windows and create a style sheet with no "working" area, or, immediately after launching QuarkXPress, before opening a document, create and save your style sheet.

CREATING A NEW STYLE SHEET

To create a new style sheet, select Edit ➤ Style Sheets. A dialog box appears giving you the option of editing the default style sheet (called Normal), of creating a new style sheet, or of importing one from another document. The default style sheet is not for general use, but rather to guide you in creating your own as necessary (see Figure 10.1).

FIGURE 10.1

Select Edit ➤ Style Sheets to get the Style Sheets dialog box. It allows you to edit an existing style sheet or create a new one.

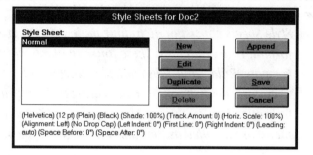

NOTE

Remember, only style sheets created with a document open will apply to that document. Style sheets created without an open document will become global style sheets.

The dialog box enables you to edit any existing style sheet. A new document has only one style sheet (Normal) and applies its programmed attributes to the text. The preset Normal style sheet values are Helvetica 12-point plain black text, auto leading with no tracking, no horizontal scaling, and 100% shading. When you modify this style sheet, all text that it applies to changes. If you modify the Normal style sheet with no documents open, the changes will apply to new documents only.

You can edit existing style sheets to suit your needs or create new ones by clicking on the New button. The New option displays the Edit Style Sheet dialog box (see Figure 10.2). This dialog box includes fields for you to input name of the style sheet and its keyboard equivalent. You must give each style sheet a unique name; of course, it is preferable to use a name that reflects the function of the style sheet (e.g., Body Copy, Heads, Subheads, etc.). A keyboard equivalent is not necessary but will save you time in production. To add a keyboard equivalent, type in the key or key combination you want to use for this style sheet.

FIGURE 10.2

When you choose to create a new style sheet, this dialog box enables you to name it and place a special key sequence to access the format from within your document.

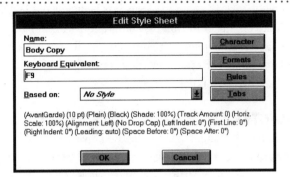

NOTE

MS Windows, being what it is, with multiple applications and font style formats available, may cause problems for you in using the Normal style sheet. You may not have the style sheet Normal, accessing a font you have loaded into your system. In this case, every time you create a new document with automatic text box, your first keystrokes may be garbage. Then you have to change the font, etc. To eliminate this annoyance, change the Normal style sheet to reflect a font you have available in your system.

The Based on pop-up menu gives you the opportunity to base a new style sheet on an existing style sheet in the inventory. If you don't want to use another style sheet as a reference, choose No Style.

TIP

Due to the amount of detail in a style sheet, you may want to save blank documents with style sheets recorded. Then if you need those style sheets, use the document as a template to develop your new material.

Information near the bottom of this box is the default information in a style sheet. It includes Character Attributes, Paragraph Formats, Paragraph Rules, and Paragraph Tabs, if any. You may include any or all of this information in a style sheet. Select and modify this information through the four buttons on the dialog box, Character, Formats, Rules, and Tabs.

THE CHARACTER OPTION IN STYLE SHEETS

Click on the Character button in the Edit Style Sheet dialog box and a typical Character Attributes dialog box appears. This is the same type of Character Attributes dialog box you can get from selecting Style ➤ Character when editing text.

All the Style command options are available in the Character Attributes dialog box. The advantage is that, as a style sheet, the attributes can be applied as a group to a specific kind of text, along with the characteristics of format, rules, and tabs. See *Chapter 8* for more details on type-style attributes and the Character Attributes dialog box.

THE PARAGRAPH FORMAT DIALOG BOX

The Formats option brings up the Paragraph Formats dialog box, which should also be familiar to you (see Figure 10.3). The Paragraph Formats dialog box is the same one that appears when you choose Style ➤ Formats.

FIGURE 10.3

The Paragraph Formats dialog box enables you to specify how each paragraph will look, including all indentation and alignment options.

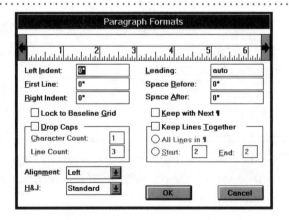

TIP

When keying a value into a numerical (measurement) field, you can use nearly any form of measurement you are comfortable with, and QuarkXPress will translate. Of course you must keep within the given measurement systems available in QuarkXPress. It is best to keep away from measurements such as "hands" or "stone" though!

The Paragraph Formats dialog box contains information for attributes such as indents, leading, spacing, alignment, and drop caps, among others.

THE LEFT AND RIGHT INDENT FIELDS

The Left and Right Indent fields give you the option of indenting paragraphs on the left or right side. The information you supply can be in any measurement system of your choice. Left Indent indicates how far the entire paragraph will indent from the left side (toward the right). The Right Indent indicates how far the entire paragraph will indent on the right (toward the left). You can apply the settings to multiple paragraphs by using a style sheet.

TIP

You may want to include a tab key (for indentation) at the beginning of the paragraph, just out of habit. Be careful, as this may be indented in addition to the first line indent you set up in this Formats section. You don't want twice the amount of indent.

FIRST LINE INDENT

The First Line Indent field is to establish the traditional indentation that goes with indenting the first line of each paragraph. Again, you can specify it in any measurement system and QuarkXPress will convert it to the existing system. You may use this concurrent with the Drop Caps option, also in this dialog box. See more information on Drop Caps later in this chapter.

LEADING

The term *leading* stems from the use of hot lead typesetting, wherein typesetters would place a strip of lead between lines of type. This would space them out, providing non-printing white space between lines of type in the paragraph. The distance between each line was called leading. The distance from the baseline of one line to the baseline of another was called line space, but as computer programs got into the typesetting business, somehow the terms got confused. Thus, today, the distance from baseline to baseline is called *leading*.

The Leading field controls leading for that paragraph. It has the same leading capability as the Leading menu command (Style ➤ Leading). Leading is usually measured in points (see Figure 10.4).

The value placed in this field must be within the range of 0 to 1080 points. Auto leading is the default. Auto leading is usually default valued at 20 percent above the point size. This is changeable through the Typographic Preferences dialog box (Edit ➤ Preferences ➤ Typographic).

FIGURE 10.4

The distance, baseline to baseline, from one line of text to another is the leading.

SPACE BEFORE AND SPACE AFTER THE PARAGRAPH

There are times in which you want to have some white space before or after the paragraph for design reasons. This is especially true if you choose not to distinguish your paragraphs with a first-line indentation. Remember, if you place space before and after, it will double between paragraphs, and you may have more space than desired.

QuarkXPress has a very handy feature that can save a lot of time. It allows you to key in the measurement system of your choice in any field requesting measurements. Once applied, the program converts it to the measurement system in use. For example, you can key in points and picas, even if the measurement field is expecting inches. You can keystroke awkward information and QuarkXPress will convert it for you (e.g., p19 represents 19 points, which would be converted to 1 pica and 7 points). If your measurement system is in inches, it will convert 19 points to 0.264 inches. This works for all of QuarkXPress measurement system options.

LOCK TO BASELINE GRID

As mentioned earlier in the book, QuarkXPress places an invisible gridwork under your text. You can display or hide the grid through the View ➤ Show/Hide Baseline Grid command. You can customize the grid by choosing Edit ➤ Preferences ➤ Typographic.

If you check Lock to Baseline Grid, it will override leading for all the text. For example, if your leading is 14, but the baseline grid leading is 12, the Lock to Baseline Grid option will split the lines to rest on every other (12 point) baseline.

An underlying gridwork is helpful from a layout point of view in that you can manipulate text to match the grid across the design. Click on this option and the text "snaps to" the baseline grid. Leave it unchecked, and items will not snap to the baseline grid.

DROP CAPS

The Drop Caps option, once checked, presents two more input fields (see Figure 10.5). They are the Character Count and Line Count.

FIGURE 10.5

The Drop Caps option, if checked, provides two more fields of information for you to interact with: Character Count and Line Count.

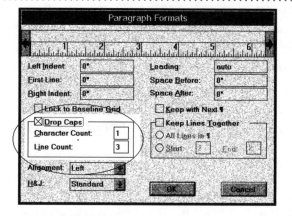

WARNING

The Drop Caps option, if active, works on all paragraphs. You probably would not want this to occur, though. It may be best to establish a separate style sheet with the drop cap option for the initial paragraph. All other paragraphs can have a similar style sheet but without the Dropped Cap. This is an excellent application for the Based on option in the Edit Style Sheet dialog box.

The Character Count determines the number of characters at the beginning of the paragraph that you want to enlarge and drop. The Line Count determines the height of the dropped character(s); that is, you must specify how many lines the enlarged character will consume (see Figure 10.6).

FIGURE 10.6
This example shows a Drop Cap of with a total drop of three lines.

Facing today's economic forecast, it has come to my attention that the touring bicycle industry is on the decline. For that reason, we are shifting our Mountain Valley manufacturing plant to deal with the more immediate trend of off-road or mountain style bicycles.

KEEP WITH NEXT ¶ AND KEEP LINES TOGETHER

To prevent paragraphs from becoming separated at the bottom of a column or a page, check the Keep with Next ¶ option. (A classic example is keeping a figure and its caption together on the same page.) To keep all lines of a selected paragraph in the same column or same page, check the Keep Lines Together option. Once checked, another small dialog box appears. This gives the alternative of having the option apply to All Lines in ¶ or of designating Start and End line numbers (see Figure 10.7).

Alignment is similar to the alignment option you had in the Style menu (Style ➤ Alignment). Its purpose is to help you align the lines of the style sheet in one of

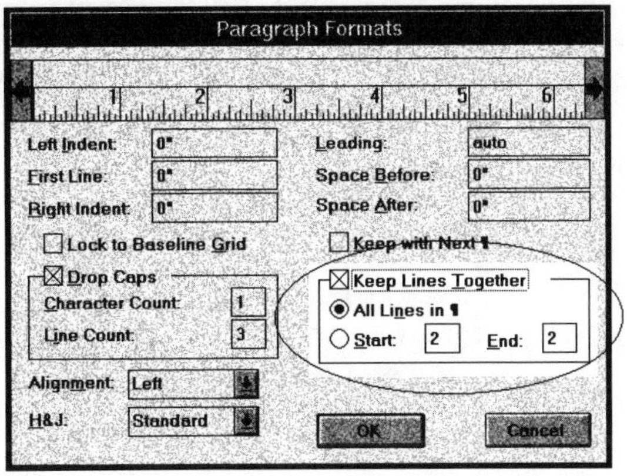

FIGURE 10.7
The Keep Lines Together option, if checked, allows you to keep all lines together in the paragraph or only specific lines.

four fashions, Left, Right, Centered, or Justified. Click on the drop-down menu and hold to select the alignment option of your choice. Once you have selected the option with your cursor, release the mouse button. Your choice will alter all lines active with this style sheet.

Be sure to consider the settings in the H & J option when determining your alignment. Regardless of your choice, the H & J setting will influence your type.

H & J OPTIONS

Click on the drop-down menu for H & J to choose from an assortment of H & J settings. These settings are established by choosing Edit ➤ H & Js. The default option is Standard, and no other options will be available if you do not create custom H & J settings.

THE PARAGRAPH RULES DIALOG BOX

Click the **Rules** button in the Edit Style Sheets dialog box to reach the Paragraph Rules dialog box. You can place rules above or below the text (of your style sheet). If you click on either option, other settings appear, allowing you to set the size, style, and location of the rule. In essence, this is the same dialog box you get when you choose Style ➤ Rules. This rule option applies only to the style sheet. You may set either or both rules options (see Figure 10.8).

FIGURE 10.8

If you check both Rule Above and Rule Below, you get specifications for lines in both areas.

Paragraph Rules
☒ Rule Above
Length: Indents ▼ Style: ▼
From Left: 0" Width: 1 pt ▼
From Right: 0" Color: ■ Black ▼
Offset: 0% Shade: 100% ▼
☒ Rule Below
Length: Indents ▼ Style: ▼
From Left: 0" Width: 1 pt ▼
From Right: 0" Color: ■ Black ▼
Offset: 0% Shade: 100% ▼
OK Cancel

NOTE

H & J is the heartbeat of good typography; without it, all characters would take on a monospaced look, like typewriters give. This is also the most difficult part of the program to get high-quality results. QuarkXPress is among the best on the market for providing quality H & J for desktop computers. It has nearly caught up to high-level electronic publishing programs in use for minicomputers and dedicated systems.

The Length drop-down menu gives you the option of making the rule as long as the Indents or Text. To choose one of these two options, click and hold on the Length drop-down menu, then select.

From Left, From Right, and Offset allow you establish line coordinates relative to paragraph text. Select the Style, Width, and Shade options from an inventory or key in your own. The Color option allows you to choose from a drop down menu of the existing color palette for that document. Add other colors through the Edit ➤ Colors option. See *Chapter 19* for more detail on color.

NOTE

At the QUI 1992 conference, several members expressed discontent with the fact you could resize text as EPS, but the linework remained unchanged. Apparently, the Rule Above and Rule Below options edit differently than type, leaving an inconsistency when resizing the EPS document.

THE PARAGRAPH TABS DIALOG BOX

Tabs enable you to place text exactly on a line and keep the position constant from one line to the next. You would use tabs when you wanted to set up your text in a column format or when you wanted to isolate a word or phrase somewhere on the line. QuarkXPress has six options for tabs: Left, Center, Right, Decimal, Comma, and Align On. Comma and Align On are new to version 3.1 (for those of you migrating to the Windows version).

NOTE

Remember, Tabulation can be used in style sheets as well as adjusted outside style sheets (Style ➤ Tabs). To differentiate between the two, the tab controls outside of style sheets are referred to as "standard" tabulation. Tabs set in style sheets will apply only to that text targeted for the style sheet. They are saved and may be reused as needed throughout your document. Standard tabs are available for a range of highlighted text only. Changes are isolated in standard tabulation. If similar changes are needed later in the document, the tab operation must be repeated for the new text.

The last option of the Edit Style Sheets dialog box is Tabs. Tabs in style sheets work that same as any tabs in QuarkXPress. Click the Tabs button to get the Paragraph Tabs dialog box (see Figure 10.9).

In this setup box, there is a special ruler that corresponds to the text box you are setting tabs within. The ruler starts at the beginning of the text box with the 0 mark. This makes it slightly different from the primary ruler that appears over your document. The primary ruler has a 0 point at the top-left edge of the document page. You must specify the type of tab stop before placing a new tab on the ruler.

There are two options available to set up each tab stop. You can visually set up each tab stop by clicking on the ruler or you can be more precise and use the numerical input for exact tab stop placement. Even when you have positioned a tab stop on the ruler, you can relocate it.

FIGURE 10.9

The tab options include aligning text Left, Center, Right, on the Decimal, on the Comma, or on a designated character (Align On).

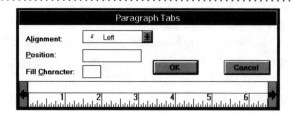

To place a tab stop in position, select one of the styles of alignment (i.e., Left, Center, Right, Decimal, Comma, or Align On). The Left alignment option means that your text, when sent to this tab stop on the line, will reside in a flush left, ragged right location at that point. Center will center the text. The Right option means that your text will stop flush right at that location on the line. Align on Decimal or Comma is a bit tricky until you experiment. With these options, your text will be centered around either decimals or commas; in other words, some of the text will come before the decimal or comma, and some after it. This is particularly good for column material such as in annual reports, where you would probably want numbers to align on the decimal or comma. The final option is Align On. Click on this option and a new field appears, allowing you to keystroke in one character. This enables you to use any single printing character as a tab stop.

After you choose the alignment option, click on the tab ruler to place the tab. You can achieve greater accuracy by keying a numerical coordinate into the Position field. After all tab stops are identified, click on **OK**.

TIP

Set each tab individually for use with a Fill Character. This way, you will ensure against having fill characters where you don't want them.

Any tab stop can have a Fill Character. The fill character will repeat as many times as necessary to fill up any white space on the line (these are often called leaders). The Fill Character field allows you to keystroke in the single character you want to use as the fill character.

TAB INDENTATION

The Tabulation setup dialog box for style sheets is very similar to the standard Tab dialog you reach from the Style menu (Style ➤ Tabs). The primary difference is in indentation controls. Tabs established outside of style sheets have indentation controls as indicated below. Style sheet tabs do not have indentation controls, left or right! In style sheets, indentation is manipulated through the use of the (Paragraph) Formats option.

NOTE

Standard tab controls available through Style ➤ Tabs have a slightly different look than tabs in style sheets. Standard tabulation includes indentation controls on left and right margins of the paragraph. In style sheets, indentation is controlled through formats.

Another difference is that the Style Sheets Tabulation dialog box does not have an Apply button. This button, in standard tabulation, enables you to see tab variations prior to final application. You can see the text move to the tabulation you have established. Standard tabs apply to existing text (that you have on the screen). Highlight a range of text, then set your tabulations. You can use Apply and see changes in your text, make adjustments, then execute. Apply is available only on the Tab commands outside style sheets (Style ➤ Tabs). In style sheets tabs, you establish criteria before inputting text.

NOTE

Since this is the only detailed explanation of tabulation, an explanation of indentation capabilities will also be presented in this chapter. Remember, indentation commands in tabulation, as detailed, are only available in standard tabulation.

You can also set up the ruler to modify indents on the paragraph. On the left side of the ruler there are a pair of triangles. The top triangle represents first line indent; the bottom triangle controls left side indent. The right side of the tabulation ruler has another triangle. It moves right side indent for the text. Any modifications made with these indentation triangles in the tabulation ruler reflect numerically in the indentation fields for Paragraph Formats. See Figure 10.10 for an indication of the indentation triangles.

FIGURE 10.10

From the Style menu (Style ➤ Tabs), set the indentation triangles in the tabulation ruler. Changes reflect in the Formats indentation fields.

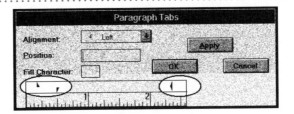

NOTE

Reference is given to QuarkXPress versions prior to 3.1 as this was an evolutionary outgrowth of QuarkXPress for the Macintosh. Many users of QuarkXPress 3.1 for Windows are also users of the Macintosh version of the software.

Another QuarkXPress 3.1 feature in standard tabulation is the Right Indent Tab. Prior to version 3.1, it was difficult to establish a flush right tab equal to the right hand margin of the paragraph. Now you can! To apply the Right Indent Tab, create a right indent by pressing Alt+Tab. This tab stop takes the characteristics of the right-most tab on the line. If that tab is flush right, the Alt+Tab will make text appear flush right at the right margin. If you have a fill character on the far right, the Alt+Tab will use that fill character.

APPLYING STYLE SHEETS

After you edit information for each style sheet, click Save to record your changes and exit the Edit Style Sheet dialog box. Now, in working on a document, you may at any time apply a style sheet. To do this, highlight a range of text to change, then select the style sheet (or key in its keyboard equivalent). You may select the style sheet first, and then key in or import the text. This new copy will reflect specifications of that style sheet. You may also show and select from options in the Style Sheet palette—choose View ➤ Show Style Sheets—(see Figure 10.11).

FIGURE 10.11

*Use the Style Sheets pal-
ette to select the style
sheets you have created.*

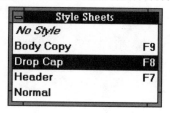

NOTE

*To select a recorded style sheet, you have three options. These
include selecting the appropriate style sheet from the submenu
in Style ➤ Style Sheets, using a keyboard equivalent that you programmed when making the style sheet, or picking the appropriate
choice from the floating Style Sheets palette (View ➤ Show Style
Sheets).*

THE SHORTCUT

Graphic designers are always looking for a better way of doing things. Here is a
better way to use a style sheet available from existing text. First, if you want to copy
all the style sheet information from an existing text area quickly (not perma-
nently), highlight a word of that text. Copy the word, which also copies all attributes (style sheet). Position the cursor where your new text should be, in
accordance with QuarkXPress procedures. Paste the copied word. Now the new
style sheet information exists where you want it. To use this, highlight the copied
word in its new location and overstrike with the text you wanted to place there.

This is a great shortcut for quick little formats—e.g., copying a particular style
and size of font and so on, especially when copying from one document to another. Open multiple QuarkXPress documents and tile them. Now you can see what
you are doing as you copy text from one document and paste it into another. After
you get the hang of it, it often is quicker than going through the procedures of
changing the font, style, size, etc.

TYPOGRAPHY

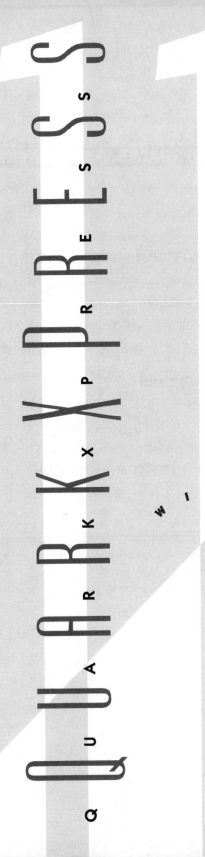

SIZE, FONT, AND LEADING

To select from a variety of measurement systems   213

use the measurements option in the General Preferences dialog box (Edit ➤ Preferences ➤ General). You can select the horizontal and vertical measurement systems independently of one another. Selection options include points, picas, inches, metric, and ciceros.

To switch between word processing and typographic leading   214

use the Typographic Preferences dialog box (Edit ➤ Preferences ➤ Typographic). This preferences dialog box includes an option for making the change specific to your needs in leading. The more popular option is Typographic. This is also the default setting.

To alter automatic leading   215

follow the same procedure for creating a style sheet as noted above, but make sure you have no document open at the time. With no document open, any style sheet you create becomes global and is accessible by any future document you may create or open.

To alter leading in the Normal style sheet (default leading)   218

you should select Edit ➤ Style Sheets, then Edit the Normal style sheet. This is the default style sheet. As you begin text work on a new text box, specifications in the Normal style sheet prevail. Changing this style sheet leading will alter your leading for all new text. Make sure you decide if you want global or only document changes and adjust according to in- structions given in *Chapter 10*.

To alter leading values in the working area without going to the menu choices   219

you should have the Measurements palette shown. Any highlighted text can be altered for leading and other variables directly in the Measure- ments palette. This is a quick way to see changes in your document and note the numerical changes (through the Measurements palette numeri- cal leading values).

To align text vertically   220

use one of the four options for manipulating the column of text material in your document. These options include alignment of text on Top, Cen- tered, Bottom or Justified. Vertical alignment is a text box attribute within the Text Box Specification dialog box (Item ➤ Modify).

The amount of space between lines of type, known as leading, is expressed in points or fractions of a point. There is no predefined rule about line space for good typography. Too much or too little leading in a paragraph is undesirable. Certain typefaces may need more or less leading due to their design. In fact, the only constant with leading is that it's measured in points, part of the printer's measurement system.

NOTE

Initial and global settings for text attributes such as size, font, etc., are established in the default style sheet called Normal. You can change this or add your own global style sheets. Global style sheets, those that apply to any document, must be created before you open a document.

THE PRINTER'S MEASUREMENT SYSTEM

In the United States, the standard for type measurement is the pica and the point. There are approximately 72 points in one inch. That would make each point approximately 0.0139 inches high. There are twelve points in a pica. Six picas equal one inch.

NOTE

The reason you find approximate numbers for the exact size of a point is that no one has ever standardized on the exact size of a point. Indeed, different typesetting equipment manufacturers use different standards for point size. However, the measurement is small enough that the rule of thumb is that there are 72 points to the inch.

SELECTING MEASUREMENT SYSTEMS IN QUARKXPRESS

In the General Preferences dialog box (Edit ➤ Preferences ➤ General), you can choose from a variety of measurement systems, including points, picas, inches, metric, and ciceros. In this way, you can use a system required by a specific project or simply the one you feel most comfortable with. A beautiful feature of QuarkXPress is that you can enter a value in any measurement system you want by including the abbreviation for that system (e.g., *in, mm*, etc.). QuarkXPress will automatically convert your entered value to the measurement system of the document.

Another measurement system available is the cicero. The cicero is a unit of measurement more prevalent in the European Didot system. A cicero is slightly larger than a pica (1 cicero equals 0.178 inches). However, the world has not standardized the size of a cicero, either, and you can customize the cicero in the General Preferences dialog box (Ctrl+Y) along with the point.

LEADING IN A QUARKXPRESS DOCUMENT

Traditionally, leading is defined as the nonprinting white space between lines of text. This came from the hot lead typesetting era when a typesetter would place strips of lead or copper between lines of type to space them out. No extra strips of lead would make the paragraph set solid. The amount of space that each line took up, including the text and leading, was known as line space.

The computer generation in the cold type era has redefined the term. Today, leading means the measurement from the baseline of one text line to the baseline of the next (see Figure 11.1).

NOTE

You can choose to use either Typographic or Word Processing styles of leading from the Typographic Preferences dialog box (Edit ➤ Preferences ➤ Typographic). The more popular option is Typographic. It measures leading from the baseline. The Word Processing option uses an older technique of measurement from the text ascent line; that is, measurement to the top cap or ascender of the next line. It is available only to keep QuarkXPress compatible with the few word processors that still use that system.

Although the standard is to use points for leading measurement, QuarkXPress will allow you to enter any value system. So if you need to specify leading in thousands of an inch, QuarkXPress is happy to oblige. Additionally, QuarkXPress will translate obscure measurements into points. This is true for all measurement systems available in QuarkXPress.

FIGURE 11.1

Leading is the distance, measured in points, from the baseline of one text line to the baseline of the next. You could also measure from the top of one line to the top of another; this is more in line with tradition (type size plus leading).

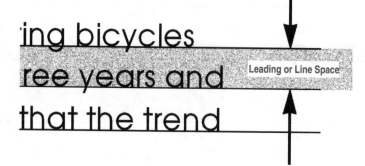

Leading or Line Space

THE LEADING RANGE IN A QUARKXPRESS PARAGRAPH

It should come as no surprise that QuarkXPress has a superior leading capability. The program allows you to enter leading values in increments as small as one-thousandth of a point! (Can you even imagine a job that would require this leading accuracy?) You make these adjustments by choosing Style ➤ Leading (Ctrl+Shift+E).

NOTE

If you try to type in a number smaller than $^1/_{100,000}$ of an inch, the leading will default to auto.

The minimum amount of leading allowed in the program is −1080 points in a minus leading situation; the maximum is 1080 in positive leading. Changing the value to 0 causes the leading to revert to its default (auto leading).

LEADING OPTIONS IN A QUARKXPRESS DOCUMENT

The QuarkXPress application gives the user three different styles of leading to choose from. The choices are automatic, incremental relative, and absolute.

AUTOMATIC LEADING

The default choice in leading is *auto* leading. You can key in text without setting any specific leading and not worry about the spacing values. You enter automatic leading in the Typographic Preferences dialog box (Edit ➤ Preferences ➤ Typographic). Set the automatic leading value in a percentage value. This percentage is relative to the type size. Set the automatic leading percentage at 20% and the total line space will be 120% of the type size on that line. Set the value at 30% and the total line space will be 130% of the type size on that line, and so on. In automatic leading mode, as you change your text size the leading changes along with it.

NOTE

*A popular value for paragraph leading is 20% beyond the type size.
That is why the default value is 20%.*

PROBLEMS WITH AUTOMATIC LEADING

Automatic leading is generally a well-liked feature, but can also have a negative
side. When there is more than one type size or adjustment on a line, the automatic
leading feature favors the largest size (see Figure 11.2).

FIGURE 11.2

*When you have multiple
sizes on a text line problems can arise with
automatic leading, be-
cause the largest text size
is favored.*

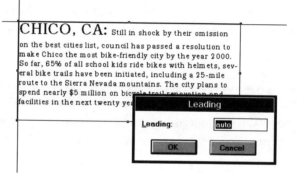

CHICO, CA: Still in shock by their omission
on the best cities list, council has passed a resolution to
make Chico the most bike-friendly city by the year 2000.
So far, 65% of all school kids ride bikes with helmets, several bike trails have been initiated, including a 25-mile
route to the Sierra Nevada mountains. The city plans to
spend nearly $5 million on bicycle trail renovation and
facilities in the next twenty years

Leading

Leading: auto

OK   Cancel

WARNING

*Leading in QuarkXPress is set on a paragraph-to-paragraph basis.
You cannot lead only one line of a paragraph separate from other
lines. The feature to use for this kind of manipulation is the
Baseline Shift option (Style ➤ Baseline Shift). This allows you to
move a highlighted range of text above or below the baseline.*

In addition, manipulated text lines, through baseline shift, play havoc with automatic leading (see Figure 11.3). Most typesetters who work with QuarkXPress will not use the automatic leading option because of possible problems later in the document.

FIGURE 11.3

This illustration repre-sents the baseline shift while in an automatic leading mode. Notice the problem with the dollar sign, elevated with Base-line Shift.

INCREMENTAL RELATIVE LEADING

The *incremental relative* leading capability allows you to add a prescribed amount of leading to the type size (e.g., +4 pt.). Just enter the number with a plus sign in the Auto Leading field (Edit ➤ Preferences ➤ Typographic). If, for example, the type size is 10 with an automatic incremental relative leading of +3, the line space would be 13 points. Change the text to 12 point and the new line space becomes 15 point (12 points plus 3 points).

As you change a value in the auto leading field of the Typographic Preferences dia-log box, it applies to all auto-leaded lines in the document. Text baselines in auto-leaded paragraphs are automatically replaced with their new value, that is, auto lead plus your value.

NOTE

Text with applied style sheet values overrides the automatic values. In leading, placing auto or incremental relative leading values for a paragraph can be overridden by placing that text as a style sheet with different leading values in its format.

ABSOLUTE VALUES FOR LEADING

The most common form of leading is *absolute* leading, which allows the user to specify the exact leading value. Then the leading value remains constant, regardless of text manipulation and size changes in the chosen area of the document. For example, if the leading were 12 points, it would remain 12 points if the text were 10 points in size or 72 points in size. The leading value for a chosen range of text remains constant, unless changed again.

TECHNIQUES FOR CHANGING THE LEADING

There are a variety of ways to adjust leading values in a document. You can highlight lines of text (click and drag technique) and change leading through the menu (Style ➤ Leading or Ctrl+Shift+E). Another way to alter leading for highlighted lines is through the leading adjustments in the Measurements palette. Click on the lead arrows (up or down) or simply overstrike *Auto*.

The auto leading value is established in the default style sheet. One of the attributes set in the Normal style sheet is that of leading. The leading option in this style sheet is "auto." Because this style sheet is the default for any new text created in a new QuarkXPress text box, the leading for new text is auto.

You can change Normal style sheet's leading option to a value more to your liking or create a new style sheet. Either way, the second method of controlling leading values is using style sheets (see Figure 11.4).

FIGURE 11.4
One of the ways to change leading is through style sheets. The Paragraph Format dialog box is accessible through Edit ➤ Style ➤ Edit ➤ Formats.

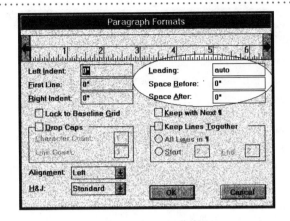

NOTE

Leading affects a single paragraph unless otherwise indicated. Click in a text paragraph with the Content tool and the entire paragraph will change through the leading options. To change multiple paragraphs, highlight a range of text. That highlighted range will change as you modify leading values.

The third method for manipulating leading values is to use the Measurement palette's leading arrows. To change leading with this palette, click on the text area with the Content tool. This ensures you are in text edit mode. Then display the Measurement palette (View ➤ Show Measurements) if it's hidden. Change leading for a paragraph by clicking on that text to position the cursor, then click on the leading arrows to add or remove leading. You can also key in an absolute number, auto, or an automatic incremental value in the field next to the leading arrows (see Figure 11.5). Highlight a range of text to change if you want several paragraphs to change leading.

FIGURE 11.5
Use the leading arrows and field.

| X: 1" | W: 6.5" | △ 0° | auto | Berkeley | 18 pt |
| Y: 1" | H: 4.633" | Cols:1 | 0 | | |

VERTICAL TEXT ALIGNMENT OPTIONS

QuarkXPress gives you four options for manipulating the column of text material in your document. You can align text with the Top, Centered, Bottom, or Justified options. Vertical alignment is a text box attribute within the Text Box Specifications dialog box (Item ➤ Modify).

The rationale behind vertical text alignment is similar to that of justifying characters on a line. In justification, there is only so much space on a line and only so many words of a selected style and size will fit; remaining space is distributed throughout the line. Similarly, in vertical alignment, only so many lines and paragraphs will fit in a vertical space of the column or text box. Any additional space is distributed throughout the column vertically.

NOTE

Vertical text alignment works within the boundaries of Text Inset, established under Item ➤ Modify. Center-aligned text will center between the top and bottom of the box. The text box fills from the center as you enter text. All remaining space fills in equally at the top and bottom of the text box or column.

If you choose Top, the lines are placed with the top of the first line positioned as specified in the First Baseline field of the Text Box Specifications dialog box (see Figure 11.6).

NOTE

The Text Inset value represents how much border or nonprinting space you want from the edge of the text box item to where your type will start. This represents a safety zone of sorts protecting your type from possibly being too close to the edge. This becomes apparent when you shade the text box or place a border frame around it. Values for the Text Inset are usually in points but may take formats from other measurement systems. QuarkXPress will translate.

FIGURE 11.6

The Text Box Specifica-
tions box allows you to
specify Vertical Alignment
options.

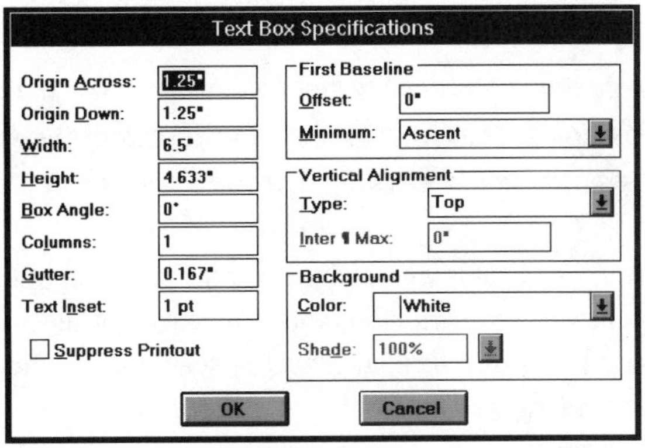

If you choose Bottom, the text starts at the bottom of the text box with remaining space located at the top. The last line in the text box will be flush with the bottom of the text box.

In text boxes specified as Justified, text lines start at the First Baseline position. The last line flush with the text inset position at the bottom of the box, and remaining lines justified in between. Justified vertical alignment allows you to specify a value of maximum distance between paragraphs in the Inter ¶ Max box (see Figure 11.7).

FIGURE 11.7

QuarkXPress allows you
to enter a maximum ver-
tical distance between
paragraphs with the Justi-
fied option in the Inter ¶
Max box. Notice how you
can input measurements
in any system and
QuarkXPress will convert
it for you. Here, points
were input.

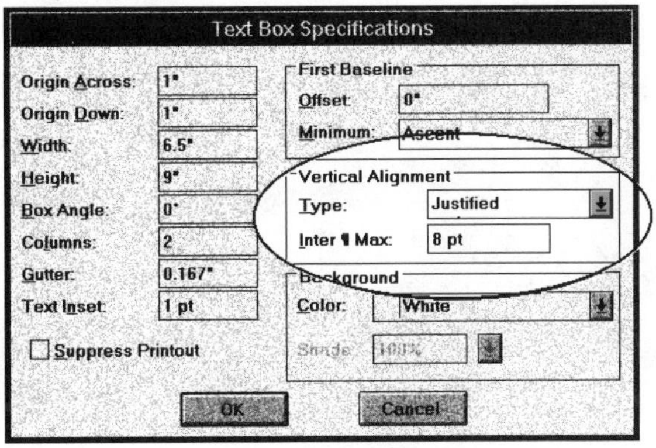

NOTE

In center-alignment, when Lock to Baseline Grid applies, text lines position so they lock to the grid increments closest to where the baselines would be if the text were truly centered.

Vertical alignment is a great timesaver for preparing your layout. Place the extra space between paragraphs as you want, electronically. Control paragraph spacing through justified vertical alignment by selecting the amount of space you allow between paragraphs. This feature works great! It takes the cut and paste out of column alignment.

KERNING AND TRACKING

To open the Tracking Table Edit dialog box   229

choose Utilities ➤ Tracking Table Edit. This dialog box enables you to select
the font and style to edit kerned values. This dialog box is similar to that of
the Kerning dialog box. Tracking values do not take type style into account.

To open the Kerning Table Edit dialog box   230

choose Utilities ➤ Kerning Edit. This dialog box enables you to select the
font and style to edit kerned values. This dialog box gives several options including the ability to import and export kerned values, key in numerical values, adjust a particular kerned pair and preview the change.

To manually apply kerning values   232

position the cursor between the character pair to kern. Alter the spacing
through one of three methods: from the Measurements palette, through use
of the menu options Style ➤ Kern or Style ➤ Character), or by the keyboard
shortcuts.

To manually apply tracking values 233

highlight the characters to alter (click and drag, or select all). Alter the spacing through one of three methods: from the Measurements palette, through use of the menu options Style ➤ Track or Style ➤ Character), or by the keyboard shortcuts.

To use the Flex Space option 234

manipulate the option in the Typographic Preferences dialog box (Edit ➤ Preferences ➤ Typographic). Flexible space is a variation of the en space that you can modify. To specify the width of a flexible character or word space, enter the value in the Flex Space width field.

You have the option in QuarkXPress of increasing and decreasing the amount of space between characters. In typesetting jargon, changing space between characters has been known as *letterspacing*. Negative spacing between two characters is *kerning*. Positive spacing between characters is *letterspacing*. Adjusting space between characters in a range, that is, several characters, lines or paragraphs, is *tracking*. The QuarkXPress application calls both positive and negative changes kerning, relative to the value you establish; it does not use the word letterspacing. This chapter explores the capability within QuarkXPress to use kerning and tracking capabilities.

NOTE

Kerning and tracking values are based on the em space. The em space is a non-printing spacing unit, measured as a square whose sides are equal to one unit of the relative point size. For example, ten-point type has an em space ten points tall and ten points wide; a twelve-point type size has an em space of twelve by twelve, and so on.

KERNING AND TRACKING IN QUARKXPRESS

Every type character has a certain amount of non-printing space on either side of it. This is based on original designs in hot metal typesetting. In this way, when two characters were next to each other, no other spacing units were necessary to prevent them from touching, when printed.

Typography today is a carry-over from a trade that is centuries old. The tools have changed, but the need for good typography remains. Good typography in today's electronic publishing industry is not different from quality standards of fifty or one hundred years ago.

Electronic publishing tools today allow you to place type characters as close or as far apart as you want. Without any manipulation on your part, type characters still have a suitable letterspacing. This is because most type characters, as in hot type, have a preset amount of non-printing white space on either side. In hot type, that non-printing space is the *shoulder* (all parts of letters in hot-lead typesetting had descriptive names). Today, type emulates the look of lead type, but not all the names apply.

In some cases, though, the defined non-printing space of a type character is not aesthetically pleasing. Typically this is the situation when two specific type characters rest next to each other. Figure 12.1 shows twenty of the more common kerning problem pairs.

Kerning in QuarkXPress is similar to its traditional predecessor. You can adjust the space between a pair of kerned characters. Where QuarkXPress departs from tradition is that it calls both positively and negatively adjusted space *kerning*.

The space between the characters is called the *kerning value*. In QuarkXPress you can input this kerning value or take it from an information table. The kerning table is a file in QuarkXPress that has a combination of various character pairs with the kerning values installed for each one, specific to the style and size of the font.

FIGURE 12.1
Twenty of the more popular kerning problem pairs

Yo	We	To	Tr	Tr
Wo	Tu	Tw	Ya	Te
P.	Ty	Wa	yo	we
T.	Y.	TA	PA	WA

Tracking in QuarkXPress is similar to kerning, but is applied to a range of characters. Information on tracking a range of characters is also available through the Tracking Edit and Kerning Table Edit dialog boxes. Like kerning, tracking can be automatic or manual.

THE RANGE OF KERNING
AND TRACKING VALUES IN QUARKXPRESS

You calculate the kerning value range in em spaces. An em space, to use the traditional phrase, is a unit of measurement relative to the point size. It is the square with sides equal to the point size; that is, in ten-point type, the em space is ten points wide by ten points tall.

The em space is another carry-over from hot lead type. Typically, to space type characters for indentation purposes, a specific non-printing "character" had to be available in the typesetter's job case. There were several sizes of these, to use depending on the need. These included the *em*, *en*, and *thin* space. The em was the square of the point size, approximately the same width as the capital *M* character (see Figure 12.2). The en space was half that wide; the thin space was about one-fifth as wide as an em. It took up about as much space as a period or comma.

As typesetting moved from metal to machine, especially computerized cold type, manufacturers began to use fractions of an em as a measuring system. They broke the em down into further divisions called units. One manufacturer may claim to kern in 54 units to the em, while another may claim 128 units to the em. The idea was that, the finer you could manipulate letterspacing, the better your typography

FIGURE 12.2

The em space is a non-printing spacing unit that is measured relative to the point size. The width and height are equal to the point size.

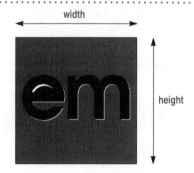

width

height

would be. It was not uncommon to have people working full-time in typesetting shops to program their own specific kerning tables with this newfound capability. Kerning was a major factor in separating the craftsman from the guy down the block who could afford to buy a cheap typesetting machine.

The typesetting industry has come a long way in a short amount of time! Now the "guy" down the street may be a woman (the industry was dominated by males for centuries), and she may have a desktop computer running QuarkXPress, which allows her to control kerning in finer increments than imagined just a few years ago. QuarkXPress kerning (or tracking) is calculated in em units and can be specified in values from −500 to 500 as measured in units of $\frac{1}{200}$ em space (see Figure 12.3). Today, the typesetting house is now a service bureau. Quality is QuarkXPress and laser imagesetter output.

FIGURE 12.3
QuarkXPress breaks the em space into 200 equal slices called units for kerning and tracking purposes.

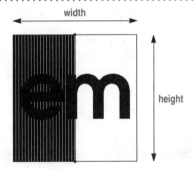

KERNING AND TRACKING TABLES IN QUARKXPRESS

Kerning and tracking are very similar in nature, but have slightly different control features in QuarkXPress. Kerning gives you capabilities to select exact kerned values for a particular character pair. Tracking meets your needs in general, modifying the font and size combination.

THE KERNING TABLE EDIT COMMAND

You open the Tracking Table Edit dialog box by choosing Utilities ➤ Tracking Table Edit (see Figure 12.4).

FIGURE 12.4

Selecting the Tracking Edit options from the Utilities menu brings up these two dialog boxes. From here, you can alter tracking values for the font of any given size.

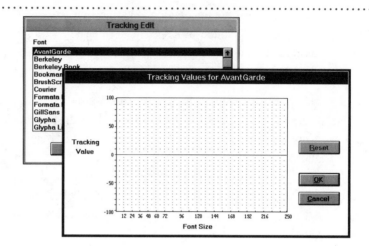

The Kerning Edit dialog box is opened similarly: choose Utilities ➤ Kerning Edit. This is also shown in Figure 12.5. This dialog box enables you to select the font and style to edit kerned values. Select the font/style combination and click on the Edit button for changes. Once the selection is made, the Tracking Values dialog box opens, specific to the font and style of your choice (see Figure 12.4).

FIGURE 12.5

To add or alter kerned pairs, select the Kern Edit option from the Utilities menu.

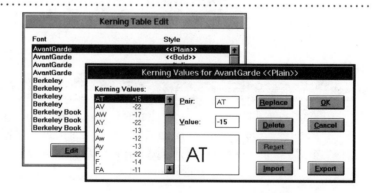

NOTE

If you type a new pair of characters in the Pair entry box, the Replace *button changes to* Add.

The Kerning Table Edit dialog box gives several options for making changes. You can choose to edit an existing character pair, create and modify a new pair, delete a kerned pair, import similar kerning values, or export these values to another file. The numerical kerning values run in $\frac{1}{200}$ em space increments. As you adjust a particular kerned pair, you can preview the change in the kerning window. Once the settings meet your satisfaction, click on **Replace** to change the pair or **OK** to exit the dialog box without changing. You can also click **Cancel**.

Information in the Kerning Values dialog box applies to the document in all situations with that pair in that font and style. So if you have edited the *WA* combination in Palatino Plain type, they will always kern at the value specified (−18 in Figure 12.5). You need not revisit the Kerning Values dialog box while working unless a character combination needs revision.

THE TRACKING EDIT COMMAND

To edit the tracking settings, select Utilities ➤ Tracking Edit to bring the Tracking Edit dialog box (see Figure 12.4). This dialog box is similar to the one for kerning, but does not have style choices. Tracking values do not take type style into account. The Tracking Values dialog box applies to each major font size group (see Figure 12.6). Click on the value bar in the graph to move the tracking values per font size. The normal tracking value is 0. Values below 0 create tight tracking, while those greater than 0 extend tracking. Once you have modified the graph to reflect your tracking preferences, click on **OK** to save the changes.

TIP

If you goof up in setting the tracking, you can click Reset *to get the default setting back; then you can try again.*

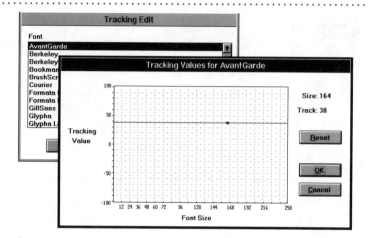

FIGURE 12.6
*The Tracking Values dia-
log box (shown for
AvantGarde) indicates
the size and tracking
value you desire. Click on
the floating "cursor" in
the graph and drag it to
the appropriate tracking
value for each size.*

APPLICATION OF KERNING
AND TRACKING CONCEPTS IN QUARKXPRESS

In QuarkXPress you can implement kerning and tracking either automatically or manually. To automatically change values, edit the appropriate dialog boxes as described above.

NOTE

*Changing kerning or tracking to one font does not change all
fonts, or (with kerning) even styles within that font. You must
make several changes for kerning and tracking.*

To manually apply the kerning and tracking values, identify the text area to alter. To change a kerning value between two characters, anchor the cursor between the two characters and change the kerning value. You can change the kerning value in one of three ways: from the Measurements palette, by using the menu options (Style ➤ Kern or Style ➤ Character), or by keyboard shortcuts. The menu options are discussed above. Let's now discuss the others.

CHANGING KERNING FROM THE MEASUREMENTS PALETTE

Display the Measurements palette (View ➤ Show Measurements) and locate the kerned pair to edit. Click between the characters to anchor the cursor. While the cursor is flashing, adjust the kerning arrows or field of the Measurements palette (see Figure 12.7). Pressing on the kerning arrows changes kerning in a predefined 10 number range ($^{10}/_{200}$ em space increments). When finished press Enter.

In similar manner, you can change the tracking of a range of characters. Start by highlighting the range of characters to track. Using the Measurements palette, change the tracking for the entire highlighted range. This range can be as small as a few characters or as large as your entire document text.

KEYBOARD SHORTCUTS FOR KERNING AND TRACKING

You can also kern and track using keyboard equivalents. Press Ctrl+Alt+Shift+} to add space in $^{1}/_{200}$ em space increments. Press Ctrl+Alt+Shift+{ to subtract space in the same increments. To track using keyboard equivalents, highlight the range of characters to alter the letterspacing. To track negatively, press Ctrl+Alt+Shift+{; to track positively, press Ctrl+Alt+Shift+}. Both track in $^{1}/_{200}$ em space increments.

To adjust kerning or tracking in 0.005 (10/200) em space increments, use the keyboard commands Ctrl+Shift+{ to decrease and Ctrl+Shift+} to increase.

FIGURE 12.7

To kern the A and W closer together using the Measurements palette, anchor the cursor between the two characters. Then click on the kerning arrows of the Measurements palette. Another method of changing the value is to highlight and replace the numerical kern value on the palette.

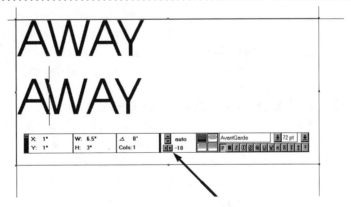

RELATED FEATURES IN QUARKXPRESS

A couple of features similar to the kerning and tracking in QuarkXPress are the Flex Space Width capability and use of Ligatures.

FLEX SPACE WIDTH

Flex space width is located in the Typographic Preferences dialog box (Edit ➤ Preferences ➤ Typographic). Flexible space is a variation of the en space that you can modify. To specify the width of a flexible character or word space, enter the value in the Flex Space Width field.

 NOTE

Remember, the en space is a portion of the em space. The en space is half as wide as the em space, but the same height (e.g., a 12 point em will have an en space 6 points wide, 12 points tall).

The flex space width is a percentage of the normal en space relative to the font and size (see Figure 12.8). You may use a percentage value ranging from 0% to 400% in 0.1% increments. The default value for Flex Space Width is 50% (relative to the en space).

To enter a breaking flexible space, press Alt+Shift+ spacebar. Enter a nonbreaking flexible space by pressing Ctrl+ Alt+Shift+spacebar.

Use the flex space width when you want to move a type character over slightly but don't want to bother setting up a tab for one occasion. It is a tool to help you manipulate type, this time through nonprinting spacing units.

LIGATURES WITHIN THE FONT

Hot type has a finite amount of space between characters. You can place the characters only so close, as the lead bodies would touch and allow no kerning. To remedy this it was sometimes necessary to saw off part of the shoulder to allow for a tighter kern. Popular type-character combinations requiring tight kerning were often molded together as one.

FIGURE 12.8

Change the Flexible Space Width value in the Typographic Preferences dialog box. Also from this dialog box, you have the option of selecting Ligature use, as available in the font.

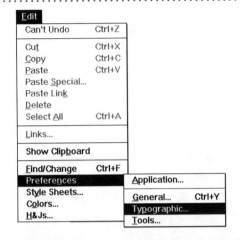

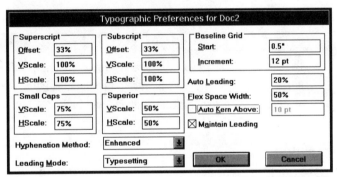

Two or more characters designed as if they were one distinct unit are called *ligatures* (see Figure 12.9). Typically, there are five f-ligatures—*fi, ff, fl, ffi,* and *ffl*— and the diphthongs æ and œ. Not all fonts (ont formats) have these available for electronic publishing. They are more prevalent in book publishing than advertising typography.

FIGURE 12.9
*Examples of ligatures
in Times Roman*

TIP

*If you are a ligature fan, you can create your own when not
otherwise available. Use the Kerning Table Edit dialog box to place
a specific pair together as you desire. You can also use this
technique for certain typographical logotypes.*

AN EXERCISE IN KERNING

To practice kerning, you can revisit your newsletter, QuickRelease, introduced earlier. Any good newsletter will have a masthead relating the title of the publication.
Any typographically correct masthead will be kerned to perfection.

NOTE

*Kerning and tracking are visually aesthetic features. There is no
specific rule regulating how much or how little space to use.*

STEP 1: ADDING THE TEXT

Key in the text that you will use for the masthead, that is QuickRelease. After typing, highlight and change the text attributes by choosing Style ➤ Character
(Ctrl+Shift+D) as follows:

- Times font

- 72 point size

- Horizontal Scale: 95%

- Style both Bold and Shadow

NOTE

In the original newsletter example, you altered the Track Amount of −15 in the Character Attributes dialog box. In this example, you will include it manually, by highlighting the range of characters and changing the Measurements palette. As you initially key in and alter your text, the two words will take up two lines. Don't worry; as you change kerning and tracking, they will condense to fit on one line.

When you are finished, click **OK** to exit the Character Attributes dialog box.

STEP 2: ADJUSTING THE KERNING AND TRACKING

Once the text is in and modified, it is time to start the kerning and tracking process. Begin by making sure you have the Measurements palette showing (View ➤ Show Measurements), as well as the Tools palette (View ➤ Show Tools).

Select the Content tool and highlight the title *QuickRelease*. Next, highlight the tracking field on the Measurements palette. Change this value to read −15, then press Enter to put your change into effect. The tracking of your masthead should instantly change. Do you notice a difference? If not, be sure the masthead is highlighted, choose Edit ➤ Undo (Ctrl+Z), and repeat. It is important that you see a difference when kerning and tracking. Feel free to play with the values experimentally to obtain better results.

After tracking, it is time to change specific kerning pairs in the masthead. Although changing the tracking cleaned up the range of characters considerably, there are still a couple of areas needing slight modification. The specific character combinations you will kern are the *Qu* and the *Re* pairs. To kern these follow the procedure outlined below:

1. Position and anchor the cursor between the *Qu* character pair.

2. Alter the kern value field in the Measurements palette to read −5.

3. Press Enter to activate the kern.

4. Position and anchor the cursor between the *Re* character pair.

5. Alter the kern value field in the Measurements palette to read −5.

6. Press Enter to activate the kern.

NOTE

Kerning and tracking are subjective values; what you see here may not be the style you prefer.

Congratulations! You have successfully kerned and tracked the characters in the newsletter masthead. The only steps left are for you to center the text and save the document file. To center the copy, highlight the characters and use the keystroke shortcut of the Style ➤ Alignment ➤ Centered command (Ctrl+ Shift+C).

NOTE

You should consider saving this example under the filename Masthead. That way, you can easily retrieve it later.

To save this file for future reference, use the File ➤ Save command (Ctrl+S). Give the file a name and change the storage location if necessary. Once the dialog box reads to your satisfaction, click on **Save**.

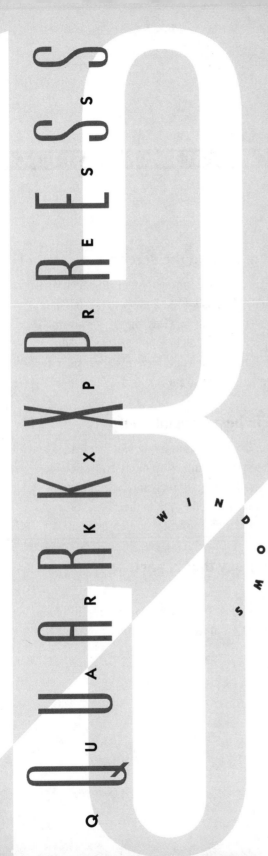

TrueType and PostScript Fonts

To help fonts render well on the screen and print better   253

invest in ATM (Adobe Type Manager). This is the program that, when loaded in your system, helps render bitmap fonts on the screen and output printer to a wider range than normally possible. Other competing programs are available on the market also.

To save storage and improve efficiency in font use   255

you should avoid duplicating fonts in multiple formats. If you have a font in one format, PostScript for example, don't redundantly load the same face in TrueType.

Do you know the difference between a *font* and a *typeface*? To understand it, you must know that the history of typesetting goes back as far as around 250 B.C., when the Chinese used ceramic stamps pressed in clay. This eventually lead to inked characters, recorded in China by Pi Sheng in A.D. 1401. Johannes Gutenberg cast his first letters from a mixture of tin, antimony, and lead in A.D. 1441. These cast letters were called *movable type* because they could be removed, stored, and reused. It is also called *hot type*, *hand-set type*, or *cast type*.

NOTE

Hand-set and its associated machine-set metal type were the mainstays of the typesetting industry until only a few decades ago. Photographic type started to catch on in the 1960s and became commonplace in the 1970s. The last linecasting machine for metal type was produced in 1971.

Hand-set type makes a distinction between the cast character and the letter impression made when printed (see Figure 13.1). The complete collection of cast characters in one size and style is a *font*. The printed image or face of the font is the *typeface*.

Most typefaces have design variations of the original layout. For example, Helvetica has Helvetica Light, Helvetica Medium, Helvetica Bold, Helvetica Italic, etc. These variations of the same basic design are the *styles*. All styles together comprise the typeface *family*.

Electronic fonts of today share much of the terminology of their hot metal ancestors, but lack the physical attributes. This causes problems for many people starting in desktop publishing. They do not have the character to pick up and hold, they don't have the opportunity to see why "set solid" is called set solid (see Figure 13.2). They can't see the lead or copper strip placed between lines for spacing. In short, people

FIGURE 13.1

*A representation of a met-
al type character, as used
in hand-set typesetting*

working in the electronic typesetting industry today have a great disadvantage to overcome: lack of hands-on experience!

FIGURE 13.2

*The leading in the left para-
graph is set solid.*

Statistics clearly show that of the 400 (average) U.S. children in fatal bike accidents each year, 65% die of head injuries. Of those adult bicycle enthusiasts polled Summer 1992, 79% always wear a helmet, 11% sometimes wear a helmet, 7% never wear a helmet and 3% rarely wear a

Statistics clearly show that of the 400 (average) U.S. children in fatal bike accidents each year, 65% die of head injuries. Of those adult bicycle enthusiasts polled Summer 1992, 79% always wear a helmet, 11% sometimes wear a helmet, 7% never wear a helmet and 3% rarely wear a

Today's electronic fonts are data stored on a disk or tape. These bits and bytes are a computer's blueprint, used to draw the face in very precise units (as small as 0.001 point increments). Capabilities of today's hardware and software blur the meanings of *font* and *typeface* to the point where the two terms are interchangeable. However, if you use history as a guide, the definition of *font* is the computer data, and the output text is the *typeface*.

FONT CATEGORIES IN ELECTRONIC PUBLISHING

Specialists in the industry categorize electronic fonts in two distinct categories, *bit-mapped* and *outline*. Bitmapped fonts are best identified as font software that enables the computer to create type images on the screen. Outline fonts are software applications that tell the printer how to form characters on the paper. Typically, outline fonts are higher quality on the printer because a laser can paint a finer line on the paper than the screen pixels on your monitor.

NOTE

Emerging as the standard in desktop laser printers is the 600 dpi printer. There is still a vast difference between the desktop printer and the quality of image from a service bureau's imagesetter, though.

The highest resolution type will come from imagesetter output, especially at the high end of the resolution spectrum—nearly 3000 dots per inch. This is far better than the resolution you have on desktop laser printers at 300 dpi or your monitor at only 72 dpi. But things change, quickly. Read on.

BITMAPPED FONTS

Bitmapped fonts are sometimes called screen fonts; that is, they look better on the screen due to the monitor's 72 dpi resolution. When these are printed, the dot resolution does not improve. Figure 13.3 shows an enlargement of the bitmapped font character. It looks terrible! It looks just as bad in print. Bitmapped fonts are best used on the screen, not in the printer.

These fonts have the following characteristics:

▸ Instructions to form characters on screen

▸ Require a lot of storage space on disk, compared to outline fonts

▸ Do not resize particularly well

▸ Primarily, but not exclusively used as screen fonts

FIGURE 13.3
A representation of a bit-mapped font character, enlarged to highlight the bits or pixel elements

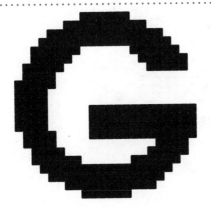

- Should be installed in all sizes you need to use (unless you have ATM—see *Adobe Type Manager* below)

- May be used for laser printers, but will show "jagged" edges (pixel rendition)—improves somewhat with ATM

- Provides an information table with character widths, which allows variable width characters, giving more true WYSIWYG

OUTLINE FONTS

Outline fonts (also known as *vector*, *scalable*, or *printer fonts*) are more precise and of higher quality, because they consist of a formula for the computer or printer to draw the character. See Figure 13.4 for a representation of an outline font character.

Outline fonts have the following characteristics:

- Mathematical formulations of the character shape using curves and lines

- Takes up less storage space on disk than bitmapped fonts

- Can be resized without degrading the character

- Are primarily but not exclusively for output to printer

- Are, in PostScript form, composed of Bézier curves

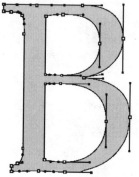

FIGURE 13.4
A representation of an outline font character. Outline fonts are usually, but not exclusively, used for output.

▶ Contain information about the size and shape of each character for the printer to use for output

▶ Allow you to print any typeface in any size, angle, and shade resolution available on the output printer, while maintaining clarity and precision

▶ May be used for screen display with ATM

OTHER VARIATIONS OF THE FONT DILEMMA

It may not be clear what type of font to use where, so here is a brief summary.

Bitmapped fonts belong on the screen only. Do not try to print with bitmapped fonts unless absolutely necessary.

Outline fonts are primarily for use on the printer. They are information groups that convert what was a bitmapped font character to a printer font character when you send the document to print. Rarely are typical outline fonts used on the screen; they are reserved for the printer.

A new form of outline font from Apple called *TrueType* allows both use on screen and in the printer. This may be the wave of the future, but now it is not widely accepted by the user community.

Adobe is countering TrueType with their own *Multiple Master Font* technology that will be used both for the screen and the printer.

From this information, the distinction between the technologies might seem clear: Bitmapped fonts for the screen and outline fonts for the printer. But that is not the way technology is moving, for several reasons. First, designers and typesetters have never been totally satisfied with onscreen font rendering because it is often not even close to the quality you can obtain in print. Competition in technology, being what it is, has brought about a new rivalry that may reshape the way type works.

NOTE

Remember, a language *in computerese means a program that someone uses to communicate with. PostScript is a language that allows your computer to communicate to a printer. It tells the printer how to recreate your design on the page using its internal laser as the drawing tool.*

PostScript is a proprietary page description language from Adobe. It is currently the dominant language in output. Apple made the decision to get into the high-resolution font business and introduced their TrueType font structure. TrueType is unique in that it is an outline font that can be used on the screen as well as for output print. Therefore, it does not have the limitations that bitmapped fonts have on the screen. Not to be outdone, Adobe, with their massive head start in this business, has taken steps to migrate PostScript in a new direction. PostScript's most recent development includes the use of what Adobe calls *Multiple Masters*. Here, a variety of custom typefaces can be generated from a single font file.

A standard PostScript printer font defines a single outline for each of its 256 characters. Each has a consistent weight, style, and width. Additional weights, styles and widths are available only on supplemental PostScript printer fonts. For example, Helvetica comes in regular, bold, and italic. To obtain Helvetica Thin, you have to buy another font specific to your needs. It cannot be redrawn from the original font through PostScript.

NOTE

A font's characteristics include its weight *(light, black, bold, plain),* style *(sans serif, serif, oblique), and* width *(condensed, regular, expanded).*

Multiple Master fonts include *master designs*, that is, several font character definitions. Each master represents an extreme in weight, style, and width. A master forms a matrix, as shown in Figure 13.5.

A special built-in utility enables the user to create a custom typeface from these elements of the master design. Not only can you create a special typeface from this grid, but each Multiple Master may be best used for a specifically-sized range of type. You could have one master best for 6–10 point type, another for 12–14, another for 14–24, and so on. This is essentially the way certain typesetting machine

FIGURE 13.5

A representation of a Multiple Master design matrix

Light condensed   Light oblique

Heavy condensed   Heavy oblique

manufacturers dealt with the quality issue in earlier digital typesetting machines. They would digitize specific masters for a specific range of sizes. As the size range changes, the computer would shift to the next set of masters. In this way, the type designer is assured of quality in any size of type produced from the original artwork of the font.

As of this writing, Multiple Master fonts are not in widespread use. The prevalent system is the traditional PostScript fonts in Adobe PostScript Type 1 format. However, this business has a way of changing nearly overnight.

APPLE'S TRUETYPE FONT STRATEGY

In 1989, Apple announced at its annual developers conference that it was developing TrueType to be included with their newest operating system, System 7. In the development of System 7, it had become clear that new strategies needed exploring that were not thought of when the Macintosh was introduced. Apple designed TrueType to help simplify font installation and management (see Figure 13.6). The goal to be compatible with every kind of printer and output device (device *independent*) and to display and print high-quality type quickly was paramount. They

FIGURE 13.6

The TrueType font dialog box is available through the Control Panel ➤ *Fonts sequence in Windows 3.1. This feature is not unique to Quark-XPress 3.1 for Windows.*

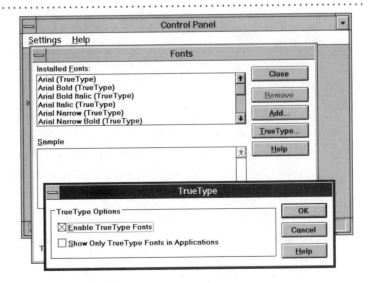

wanted TrueType to be powerful and flexible enough to handle complexities of many world languages, not just the Roman alphabet. Finally, their goal was to design a type format to work on computer platforms other than Macintosh.

With the help and support of font vendors, Apple developed TrueType and shipped it in March 1991. Shortly thereafter, Apple and Microsoft entered an agreement whereby all new Windows versions would support (even embrace) TrueType font technology. Thus, when installing fonts, a great deal of thought was given to installation of TrueType fonts and making them the sole font option, at the user's discretion. See the Font installation option in your Windows 3.1 Control Panel.

NOTE

This may be sheer speculation, but it seems that Apple and Microsoft teamed to break the "parasitic" relationship of Adobe toward their respective companies and the industry as a whole.

BITMAPPED VS. TRUETYPE FONTS

TrueType is an outline font technology. As described earlier, an outline font details all the characters as a series of mathematical lines and curves. PostScript uses Bézier curves for drawing the character, while TrueType uses a particular mathematical equation known as the *quadratic curve*. Quadratic curves are easy to compute and scale on the computer. TrueType enables conversion from other forms, such as the Bézier curves into quadratic curves, thus allowing type vendors to translate font libraries into TrueType format.

Because outline font information consists of mathematical formulas, it is easy for the computer to scale and reshape the font. Bitmapped fonts cannot be mathematically expanded or reduced, though, without the character showing the "jaggies." To resize properly, you must install a specific bitmapped font for each type size you want to use.

In the early days of the personal computers, there were only bitmapped fonts and dot-matrix printers. Apple introduced the LaserWriter printer in 1985 and quickly found that the bitmapped technology was insufficient. The decision was to continue bitmapped fonts for screen display but allow laser printers to use the Adobe

PostScript outline fonts. The LaserWriter contained its own outline version of the fonts displayed on the screen, scaled and positioned characters according to print instructions, built an entire page in memory, and then printed the page.

Using outline font technology, printers were able to smoothly reproduce any font at any size. Meanwhile, Mac users were still working with designs of bitmapped fonts on the screen. Resized bitmapped fonts distort so designers had difficulty seeing what they would get.

To counter these problems, Apple decided to create TrueType. Instead of addressing the deficiencies of bitmapped screen fonts only, Apple designed TrueType to work as both a screen *and* printer font. This gives high-quality, accurate, on-screen type display the same priority as it has for printed display. You can tell if there are any TrueType fonts in your system if the font icon has multiple characters.

HOW FONTS WORK

Both TrueType and PostScript fonts work in similar manner. They contain a powerful instruction set that takes orders from the user. These orders consist of manipulations you give in the application; for example, you may want the type to be larger or narrower. Give the instruction and the font manipulates to obey. These instructions dictate the size, quality, and resolution of the final character. In PostScript, the character results in printed form. In TrueType, the form is both on screen and in print.

NOTE

Hinting is a programmer's method of telling the type designer how to place subtle differences in the type character. Fonts with hinting can have more manipulation by the type designer, compared to those without hinting.

These font formats provide type designers with *hinting* controls (see Figure 13.7). Hinting comes in high-level and low-level features that enable designers to control global characteristics such as the width of a character stem. This gives more control to the type designer to display the original design as intended.

FIGURE 13.7

To a type designer, the advantage of hinting allows them to customize a design for output. For everybody else, hinting means little but is required to make the laser type look good.

Low-level hinting information is particularly important for displaying screen font characters. As you type, the computer notes the font and style in use. It then refers to the TrueType outline for the chosen character and scales it to the correct point size. Then it overlays a grid representing your display monitor resolution and each cell in the grid. Hinting information is used to position pixels on the grid to fit the character outline as best as possible. The resulting pixels are turned black and the character appears on the screen (see Figure 13.5).

MIXING TYPE FORMATS

Multiple font formats can coexist in the Windows environment. You can use TrueType, bitmapped, and outline fonts all at the same time. Under Windows 3.1, the PC follows a hierarchical order in determining what a character will look like on screen. Specifically, the system looks first to see if there is a predrawn bitmap that matches the font and size chosen. If none is found, it then looks for a TrueType version (assuming you chose the TrueType preference in the Control Panel). If a TrueType version cannot be found, the system looks for an Adobe PostScript Type 1 font of the same typeface. It should stored in the proper location according to path information for fonts. The system uses ATM to convert the Type 1 outline format to a form it can display on the screen. If the Type 1 outline and ATM cannot be found, your screen font becomes "dysfunctional."

ADOBE TYPE MANAGER

A new technology called Adobe Type Manager (ATM) uses outline font information from printer fonts to emulate outline fonts on the screen. Without the need of each size having its own master, ATM allows outline fonts to be used as screen fonts. ATM still requires bitmapped screen fonts in sizes under twelve points. However, larger than twelve-point type is drastically enhanced in its screen appearance with ATM (see Figure 13.8).

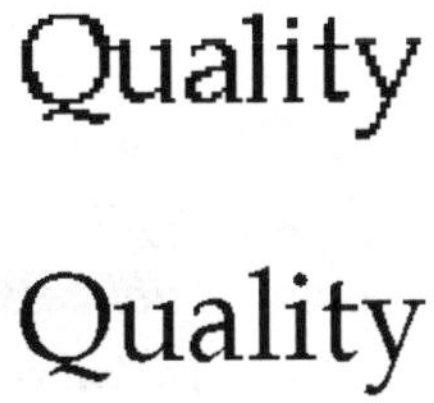

FIGURE 13.8

Here is how screen fonts may appear with and without Adobe Type Manager (ATM) properly activated.

Quality

Quality

NOTE

A master *is the original design of the type character, as generated by the type designer. From this master the designer can create variations, such as larger or smaller sizes, condensed or bold type, etc. Think of it as something similar to a master mold.*

The two primary advantages of ATM are:

▶ Screen representations of fonts can be created using outline fonts, giving a better screen image of type.

▶ Bitmapped fonts are needed only for reproducing special sizes under twelve points, drastically cutting font storage requirements.

ATM has the capability to use existing fonts in both bitmapped and outline format, in particular PostScript fonts. This has become very popular in view of the investment many have in PostScript font libraries.

ENCRYPTION, FORMATS, AND MORE HINTING

It is difficult to make type look good in low-resolution situations. When outline fonts are scaled down, there are fewer pixels to draw the character. The same problem is true in low-resolution printers. When you get down to the point that the thickness of one pixel can make or break the look of your characters, you have inconsistent quality in type. Both TrueType and PostScript have *hints*, that is, algorithms that are part of the font and improve its ability to produce good-looking letters.

NOTE

There are Type 1, Type 2, and Type 3 formats. Types 1 and 3 are available to the general public. Type 2 was for certain proprietary purposes and never released for general public use. The difference between Type 1 and Type 3 is in the encryption capabilities. Type 1 format allows encryption, while Type 3 formats do not.

Encryption is the process used to protect certain code information in fonts and other computer files in general. Type 1 fonts are rarely encrypted any longer since Adobe released the font format in March 1990. Prior to that time, Type 1 font formats included the ability to allow encryption, thus hiding specific hint information. When hint information was encrypted, the key differences were kept from would-be software pirates. Designs remained intact and no copies were made. Competition forced Adobe to stop encryption techniques and open the market for everyone. This allows for a more open environment in the font technology and is one method to keep PostScript fonts popular in view of competition from TrueType.

WHICH IS BETTER, TRUETYPE OR POSTSCRIPT?

What factors determine which font format is better? It primarily boils down to cost, speed, and output quality. Cost factors deal with how much you have already spent on your existing type library, and how much has your service bureau already invested in theirs. You don't need any new hardware technology to utilize either

PostScript or TrueType; or do you? Sooner or later, everyone must upgrade his hardware. New printers are being built with both PostScript and TrueType capabilities. Currently, because PostScript has sold over the past few years, it is more popular, at least with those users who have established an expensive type library. Therefore, there are a great number of PostScript printers on the market. However, TrueType does not need PostScript printer capability, which lowers printer costs, so look for more people saving money on printer hardware and compensating with TrueType font. Generally, as TrueType becomes more entrenched in the market, especially with the Microsoft Windows buy-in, look for it to become the font standard.

What about speed? Which format draws faster on screen? Which one works faster in the output device? Well, both formats, TrueType and PostScript with ATM, perform poorly on slower processors. Don't even bother with older processors, such as in the XT (8086/8088) and AT (80296) class machines. You've got better things to do with your life! The minimum standard for operation with either product is the 386SX. The reason for the critical nature of your computer's microchip speed is that all processing is done at your local computer. The exception is if you are connected to a network in which a dedicated system other than your own processes font information. PostScript is dependent on more factors for output than is TrueType. If you have the option of running a Windows system outputting to a desktop printer for proofs, the non-PostScript printer with TrueType fonts will perform much faster than the comparable PostScript laser printer with PostScript fonts.

In the Service Bureau setting, the early laser typesetters for electronic imaging were PostScript. From that time forward, PostScript has continued to evolve and become the standard page description language for imagesetters. This will have little or no impact on your work, regardless of what kind of font you use, because a good service bureau will have a full complement of both PostScript and TrueType fonts available to run customer jobs.

As for screen speed, the best thing you could do for either font format is to use a direct bus card which speeds screen refresh. In the Windows environment, on PCs and PC clones, the drawback is the processor speed to screen redraw. You can have the fastest PC on the market, but if you haven't taken extra steps to accelerate the screen redraw, the image will still come up slow, and thus your productivity is compromised. As for the font formats, reports from various trade publications imply that PostScript with ATM draws characters on the screen faster than TrueType; however, this is primarily a function of hardware and is subject to quick changes due to progress in that technology.

On the quality issue, both formats print to screen well, perhaps a bit too well. True-Type may have a tendency in certain situations to sacrifice type design to draw a better screen rendition. In general, quality of output is pretty much a draw. You have to make your own decision here.

NOTE
Much of what is presented here may be out of date within a couple of years! That's the way the industry is progressing. Imagine, the "desktop publishing" era has only been around for a few years and look at what strides have been made already.

The conclusion? All indications are that new users of this technology will tend to migrate to TrueType fonts, due to the acceptance of Windows 3.1 in this area. Those individuals who have a history of working with the graphic design and printing industries may have established a library of PostScript fonts and wish to follow that lead. Only time will tell if one standard will dominate over the other or if some new emerging standard, such as Multiple Master Fonts, will emerge.

14

More Typographic Maneuvers

To form a new text box 260

select the Text Box tool from the floating Tool palette. Move the cursor to the working area of your document, and actual location does not matter here. Click and drag the mouse button; drag to the opposite corner, forming a rectangle. Then release the mouse button.

To adjust size of the text box 261

use one of several methods available. You can click on the "grab bar" of the item and drag it (use the Content or Item tool), resizing the box as you drag. You can key in size values in the Measurements palette or the Modify dialog box (Item ➤ Modify).

To manipulate the First Baseline area of a text item 264

click on the text box item with the Content or Item tool to identify it. Select the menu option Item ➤ Modify. The Text Box Specifications dialog box allows you to edit values for First Baseline area of that text item.

To alter the text item background 264

click on the text box item with the Content or Item tool to identify it. Select the menu option Item ➤ Modify. The Text Box Specifications dialog box allows you to edit the item's background color and shade.

To lock or unlock the location of a text item   265

click on the text box item with the Content or Item tool to identify it. Select the menu option Item ➤ Lock (or Unlock).

To manage widow and orphan control for text   266

choose Style ➤ Formats. The Paragraph Formats dialog box appears with control options for widow and orphan controls.

To use the Find and Change option for changing attributes   272

first, select the standard Find and Change dialog box (Edit ➤ Find/Change). Then click on the Ignore Attributes option. This opens the dialog box to a larger area including selection of font, style, etc., enabling you to not only search and replace text, but also control that text's attributes as well.

There are typographic features of QuarkXPress that are not easily categorized under the word processing or typographic headings we've covered so far. This chapter encompasses typographic maneuvers for text boxes, paragraph controls, hyphenation, and other special timesaving features.

NOTE

The only place you can enter text in a QuarkXPress document is in a text box. You can key it in or import it from another source, but type will go only into a text box. Once the text is in the text box, you can edit it with the Content tool only.

MODIFYING A TEXT BOX

So far you have been shown how to use text within a text box, as well as how to import, export, color, and shade it, but do you really know how to manipulate that box yet? Here are some basics often overlooked when first starting the QuarkXPress document.

NOTE

Items created on a master page will become master items and will appear on related document pages. Items created on a document page will show only on that document page.

CREATING AND RESIZING A TEXT BOX

To form a new or additional text box, select the Text Box tool. Click and drag to the opposite corner to form a text box. Release the mouse button. The exact size of the text box is not critical, since you can resize it at any time. You resize item boxes in one of three ways.

‣ Make manual changes through dragging the item's grab bars, a common Windows maneuver.

‣ Make precise changes in the Measurements palette

‣ Make precise changes with the Item ➤ Modify option. Identify the text box and select Item ➤ Modify. This brings up the Text Box Specifications dialog box, an outstanding feature of QuarkXPress that enables you to edit numerical coordinates of the item.

Precision is typically down to three decimal places in many fields in the Text Box Specifications dialog box.

THE TEXT BOX SPECIFICATIONS DIALOG BOX

Depending on what item you identify, Item ➤ Modify brings up different dialog boxes. See Figure 14.1 for the various dialog boxes for each item type.

Select the text box and Item ➤ Modify to bring up a dialog box entitled *Text Box Specifications*. You can manipulate this text box and its contents in a variety of ways.

LOCATION AND SIZE VALUES

The first four fields in the dialog box deal with the placement and size of the item. The Origin Across and Origin Down values position the top-left corner of the text box, relative to the 0,0 ruler position. If the 0,0 ruler position changes, these values will automatically change also. The next two values are the Width and Height values. Typically the text box is a rectangle, whose dimensions are reflected here. Similar to other QuarkXPress dialog boxes, you can enter values in any combination of measurement systems and the program will translate them for you. In Figure 14.2, a value has been entered in the Origin Down box that is actually a hybrid of inches and points.

The Box Angle value is the rotation value of the text box. In QuarkXPress you can rotate the text box along with its contents a range of −360–360°, in increments as fine as 0.001°. The default rotation is counterclockwise. A positive number in the Box Angle value rotates the text box counterclockwise; a negative number rotates

FIGURE 14.1

Each type of item (line, groups, picture box, text box) brings up a different Specifications dialog box, as shown here.

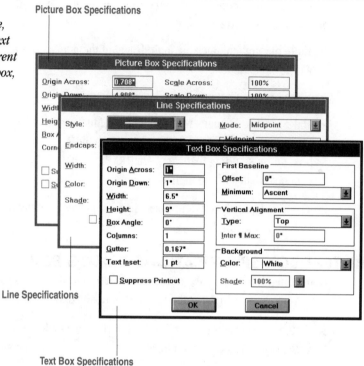

Picture Box Specifications

Line Specifications

Text Box Specifications

the text box clockwise. You can also rotate the text box manually using the Rotation tool or through the Rotation field on the Measurements palette.

TIP

If you want to make money, you must spend money. The best way to work with QuarkXPress is to spend your money on a fast PC with a large monitor and an accelerated, high-resolution graphics card. Remember, QuarkXPress is a production tool. The rule of the game is that whoever gets production out quickest with the highest quality and lowest cost is the winner!

Another interesting feature of QuarkXPress's rotation capability is that you can edit rotated text. This advantage meets with mixed admiration, though. It does save

FIGURE 14.2

QuarkXPress will translate any measurement system combination (almost) that you throw at it. Here a combination of inches and points is placed in the Origin Down and Width values.

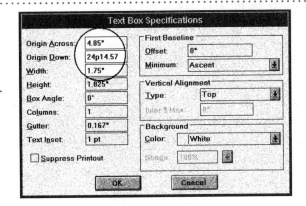

time, in that you don't have to unrotate text or go to some dialog box to edit. In many cases, however, rotated text is difficult to read onscreen, making fine detail editing cumbersome. This problem is mostly a function of your hardware. If you have a standard PC arrangement, perhaps the resolution of the monitor and card are insufficient to read small type at an odd rotation angle.

COLUMNS AND THE GUTTER

The next two field values in the Text Box Specifications dialog box are for Columns and Gutter. These values are similar to the ones you set when creating a new document (in the New dialog box). Values in the New dialog box affect the entire document. In contrast, values in an active Text Box Specifications dialog box change only that item. You can have from 1 to 30 columns and the gutter value can range from 0.042" to 4".

TEXT INSET

The Text Inset value represents how much border or nonprinting space there will be from the edge of the text box to the type. This represents a buffer zone of sorts in that it assures your type will be a minimal distance from the edge. This setting is especially important when you shade the text box or place a border frame around it. Values for the Text Inset are usually in points but you can use other measurement systems. QuarkXPress will translate.

SUPPRESS PRINTOUT

Use this handy check box to prevent the contents in this particular Text Box item from printing. This option will not affect other items on the page. Apply Suppress Printout for occasions when you don't want printed text immediately. An example of this might be a textbook where you want to have a student edition and have teacher's notes non-printing for the student. You can print out a distinct copy for the teacher's edition. Another occasion to use this option may be in an editorial situation when the editor wants to leave notes to the author, artist, etc., that you would not want to print. You may even want to highlight these notes in a color!

FIRST BASELINE

The First Baseline area of the dialog box controls where the paragraph will start. The Offset value represents the first line's starting location from the top of the text box. Values in this field can range from 0″ to 2.665″. It takes only positive values. You can key the measurement from the Ascending characters, Cap Height or Cap + Accent characters in the Minimum pop up menu.

WARNING
Use caution when you apply a First Baseline value, as it may be affected by the Text Inset (the amount of space the text has on all for sides of a text box). These two variables, First Baseline and Text Inset may have a dramatic influence on each other if used simultaneously.

Cap Height is equal to the height of a zero (0) in the font of the largest character on the first line. Cap + Accent is that space *plus* the space needed for an accent mark *above* the Cap Height. Ascent is equal to the height of the ascenders (see Figure 14.3) in the font of the largest character on the first line of text.

VERTICAL ALIGNMENT

Vertical Alignment handles the alignment of text material within the text box. It works just as Vertical Alignment did when you explored it in *Chapter 8*. The Type pop-up menu enables you to specify the alignment: Top, Bottom, Centered, or Justified. Choose Justified and a value field appears for placing the inter-paragraph

FIGURE 14.3

You use the first baseline area to specify the particulars of your typeface with respect to the height of its ascenders and descenders, as well as cap height and point size.

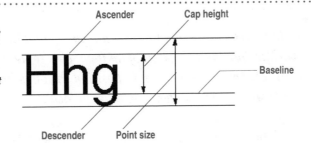

spacing (called Inter ¶ Max). This is a maximum spacing value between paragraphs as they align vertically to fill the text box. Values here range from 0″ to 15″.

BACKGROUND

The background color option shades the text box background, not the type itself, with the chosen color. You can pick colors from the existing document color palette. Edit this color palette through Edit ➤ Colors. Shades are represented in values of 10%, but you may key in your exact value in the field as necessary. The default color is white and has no shade available.

THE MEASUREMENTS PALETTE FOR EDITING THE TEXT BOX

The Measurements palette is another way to position the text box. It includes values for position, size, rotation, and columns. If there is any text in a text box, the Measurement palette also has information on font, style, size, leading, and alignment. To edit the selected text box item from the Measurements palette, simply highlight the value you wish to change, key in your replacement and press Enter. In some cases, you can manipulate arrows or choose from pop-up menus.

LOCKING AND UNLOCKING ITEMS

If you have placed an item on the document page and don't want it to move, you can lock it in position. This is handy when working on a complex layout where the slightest error would mean trouble. If you inadvertently click on an item to move it a pixel or two, it might destroy your layout.

NOTE

At times, relocation of an item is unwanted and inadvertent. To avoid accidental movement of an item, choose Item ➤ Lock (Ctrl+L). This fixes the item in position so you cannot move it. If you wish to move the item you must unlock it first.

To ensure no surprises, anchor important items with the Lock option under the Item menu (Ctrl+L) once you've settled on their final positions. Anchoring items will not prevent you from editing their contents. It only anchors the box, text or picture, containing these items. You can unlock and move it at any time.

MORE PARAGRAPH CONTROL FEATURES

There are two more features for paragraph control you have yet to meet. These include widow and orphan control and initial caps.

CONTROLLING WIDOW AND ORPHAN LINES

First, you may want a refresher on just what widows and orphans are, typographically speaking. They are undesirable effects that fall at the end of a paragraph. A *widow* is a single word in a line by itself, ending a paragraph or starting a page. An *orphan* is a single or partial line at the beginning of a column of type, carried over from the previous column. You can eliminate these manually or use automated settings that help prevent widows and orphans from occurring in the first place.

WARNING

Use of automatic widow and orphan control in the Paragraph Formats dialog box could place entire paragraphs on the next page, leaving a gap in the previous page. This may present an unwanted effect in vertical justification.

FIGURE 14.4

The Paragraph Formats dialog box is the same dialog box you encountered when working with style sheets.

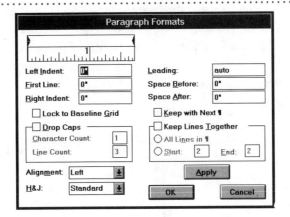

To specify the way lines and paragraphs stay together, choose Style ➤ Formats. The Paragraph Formats dialog box will appear (see Figure 14.4). To keep selected paragraphs grouped with their successors, click on Keep with Next ¶.

To keep all lines of a particular paragraph together (avoiding orphans and widows), check Keep lines Together, then click on All Lines in ¶. When you click All Lines in ¶ QuarkXPress treats the paragraph as an indivisible unit.

HOW TO CREATE THE AUTOMATIC INITIAL CAP

An *initial cap* is the first character or word of a paragraph enlarged to create a special visual effect. QuarkXPress enables you to create this effect several ways, including initial drop caps, initial cap styles, hanging caps, and raised caps.

You must begin by selecting the paragraphs for which you want an initial cap. Typically, you do this by anchoring the cursor within a single paragraph or highlighting a range of paragraphs. The checkbox for initial caps is in the Paragraph Formats dialog box (Style ➤ Formats) as shown in Figure 14.4. Check the Drop Caps option to identify from one to eight characters to alter.

Click on Drop Caps and the dialog box changes to reflect your new choices. You can select the number of characters to drop as well as the number of lines to drop them. The value for line count must be between 2 and 8. You can also increase or decrease the size of a drop cap by highlighting and specifying a percentage in the Measurements palette (see Figure 14.5).

FIGURE 14.5

The default Drop Caps op-
tion in the Paragraph
Formats dialog box gives
the initial cap an out-
standing look. Change the
percentage in the Meas-
urements palette to
increase or decrease the
size of the initial cap.

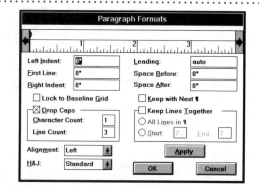

The drop cap percentage

HYPHENATION AND JUSTIFICATION

Justification is a complex process whereby the computer determines how many characters will fit on the line. It takes into account the possibility that the last word on the line can be hyphenated. Regardless, a certain amount of extra (non-charac- ter space) remains. In justification, that extra space is distributed throughout the line, first between words and then between characters. If properly distributed throughout the line, the text appears flush left and flush right (justified). This option usually requires hyphenation to work best. That is why the two are known together are *H & J*.

NOTE

You can include H & J specifications as part of a style sheet's paragraph format. Then you can apply specific H & J settings to various parts of your document as necessary.

SPECIFYING WORD AND CHARACTER SPACING RULES IN JUSTIFICATION

The way in which the program distributes extra space is governed by the settings in the Hyphenation and Justification (H & J) dialog box (see Figure 14.6), which you can see by choosing Edit ➤ H&Js, choosing an H&J file, and clicking Edit.

NOTE

QuarkXPress allows you to control word and character spacing in several ways. These include H & Js, kerning and tracking, standard kerning tables, and customized tracking tables.

The Justification Method area of the dialog box allows you to specify minimum, optimum, and maximum values for both word and character spacing. The justification process uses these values to determine where to add extra space. The minimum spacing value indicates the smallest amount of space allowed between characters or words. In order for the computer to get the best possible fit of characters on the line, it sometimes must squeeze words and characters together (or stretch them apart). The minimum value is the absolute smallest space you allow in this process, while the maximum value is the absolute largest space allowed between words or characters.

FIGURE 14.6
*The Edit Hyphenation and
Justification dialog box*

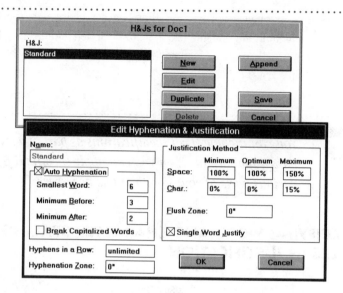

The optimum value is the best possible value for spacing. This is the most desirable because it is the most typographically correct.

H & J specifications for the QuarkXPress document are paragraph attributes. This means that you can apply one set of values to one paragraph and another set of values elsewhere. Different paragraphs may have different needs.

THE FLUSH ZONE

This sounds ominous! The Flush Zone option enables you to specify the area within which the last word in the last line of a justified paragraph must fall to justify. If you were to enter, for example, a value of 1″ in the field, this would mandate that the line be within 1″ of the right indent margin for justification allowance. Otherwise, the text will default to flush left.

NOTE

Justification allowance *is that zone at the end of the line that allows the computer to either place more text or consider justification with no more text on the line. If justification is appropriate, the extra (non-text) space on the line is distributed, first between words, then between characters, if necessary.*

MULTIPLE HYPHENATION SPECIFICATIONS

The Edit Hyphenation and Justification dialog box also gives you a choice of automatic or manual hyphenation. Check the Auto Hyphenation option and you can specify values for the smallest word to hyphenate, minimum number of characters before a hyphen, and the minimum number of characters after a hyphen. Leave this option unchecked to hyphenate manually.

WARNING

Although H & J follows preset rules for hyphenation for English, it is sometimes incorrect. Careful proofreading is always advised.

In the same dialog box, you also have control over the *hyphenation zone*. That is, you can determine where the hyphens are to be in the line. You may want to force-justify text up to a half inch from the end of the line; if so, place that value in the Hyphenation Zone field. This gives you more control over the text within that ½″ zone, countering inappropriate automated hyphenation. Also, you can control how many successive hyphenated lines your copy has.

NOTE

For good typography, do not hyphenate more than two lines in succession. This condition is know as a stack *or* ladder *and should be avoided.*

THE FIND AND CHANGE OPTION

If you have followed along in the book and tried each new feature as introduced, there's very little left, at least in the type manipulation area. Here is one holdout; it is use of the Find and Change feature. Use this for text replacement (search and replace) and, as an added bonus, can also change type attributes!

NOTE

The Find and Change feature is a standard Windows feature; the function and design of Find/Change is dictated by Windows, not by QuarkXPress.

A typical word processing feature that QuarkXPress incorporates is the Find/Change option. Select this by choosing Edit ➤ Find/Change or by using the keyboard shortcut Ctrl+F (see Figure 14.7). As you would expect, the Find/Change option allows you to find a string of text with the options of matching the whole word or just part and of including case sensitivity. You can use this to search for a particular word or phrase without making changes or you can take advantage of the Change to aspect of the dialog box to replace the phrase with a new one. Click on Find Next and it will search forward through the document to find the information you seek.

FIGURE 14.7

The Find and Change dialog box

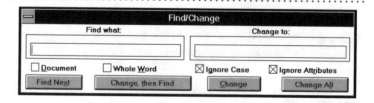

USING ATTRIBUTES

Click on the Ignore Attributes option, and the dialog box opens to an array of Find and Change features (see Figure 14.8). You can search and replace not only text,

FIGURE 14.8

The full Find/Change dialog box with attributes

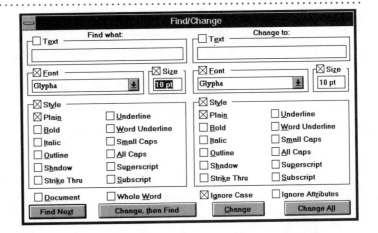

but also the font, size, and style. You can search for any or all of these attributes independently. Use this to search for only 12 point text in the document and replace it with 10 point text; search for bold text and replace with italic. Any combination is acceptable.

TIP

When working on a situation involving text, use a shortcut of popular words in your keystroking. For example, in this book, the word QuarkXPress *is used often. Rather than typing this repeatedly, the author used the code* QX. *After all input, the Find/Change option allowed a quick replacement of* QX *with* QuarkXPress. *That is also why you never hear the software referred to simply as XPress!*

GRAPHICS AND PICTURES

15

Manipulating Pictures and Graphics

To draw a square picture box or circular oval 281

hold down the Shift key as you draw or resize the graphic box.

To create any of the four picture box shapes 281

select the appropriate tool from the Tools palette. Then click and drag (to the opposite corner) to create the picture box.

To help clarify your import possibilities 283

it may be useful to know a little about graphics. There is a difference in file formats and the types of graphics that applications produce. A file format is the method or structure that the image data is recorded in. You can use the same file format for more than one kind of graphic image. The type of graphic (bitmapped or object oriented) determines quality of the picture.

To double the quality of imported TIFF and RIFF screen images 286

hold down the Shift key as you import the graphic. These images normally reproduce on the screen at 36 dots per inch (dpi), but you can raise that to 72 dpi by this technique.

As stated earlier, QuarkXPress is centered around the concept of *items* (text boxes, picture boxes, lines, and groups). This section of the book discusses the picture box and its capabilities.

To use a graphic or picture element in QuarkXPress, you must first create a picture box in which to place that element. These picture boxes come in a variety of shapes, as do graphic elements. One common thread in all picture box shapes is that they must originate from the picture box tools on the Tools palette.

PICTURE BOXES IN QUARKXPRESS

All pictures, including charts and graphs, as well as the obvious photograph, help bring a page layout to life. They add emphasis and they communicate to the reader, often enhancing the surrounding text. QuarkXPress allows you to import a variety of picture formats including scans, paint, draw, and illustration graphics. After importing a graphic, you can resize, reposition, and manipulate it in several ways.

NOTE

An active picture box is one that you select then modify through Item ➤ Modify. You can only modify one box at a time (the active one).

THE TOOLS PALETTE AND PICTURE BOX CREATION TOOLS

To incorporate pictures or graphics, you must first create a picture box, since all pictures must be contained in a picture box. The way you create a picture box in QuarkXPress is to use one of the four picture box creation tools in the Tools palette.

NOTE

A polygon picture box must have at least three sides.

Each picture box tool has its own shape, because in most cases, pictures will rest within text; that is, text will flow around a picture item in some way. As these two items mix, there are considerations of *layering* and *runaround*, which are the focus of *Chapter 16*.

NOTE

To specify a corner radius (the radius of each corner of the rectangle), for an active picture box, use the Corner Radius field of the Picture Box Specification dialog box (Item ➤ Modify). You can also use the corner radius icon in the Measurements palette. This is the icon that looks like a curved corner. You can overstrike its numerical value to change the radius.

To create any of the four picture box shapes, select the appropriate tool from the Tools palette. Then click and drag (to the opposite corner) to create the picture box. Just as with text boxes, picture boxes can be resized or relocated manually or numerically. Do not be concerned with detail initially. There are four picture box shapes to choose from, the Rectangular Picture Box, the Rounded-corner Rectangular Picture Box, the Oval Picture Box, and the Polygon Picture Box (see Figure 15.1).

NOTE

To draw a perfectly square or perfectly circular picture box, hold down the Shift key as you draw or resize the graphic box.

You can manipulate picture boxes in the following ways:

▸ Use the Item or Content tool to alter the box shape by clicking and dragging the grab bar

FIGURE 15.1

You can draw any of four picture box shapes: a rectangle, a rounded rectangle, an oval, or a polygon.

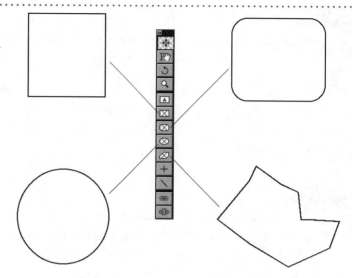

- Move the box through click and drag of the Item tool (click on the body of the box, not the grab bar)

- Reposition graphic or picture elements inside the box with the Content tool (click and drag the element, not on the grab bars)

- Rotate picture boxes using the Rotation tool (this works the same as with text boxes)

- The Measurements palette gives information about location, size, and rotation of the box, which you can alter to change it

- Select Item ➤ Modify for the Picture Box Specification dialog box and adjust the settings to your liking

NOTE

Hold down Ctrl and double-click with the Item or Content tool on an item box and the Specifications dialog box appears.

TYPES OF GRAPHICS AND FILE FORMATS

To help clarify your possibilities with QuarkXPress, it is useful to know a little about graphics. There is a difference in file formats and the types of graphics that applications produce. A *file format* is the method or structure that the image data is recorded in. You can use the same file format for more than one kind of graphic image. The type of graphic (bitmapped or object oriented) determines quality of the picture.

TYPES OF GRAPHICS

There are two generic types of graphic images used in the personal computer environment. They are *bitmapped* and *object oriented* (raster). The bitmapped image is the older of the two types. Perhaps the easiest way to understand bitmapped is with the dot or pixel, as images appear on the computer screen. Each image consists of a series of dots or pixels used to paint the picture on the monitor. In bitmapped graphics, the dot-composed images are created as dots on the printer. Early in the desktop computer revolution, there were no laser printers and the dot-matrix printer was dominant. Bitmapped graphics print well in dot matrix, partly because the image is composed of dots. Also, people didn't expect terrific quality. Today, more sophisticated technology is used and bitmapped graphics show excellent dots. The problem is, now people have certain standards of quality and they don't want the dots. They want perfect images from the printer.

The object oriented graphic is higher quality, both onscreen and in print, because it draws from a series of mathematical formulas composing the look of the image. When the graphic is resized, the formulas recalculate the best look of the image. The output is near perfect, no "jaggies", especially on imagesetter output. The processor that calculates the object oriented images for imagesetting is called the *RIP*, which stands for Raster Image Processor.

IMPORTING VARIOUS FILE FORMATS

In QuarkXPress, you first must create the picture box, then import a picture or graphic element from another file or paste from the clipboard. The graphic file is usually generated from another application outside QuarkXPress. You can use files from a variety of software types, including draw, paint, illustration, and scanned images.

As cross-platform computer practices grow in various industries, you can expect to see new file formats. There are two ways to anticipate this probability. First, you should communicate with your clients and users of the "other" computer platform to see whether their software can store in a compatible form. If it cannot, then bring data in by disk, modem, network, etc. The second method is to find a translation program. These programs enable you to translate from one foreign file format to a more familiar one. In most cases, any file format can convert to another usable format. At times it may take a couple of translations, but with perseverance you will prevail.

QuarkXPress is a cross-platform software product. It was first written for the Macintosh environment and recently was released as a Windows compatible software product for the PC line of computers. Because of this, versatility with file formats is mandatory. QuarkXPress for Windows imports pictures of the following types and extensions:

TYPE	EXTENSION
Bitmap	.BMP, .DIB, .RLE
CompuServe GIF	.GIF
Computer Graphics Metafile	.CGM
Encapsulated PostScript	.EPS
HPGL	.PLT
Macintosh PICT	.PCT
Micrografx Designer	.DRW
Paintbrush	.PCX
Scitex	.CT
TIFF	.TIF
Windows Metafile	.WMF

Here is a closer look at a few of the popular formats.

THE BITMAPPED AND PAINTBRUSH FILE FORMATS

Some applications create bitmapped images made of dots or screen pixels. These images are unique in that resized images appear to be larger bits, unlike other file formats in which the image as a whole enlarges. Bitmapped and paintbrush images are simply a collection of dots that compose the graphic image. These dots are pixels (picture elements) on your screen. These images are typically the lowest resolution quality for printing purposes.

TIFF IMAGES

A popular file format for PC and Mac computers is *Tagged Image File Format*. Like paint files, TIFF images are bitmapped, but they are resizable. They can be any size and have any resolution. Typically, scanned images are stored as TIFF images. TIFF images are commonly black-and-white or grayscale, but a few programs support color TIFF images.

NOTE
You can convert pictures when importing through keyboard commands. Hold down Ctrl while importing a TIFF grayscale to convert it to TIFF Line Art. To convert TIFF line art to TIFF grayscale, hold down the Alt key during the import. Hold down Ctrl and import to convert TIFF Color to TIFF grayscale.

TIFF formats are a standard on many different computer platforms, but not all TIFF images produced on these different platforms are alike. IBM TIFF images differ slightly from Mac TIFF files, due to the different data storage conventions used by each computer; these must be converted when moving from one platform to another. Several programs with TIFF images include a conversion utility (a growing concern in cross-platform production), which translates IBM to Mac and vice versa.

TIFF images can be quite large. It is common, for example, for a full-screen image in TIFF to take up nearly 900K on disk. It may be impractical to include in your document at that size. Therefore, QuarkXPress stores and displays TIFF images in the lower-resolution PICT format. The higher resolution TIFF image must be accessible to QuarkXPress, but not within the same file as your document. The original file links with a lower resolution image in the document. To send documents with TIFF images to a service bureau, you must also include the original high-resolution file for the imagesetter. If you fail to do this, you will get a bitmapped image (lower resolution) of the picture.

THE RASTER IMAGE FILE FORMAT

Similar to TIFF, the *Raster Image File Format* (RIFF) is a high-resolution image format designed for quality output. TIFF and RIFF images print well on imagesetters, which use photographic paper and high-quality laser exposure, yielding "continuous" tones at nearly 3000 dpi.

NOTE

Typically, TIFF and RIFF representations reproduce on the screen at 36 dots per inch (dpi). You can increase the screen resolution of the picture to 72 dpi by holding down the Shift key as you import the graphic.

ENCAPSULATED POSTSCRIPT GRAPHICS

PostScript files with a screen preview are *Encapsulated PostScript* (EPS) files. This is the higher-level drawing file format used by such programs as Illustrator and Freehand. QuarkXPress also creates EPS files through File ➤ Save Page as EPS.

The EPS format, like TIFF, is equally popular in the Mac and IBM communities. In fact, the two platforms can communicate without conversion with EPS files. This is due, in part, to the presence of PostScript in the desktop computer marketplace.

EPS files tend to be large. Therefore a lower-resolution representation of the image displays while high-resolution data resides in file for output calculations. EPS file names are shown in the QuarkXPress Picture Usage dialog box (Utilities ➤ Picture Usage).

PICTURE MANIPULATION IN QUARKXPRESS

If you take the word *picture* to include all graphic images, QuarkXPress has a wide variety of methods for importing, storing, manipulating, and printing pictures. The previous section presented graphic descriptions; now you can bring them into play!

NOTE

Many people working with QuarkXPress speak of it with words like "having fun." Maybe this is because it gives you the freedom to imagine better graphic solutions. It's a philosophical point, but imagination and fun are mandatory in graphic design philosophy.

IMPORTING PICTURES

As noted earlier, you can import pictures from a variety of file formats. To do this you must perform the following steps:

1. Make sure there is the graphic somewhere in your system to import. It can be on file on a floppy disk, on your hard drive, on a network connection, or whatever, but it must be accessible.

2. Create a picture box with one of the four picture box creation tools from the Tools palette. The size and location of the box is not critical yet, since you can relocate or resize later.

3. Using the Content tool, click on the new picture box to select it. You can import graphics with the Content tool and the picture box combination only (see Figure 15.2).

4. Select File ➤ Get Picture or simply use the keyboard equivalent Ctrl+E. This brings you to a dialog box where you can choose the file to import (see Figure 15.3).

5. Search through the dialog box to locate a graphic file to import. Clicking on **Preview** presents a rough representation of the image.

6. Press Enter or click on **Open** to import.

FIGURE 15.2

You can edit or import the picture box contents with the Content tool.

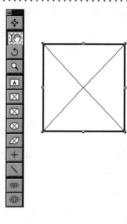

FIGURE 15.3

The Get Picture dialog box allows you to select a picture file to import.

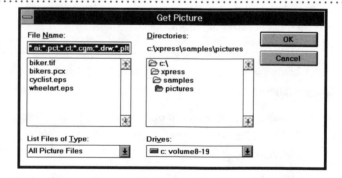

As your image imports there is a good chance that it isn't quite what you expected. Perhaps the screen image has low-resolution quality. That does not necessarily relate to print quality. Remember, there may be a linked high-resolution image tagged to that graphic box for printer purposes.

Another observation: The image and picture box have no apparent correlation in size or ratio. You may import a large picture into a small picture box, or a square picture into a rectangular box. Remember, when you created the picture box, its initial size and location weren't important. The size and positioning of both the picture and the picture box can be controlled independently of each other.

NOTE
If your picture box appears empty after graphic import, it probably means that a blank area of the picture falls on the window area of your picture box. Try using Ctrl+Shift+M to center the image in the middle of the picture box. This will start your manipulation of the graphic to fit it in the picture box.

Another situation that may arise is that of the image nearly, or even completely, missing the box "window." The fix for this is a simple adjustment of moving or resizing.

MODIFYING THE IMPORTED GRAPHIC AND PICTURE BOX

Once the image imports to the picture box, you can make modifications. Which one you change first depends on your layout and the graphic image. Here, you can take the approach of reshaping the box first, as the examples shown are too small for the existing picture box.

NOTE
To immediately resize the imported graphic to fit the size of the picture box, key Ctrl+Shift+F. If you don't like the result, immediately press Ctrl+Z (Edit ➤ Undo).

Figure 15.4 demonstrates how to enlarge the picture box manually. Use either the Content tool or the Item tool to enlarge the box. Resizing the box will not distort the image itself.

Other picture box controls are in the Measurements palette and the Picture Box Specifications dialog box (discussed later in this chapter).

FIGURE 15.4

*You can manually extend
the picture box by drag-
ging one of the grab bars.*

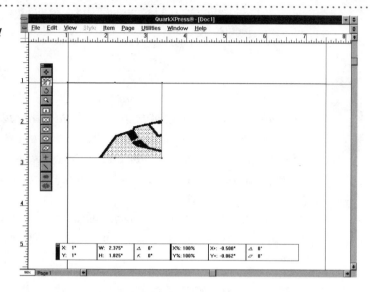

NOTE

*To reposition the graphic element inside the picture box, use the
Content tool. This tool changes the cursor to a hand icon when
over a picture box. You should click on the picture with the hand
icon and drag it as necessary. This does not change the size or
aspect ratio of the picture; it only slides it around inside the
picture box.*

Manual resizing of the picture box allows you a quick look at the box in relationship to the graphic it holds. As you can see in Figure 15.5, the box is much larger
than the graphic. It will have to be resized, and perhaps the graphic should also be
resized. To adjust size of the box, again, drag grab bars until the picture is
"framed" to your satisfaction. To adjust the size of the graphic image, use the Picture Box Specification dialog box.

FIGURE 15.5

After enlarging the picture box, you can view the entire graphic image.

THE PICTURE BOX SPECIFICATIONS DIALOG BOX

Select the picture box and choose Item ➤ Modify for the Picture Box Specifications dialog box (see Figure 15.6). This dialog box is the most extensive area for manipulating the picture box numerically. You could also use the Measurements palette, but it is not as inclusive for all picture box values.

NOTE

Oval and Polygon Picture boxes do not have the Corner Radius field showing in the Picture Box Specifications dialog box.

The first six fields on the left in the PBS dialog box have similar value areas to that of the Measurements palette. They tell the location (origin down and origin across of the box), width and height, rotation angle, and corner radius (if applicable). Changing any of these values will affect the picture box accordingly.

FIGURE 15.6

*The Picture Box Specifica-
tions dialog box*

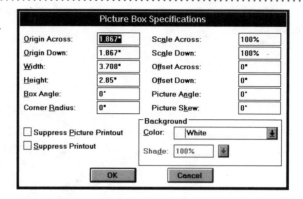

Box Angle (rotation) values range from −360° to 360° in 0.001° increments. Corner Radius values range from 0″ to 2″. The Corner Radius field is not available for
oval or polygon boxes.

NOTE

Keeping the aspect ratio *constant means that when the width of an
item changes in size, its length changes by the same percentage.
For example, if a 2″ by 3″ box were reduced 50%,* both *the width
and height would be reduced by 50%, leaving you with a 1″ by
1¹/₂″ box.*

In the second column of the PBS dialog box, you have scaling values. Scale Across
modifies the picture box in a horizontal scale. Scale Down modifies the box in a
vertical field. Scale values for either field range from 10% to 1000% in 0.1% increments. You can maintain the same *aspect ratio* by placing equal values in the
Scale Across and Scale Down fields.

NOTE

Offset values are relative to the position of the box origin. They do not necessarily reflect measurements from the ruler or relative document location.

To numerically reposition the picture within the active picture box, use the Offset Across and Offset Down fields. A positive value in the Offset Across field moves the picture to the right; a negative value moves it to the left. In the Offset Down field, a positive value moves the picture down, while a negative value moves it up.

To rotate the picture within the box (while leaving the picture box unrotated), use the Picture Angle field. You can rotate the picture in a range similar to that of the box angle. Values range from −360° to 360° in 0.001° increments.

You can slant the picture within the picture box by entering values within the Picture Skew field. Values for skew range from 75° to −75° in 0.001° increments. Positive values slant to the right and negative values slant the picture left (see Figure 15.7).

The Background area of the PBS dialog box enables you to apply color and shade to the picture box. Even if the picture is not in color, you can add background color through this area of the dialog box. Colors listed in the pop-up menu include those on the document's system palette. Add or edit using Edit ➤ Colors. (See *Chapter 17* for full details in this area.) Shade modification values range from 0% to 100% in 0.1% increments. You can choose from a pop-up menu or just type in the value.

To prevent an active picture box and its contents from printing, check the Suppress Printout option. To print the picture box but not its contents, check the Suppress Picture Printout box. These two options are timesavers when dealing with complex graphic images, which can seem to take forever to image.

NOTE

It is important to keep in mind that when the Item tool is selected, Cut, Copy, Paste, Clear, and Delete all work on both the item and its contents. When the Content tool is selected, these commands work on the contents of the box alone.

Use the Item tool and Cut (Edit ➤ Cut) to remove an active picture box and its contents. Cut will place the removed item and its contents on the Clipboard. The Copy option places a duplicate of the selected item and its contents on the Clipboard. Paste places a copy of the Clipboard's contents in the center of the current screen. Activate the picture item with the Item tool, and the Clear option removes the item with its contents. Use the Content tool, and Clear removes only the contents of the item, leaving the picture box itself. Delete removes the picture box and its contents (similar to using the combination of Item tool and Clear).

FIGURE 15.7
*These photos illustrate
the various picture box
manipulation techniques
at work.*

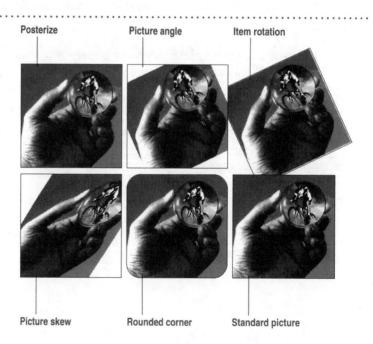

OTHER PICTURE CONTROL TECHNIQUES

Along with the manipulation methods mentioned, there are a few remaining techniques accessed from menus. These include the use of the Style menu items. When a picture box is active and the Content tool is selected, the Style menu takes on a new look, specifically for picture boxes. Options include addition of color and shade to the image; the ability to make a picture appear negative; contrast variables and screen choices for printing.

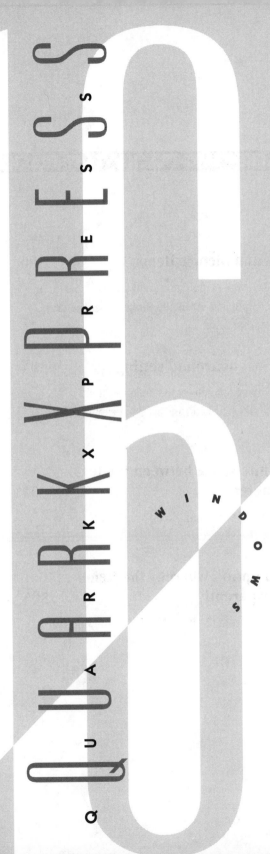

COMBINING TEXT AND GRAPHICS

To combine text items and picture items 300

you must take into consideration each item's runaround and layering effects. Both of these can be manipulated through options under the Item menu options.

To use the Item mode of runaround setting 301

leave the runaround options unchanged (this is the default setting). This will allow a normal runaround, whereby text runs around graphic objects or other text items.

To place a non-type white space between the text and the text box perimeter 304

use the text inset field in the Type Specification Box dialog box (Item ➤ Modify or Ctrl+M).

To create a runaround option whereby the items appear to overlap transparently 305

select the runaround option NONE from the Item ➤ Runaround options.

TRACKS

There are two major areas of consideration when combining text and graphics: *runarounds* and *layering*. Runarounds refer to the effects you can get in QuarkXPress when you place an item (typically a picture item) in the middle of text. Layering involves organizing multiple items on top of one another on the document page. Each item takes up a new layer, like a tissue overlay over a mechanical layout. Each time an item is resized, moved, or changed in any way, it goes to the top of the stack. Layering can be somewhat frustrating for the beginner and can cause problems for anyone if not handled properly.

RUNAROUND TEXT AND GRAPHICS

QuarkXPress treats a *runaround*, or *text wrap*, as the way in which text flows with respect to items and pictures placed in front of the text. When you choose to run text around a picture, there are variations to consider. You can elect to run text around the picture box perimeter or the frame; you may want to run text around the picture itself. In any event, there is an assortment of runaround variables that must be set. Variables can be selected for any item: picture box, text box, line, or group. The manner in which you combine these runaround variables determine your results.

NOTE

Think of Item mode with runarounds as being similar to oil and water. Pour oil in water and the water makes room for the oil; it does not mix with it. In a similar way, when you place a text or picture box over another text box, the text moves away, like water from the oil.

Usually you run text around either picture or text boxes. It is rare that you run text around lines or grouped items, although certain graphic designs may require it. QuarkXPress offers a variety of runaround techniques, including the categories of None, Item, Auto Image, and Manual Image. You'll find these options in the Runaround dialog box for an active item (Item ➤ Runaround), which is where you control most of the parameters of runarounds (see Figure 16.1).

FIGURE 16.1

The Runaround dialog box for an active item

Runaround Specifications	
Mode:	Item
Top:	1 pt
Left:	1 pt
Bottom:	1 pt
Right:	1 pt
Invert	
OK	
Cancel	

TEXT BOX ITEMS WITH RUNAROUND MODE: ITEM

Item mode is the default runaround setting (see Figure 16.2). This option forces the text to wrap around the graphic object by a prescribed distance on all sides.

If two text box items are involved, the text of one item box runs around the text of the newer text box item. As you create a text box, it is placed on the top layer of other elements in your design. Previous text may wrap around this new text element as if it were a picture box. The default offset value in the Item mode is 1 point on each side. Here, a small text box is positioned over another text box.

NOTE

With text boxes, you have only the Item and None modes for runaround. With picture boxes, though, you can select from all four runaround options.

The active text box is shaded, with reduced type. Notice that the text in the larger box has moved out of the way to make room for the smaller one.

FIGURE 16.2

The smaller text box is placed on the larger. The smaller box is active and shows Item runaround mode.

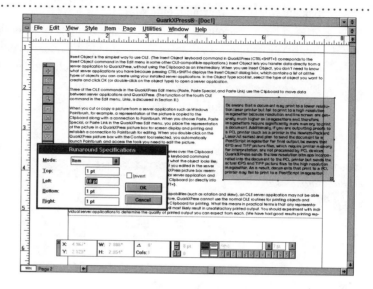

The combination of your item runarounds may initially lack the quality you want. Certain combinations of items with runaround items cause text to flow odd on any or all sides of an item. To help this, you can be selective of runaround distances on each side of a runaround rectangle. Certain "tweaking" of the runaround specifications will eventually give you a pleasing result (see Figure 16.3). Note that the left value is the only one changed, but it is a more pleasing layout of two runaround items.

One runaround problem for many new users of QuarkXPress is that of the three-sided runaround (see Figure 16.4). This is not a glitch in the runaround; it was planned! Think about it: In a one column layout, would you really want type broken up with a graphic image in the middle? No! The best way to handle four-sided runarounds is to have multiple columns, as discussed later in this chapter. The blank area in a three-sided runaround may be to the left or to the right of the runaround area, depending to how close your runaround item is to a given margin.

FIGURE 16.3

Placing more offset space on the side will give a pleasing runaround.

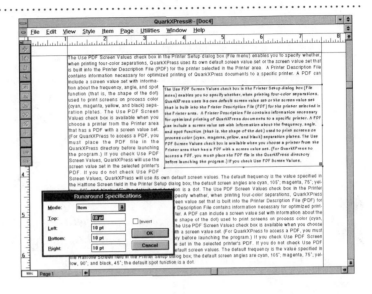

FIGURE 16.4

The three sided run-around for single columns of type

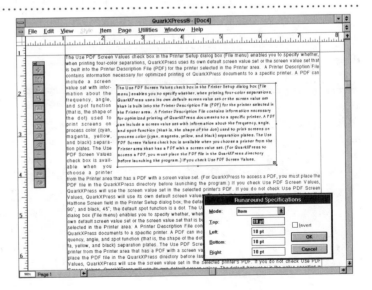

QuarkXPress does not allow you to design poor typographic conditions by using a four-sided runaround for single columns of text. When asked whether they would "fix" this condition, the Quark people answered *no!*

Incorporating text and picture boxes with Item mode works much like text on text runarounds, except that the picture doesn't actually move out of the way; it is simply covered up. Figure 16.5 shows a shaded text box placed over a picture box. The picture box contains a PICT item and does not move away. You should expect this result for any format of picture item.

TIP

If you want to put some white space between the text and the text box perimeter, use the text inset field in the Type Specification Box dialog box (Item ➤ Modify or Ctrl+M).

Notice that in Figure 16.5, the runaround values are 10 points on all sides. One problem you may encounter with runaround value is when a text box positions over a photograph, such as in the example. The picture does not break apart for

FIGURE 16.5

Picture boxes running around text work a little differently. The picture does not displace to make room for the text; rather, the text box just covers up a portion of the figure.

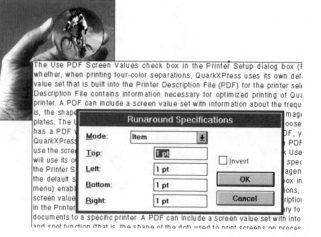

runaround. Therefore, the runaround values chosen, such as in the example, are of little significance.

TEXT BOX ITEMS WITH RUNAROUND MODE: NONE

Perhaps the best way to understand the None runaround mode is to visualize the type (or graphic) being on clear acetate. The image appears with a transparent background, allowing you to see other "layers" or items beneath it. This can get quite confusing, if you see several layers at once.

Figure 16.6 demonstrates what happens to the small, shaded text box when it is placed on another text box and the runaround mode is changed to None. At first there doesn't appear to be much difference from previous examples, unless you had to read the larger box text!

Because the example in Figure 16.6 is shaded, you cannot see the two layers simultaneously. Shading acts as an opaque coloring on the item. No shading or coloration would render the item background as transparent.

To demonstrate this, there is a third, non-shaded text box in Figure 16.7. This new text box is simply a headline reading *Runaround Set to None*. It appears to be transparent; you can see through the background to the type behind it. The text in

FIGURE 16.6

When the runaround mode for the small, shaded text box is set to None, the larger text box becomes impossible to read, since the text continues "behind" the smaller runaround box.

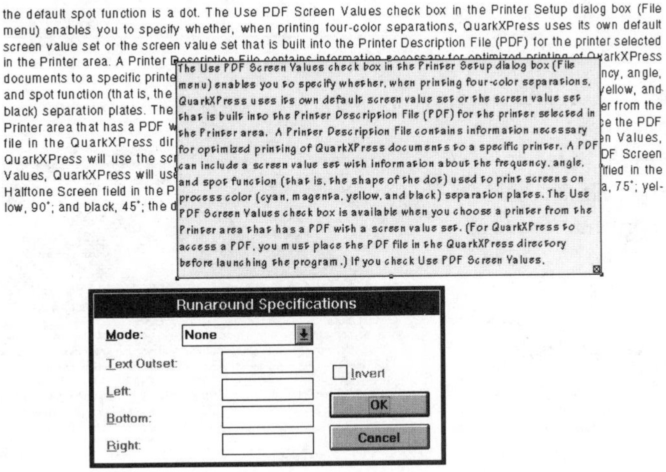

the default spot function is a dot. The Use PDF Screen Values check box in the Printer Setup dialog box (File menu) enables you to specify whether, when printing four-color separations, QuarkXPress uses its own default screen value set or the screen value set that is built into the Printer Description File (PDF) for the printer selected in the Printer area. A Printer Description File contains information necessary for optimized printing of QuarkXPress documents to a specific printer... and spot function (that is, the... black) separation plates. The... Printer area that has a PDF w... file in the QuarkXPress dir... QuarkXPress will use the sc... Values, QuarkXPress will us... Halftone Screen field in the P... low, 90°; and black, 45°; the d...

The Use PDF Screen Values check box in the Printer Setup dialog box (File menu) enables you to specify whether, when printing four-color separations, QuarkXPress uses its own default screen value set or the screen value set that is built into the Printer Description File (PDF) for the printer selected in the Printer area. A Printer Description File contains information necessary for optimized printing of QuarkXPress documents to a specific printer. A PDF can include a screen value set with information about the frequency, angle, and spot function (that is, the shape of the dot) used to print screens on process color (cyan, magenta, yellow, and black) separation plates. The Use PDF Screen Values check box is available when you choose a printer from the Printer area that has a PDF with a screen value set. (For QuarkXPress to access a PDF, you must place the PDF file in the QuarkXPress directory before launching the program.) If you check Use PDF Screen Values,

Runaround Specifications

Mode: None

Text Outset:
Left:
Bottom:
Right:

Invert
OK
Cancel

the other two boxes does not move away from the new item, because it is set to None runaround mode. This can be either good or bad for your layout.

Figure 16.8 shows how the None mode works for several items. The unshaded text boxes appear transparent. The shaded box still appears to be opaque, and the text behind it is still unreadable. The picture is the bottom layer of this stack. Since the picture consists of all pixels in a PICT graphic, there is no background to have transparent. Therefore, setting the runaround to None for the graphic element is meaningless. If placed on the top layer it would completely cover the text beneath it. Layering can get to be a problem when working on a complex layout.

FIGURE 16.7

The third text box has no shading and is set to the None runaround mode. Thus you can see both text boxes "beneath" it.

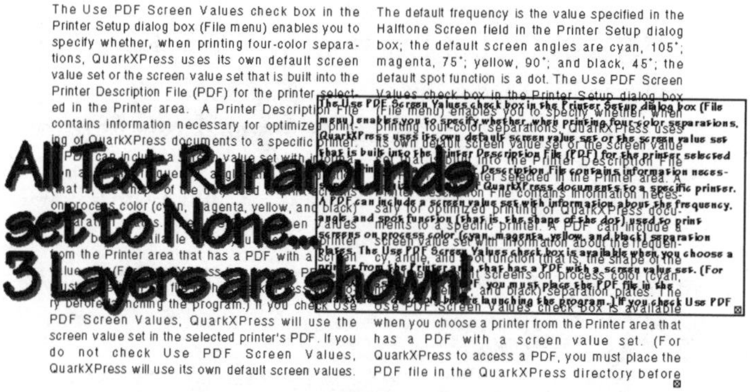

FIGURE 16.8

Using the None runaround mode with text over text items and over picture box items can lead to fairly complicated (and not always aesthetically pleasing!) layouts.

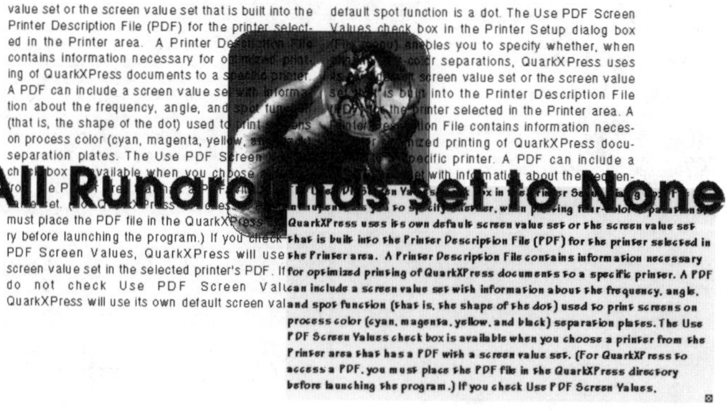

PICTURE BOX ITEMS SET TO RUNAROUND MODE: ITEM

In a manner similar to text boxes, picture boxes with the runaround mode set to Item (the default) disperse text "behind" them. In Figure 16.9, the example has a photo inside a picture box, placed in a two-column layout. The corners are rounded to demonstrate slight type wraps near the corners. Given that this is not a perfect square, a new field shows in the Runaround Specifications dialog box: *Text Outset*. This setting generally takes care of any odd shaped item box and treats all sides equally. Rounding the corners on this rectangular box makes it similar (at least to QuarkXPress) to an oval picture box.

As you can see, with a text outset value of 10 points, there is a noticeable white border around the graphic restricting text flow. This is not good typography, because some type lines need adjustment, some *TLC*. You can provide this in a number of ways, including adjusting the runaround outset, the photo box size, etc.

Notice too, that this is a two column layout and the runaround appears to take place on all sides. The runaround is still a three-sided layout, but with two columns it gives you the illusion of four sides. The type is readable in a two column layout where it would not have been in a single column with similar runaround.

FIGURE 16.9

A graphic with the runaround mode set to Item with a text outset of 6 points is placed over two columns of type.

The Use PDF Screen Values check box in the Printer Setup dialog box (File menu) enables you to specify whether, when printing four-color separations, QuarkXPress uses its own default screen value set or the screen value set that is built into the Printer Description File (PDF) for the printer selected in the Printer area. A Printer Description File contains information necessary for optimized printing of QuarkXPress documents to a specific printer. A PDF can include a screen value set with information about the frequency, angle, and spot function (that is, the shape of the dot) used to print screens on process color (cyan, magenta, yellow, and black) separation plates. The Use PDF Screen Values check box is available when you choose a printer from the Printer area that has a PDF with a screen value set. (For QuarkXPress to access a PDF, you must place the PDF file in the QuarkXPress directory before launching the pro-

gram.) If you check Use PDF Screen Values, QuarkXPress will use the screen value set in the selected printer's PDF. If you do not check Use PDF Screen Values, QuarkXPress will use its own default screen values. The default frequency is the value specified in the Halftone Screen field in the Printer Setup dialog box; the default screen angles are cyan, 105°; magenta, 75°; yellow, 90°; and black, 45°; the default spot function is a dot. The Use PDF Screen Values check box in the Printer Setup dialog box (File menu) enables you to specify whether, when printing four-color separations, QuarkXPress uses its own default screen value set or the screen value set that is built into the Printer Description File (PDF) for the printer selected in the Printer Description File (PDF) for the printer selected File c printin

PICTURE BOX ITEMS SET TO RUNAROUND MODE: NONE

What do you think happens when you place a picture over text items and have the picture box set to None runaround mode? Right, you can't read the text. Maybe this is a problem, maybe not. Depends on the client, right?

In theory, placing a picture box (with Runaround: None) over a text box will simply make the picture background transparent. However, if you are working with a photograph, as in Figure 16.10, with no "background," None has no effect.

What if you were using a different graphic, a non-photo type? The results might be a bit different. Try it! When you place runaround to None, the graphic background should *appear* transparent. The graphic foreground is shown and appears as if it were on the top layer, over previous elements on the document page.

AUTO IMAGE MODE

Auto Image is a runaround mode that is designed for picture box items. It cannot be applied to text box items. The idea behind Auto Image is that you can have QuarkXPress automatically determine where the type will run around your graphic. Simply place the runaround mode on Auto Image, set the text outset, and

FIGURE 16.10

Placing a bitmapped graphic in a picture box with runaround mode set to None covers the text, because in a photo, there is no background that can be set to "transparent."

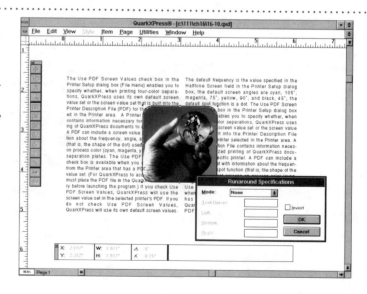

you're done! The only problem is that it doesn't do much for photographs. See Figure 16.11 for results in placing a photograph in a picture box set to Auto Image.

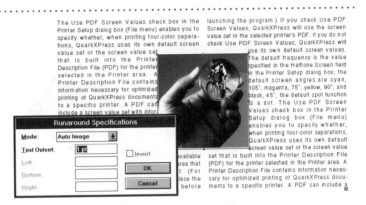

The Use PDF Screen Values check box in the Printer Setup dialog box (File menu) enables you to specify whether, when printing four-color separations, QuarkXPress uses its own default screen value set or the screen value set that is built into the Printer Description File (PDF) for the printer selected in the Printer area. A Printer Description File contains information necessary for optimized printing of QuarkXPress documents to a specific printer. A PDF can include a screen value set with infor

launching the program.) If you check Use PDF Screen Values, QuarkXPress will use the screen value set in the selected printer's PDF. If you do not check Use PDF Screen Values, QuarkXPress will use its own default screen values. The default frequency is the value specified in the Halftone Screen field in the Printer Setup dialog box; the default screen angles are cyan, 105°; magenta, 75°; yellow, 90°; and black, 45°; the default spot function is a dot. The Use PDF Screen Values check box in the Printer Setup dialog box (File menu) enables you to specify whether, when printing four-color separations, QuarkXPress uses its own default screen value set or the screen value set that is built into the Printer Description File (PDF) for the printer selected in the Printer area. A Printer Description File contains information necessary for optimized printing of QuarkXPress documents to a specific printer. A PDF can include a

Runaround Specifications

Mode: Auto Image

Text Outset: 1 pt

Left

Bottom:

Right:

☐ Invert

OK

Cancel

vailable
rea that
t. (For
lace the
before

NOTE

In Item mode, the runaround goes around the item's box. In Auto Image or Manual Image mode, the runaround goes around the graphic, not the box. That is why Auto Image and Manual Image are available for picture boxes and not text boxes.

Auto Image is a bit improved in Figure 16.12. See how the text delicately wraps around the graphic image, not just the perimeter picture box. Okay, it doesn't look that great! A little *TLC* again? In the event that you have images spread between two columns and you want the text to wrap tightly around the picture, change the alignment to *Justified*. In the example, alignment is set to be ragged on the right. This will never wrap tight around the picture.

MANUAL IMAGE MODE

If you want something done right, you have to do it yourself. To have total control over your type, or at least as much as a computer allows, select the Manual Image runaround mode. This allows you to specify where the text will wrap around your

FIGURE 16.12

Use of a graphic element (non-photo) with Auto Image mode of run-around. Notice how the text wraps around the image itself rather than the picture box perimeter.

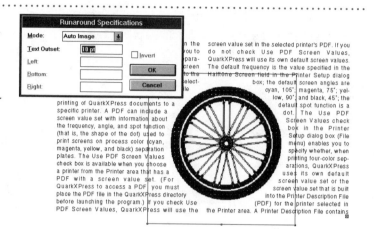

graphic element. Figure 16.13 shows the example getting closer to acceptable, but not quite there yet!

FIGURE 16.13

To have more precise control over the runaround of text, select the Manual Image mode.

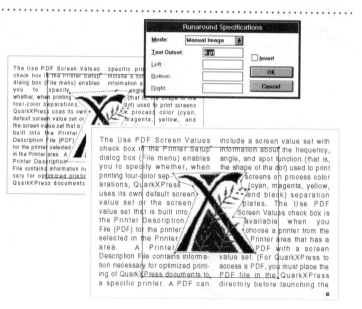

A close-up view of Manual Image runaround mode shows that it places dozens of tiny grab handles around the graphic image or images within your picture box (see Figure 16.14). The type projects through the boundary of the picture box and is stopped by the new manual boundary around the picture (not the box). You can relocate these grab handles through click-and-drag. If no grab handles are available where you want one, hold down Ctrl and click on the outline; a new grab handle will appear, which you can relocate. To delete an unwanted grab handle, position the cursor over it, hold down Ctrl and click the mouse button.

INVERTING TEXT, AGAIN!

You were briefly introduced to the idea of inverting text earlier in the book. The concept is not well-liked by many QuarkXPress users. Maybe because it is rather difficult to use effectively, or maybe it is rejected because type often looks bad when inverted.

Since we are discussing runarounds, here is another quick look at inverting text to fill a graphic shape. Follow these steps:

1. Create a filled column of text, or better, two columns of text. The Invert appearance will look better if you make the text alignment *Justified* (Style ➤ Alignment).

FIGURE 16.14

A close-up of Manual Image runaround mode shows the grab handles you can use for fine control on text runaround.

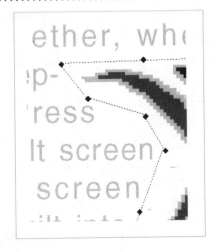

2. Create a picture box and import a graphic into it. Bring it in from some other source such as the Scrapbook or import from a stored file.

3. Position and resize the picture box and graphic to where you want the inverted text to reside.

4. To have the text fill the shape of a graphic you've just imported, click on the graphic to make it active.

5. Select Manual Runaround (Item ➤ Runaround).

6. Check the Invert option in the Runaround dialog box.

7. Click on **OK** and, voila! Your type takes the shape of the graphic. Unfortunately you can't see it because the graphic is blocking your view.

8. Click on the graphic and its picture box to activate it.

9. Press the Delete key to remove the graphic and see your text in its shape. The graphic should disappear, leaving you with a lot of type that may be difficult to read, in whatever shape your graphic was (see Figure 16.15). Enjoy!

LAYERING

As promised at the outset of this chapter, you were to have both runarounds and layering. For the most part, layering was introduced subtly throughout the chapter; you really cannot function well in runarounds without it.

TIP

To select a particular layer, click on it while pressing the Ctrl+Shift+Alt keys. This allows you to jump systematically through each layer.

As items rest on the same geometric space in the layout, they take up layers. Each item created on the layout adds a layer. If Runaround is set to Item, the item is opaque and elements beneath it move out of the way. If on different layers, opaque objects block the view of items "beneath" them. One way to deal with this is to keep sending the item on the top layer to the back. The Item ➤ Send to Back and ➤ Bring to Front options help you relocate items on their respective layers.

FIGURE 16.15

Inverting text to fill a graphic shape

The Use PDF Screen Values check box in the Printer Setup dialog box (File menu) enables you to specify whether, when printing four-color separations, QuarkXPress uses its own default screen value set or the screen value set that is built into the Printer Description File (PDF) for the printer selected in the Printer area. A Printer Description File contains information necessary for optimized printing of QuarkXPress documents to a specific printer. A PDF can include a screen value set with information about the frequency, angle, and spot function (that is, the shape of the dot) used to print screens on process color (cyan, magenta, yellow, and black) separation plates. The Use PDF Screen Values check box is available when you choose a printer from the Printer area that has a PDF with a screen value set. (For QuarkXPress to access a PDF, you must place the PDF file in the QuarkXPress directory before launching the program.) If you

check Use PDF Screen Values, QuarkXPress will use the screen value set in the selected printer's PDF. If you do not check Use PDF Screen Values, QuarkXPress will use its own default screen values. The default frequency is the value specified in the Halftone Screen field in the Printer Setup dialog box; the default screen angles are cyan, 105°; magenta, 75°; yellow, 90°; and black, 45°; the default spot function is a dot. The Use PDF Screen Values check box in the Printer Setup dialog box (File menu) enables you to specify whether, when printing four-color separations, QuarkXPress uses its own default screen value set that is built into the Printer Description File (PDF) for the printer selected in the Printer area. A Printer Description File contains information necessary for optimized printing of QuarkXPress documents to a specific printer. A PDF can include a screen value

NOTE

Beginners seem to have a great deal of trouble mastering the layer concept in QuarkXPress. If you are having problems, keep up the practice, don't lose patience, and remember, you are in the majority of QuarkXPress users (frustrated). Some suggestions have been made to Quark to change the layers to a tangible, such as a numerical layer, as used in some other software products. Until something like that happens, keep your cool and keep pressing Ctrl+Shift+Alt to go through each layer.

As you have seen from the previous examples in this chapter, layering can affect the quality of your layout. It becomes even more important as you incorporate runarounds.

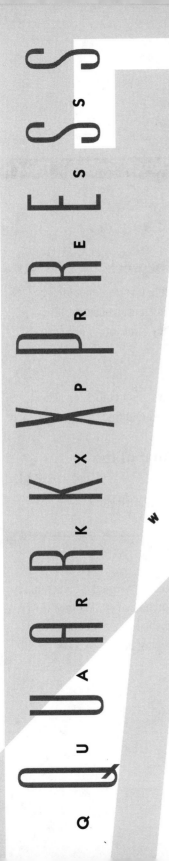

Color Concepts

FAST

To avoid surprises in preparing color work 319

talk to your print sales representative before getting involved in color prepress activities. Your printer may have techniques or procedures they have found to be best for their production that they want you to follow.

To add impact to your newsletter 320

don't be afraid to use color. You can add one or two spot colors for accent, without the fear of costly four-color separations and multiple press runs.

To match color on your monitor to that of the output printer 321

consider using TruMatch. This is one of the color options within QuarkXPress.

To use color in QuarkXPress 323

you need to boost your computer and monitor's color potential. You get this color monitor capability through the Video RAM memory (VRAM) in your computer, or through a separate color "card" installed in the computer. This card should be properly matched to a high quality monitor.

TRACKS

In the world of color there are a few definitions that try to qualify or quantify the mysterious. Although experts use these terms, when all is said and done, color is left to the consumer. In the business of printing and publication, that consumer is often the client. You may have studied color as presented by historical experts—Maxwell, Munsell, or others who mapped out the strategy of color—but who is really the expert in print production? That's right, it is the client. Remember as you see new gadgets and techniques, color is not always the same on all equipment or to all people.

NOTE

Color will appear different on the monitor (your computer's screen), on a proof, and on the final print. Don't be surprised if you design something in color and the print is different from what you expected.

THE MAKEUP OF COLOR

There are several historical figures and systems that artists and designers study to gain an understanding of color. Regardless of the system, there seems to be a trend in the vocabulary they use in describing the color system. Granted, these descriptions follow a variety of names, but they all seem to boil down to four areas. These color definitions include: *hue*, the qualitative value or richness of the color; *saturation*, the purity of the color; *chroma*, a relationship of color to levels of gray; and *brightness*, the amount of light that is transmitted through a transparent color or reflected from an opaque color.

NOTE

Other names for hue include tone, tint, *or* tonality. Chroma *may be called value or lightness.*

Color comes in a variety of forms, including transmitted or reflected, additive, and subtractive. The problem you have in electronic prepress is that there is no international standard for color. Also, you have a variety of mechanisms interpreting color. These include color scanners, still video cameras, your monitor, the software application, your color printer or proofing system, imagesetters, and, of course, the printing press. Also keep in mind that the biggest variable in color is the person operating the piece of equipment. In this business, it seems that no two people judge color alike, and if they do, their opinion differs from that of the client!

WARNING

Color means different things to different people. To avoid surprises, talk to your print sales representative before getting involved in color prepress work.

In the print production cycle there are the following variables that may affect color rendition:

- Incorrect screen tint values
- Register
- Wrong process color inks
- Press dot gain
- Pressmanship
- Paper color
- Run sequence

- Plate quality

- Press color control

- Color viewing conditions

- Press layout

- Condition of equipment

THE COLOR MODELS OF QUARKXPRESS

Although this chapter isn't going to be a "magic bullet" for your color problems, QuarkXPress has many practical color applications. QuarkXPress 3.1 supports six color models in base form (XTensions may add to these models). These color systems are Pantone, FocolTone, TruMatch, HSB, RGB, and CMYK.

NOTE

A process color is a color used as the basis for four color printing. Magenta, cyan, and yellow are process colors. These transparent inks, when used in the proper combinations, simulate full color for printing. Black is usually the fourth ink used in four color printing although it is not considered a process color.

PANTONE COLORS

A popular color system often specified by graphic designers for spot color and multicolor print jobs is *Pantone*. This is a system of colors from Pantone, Inc., which is part of the overall system including the Pantone Matching System (PMS). A Pantone color can be specified as either a spot color or a process color (see note). Traditionally, Pantone colors were available through color swatches that designers placed with their camera-ready artwork. This would be an indicator to the printer that the specified ink color is to match the given Pantone color swatch.

Colors used on only a single item, area, or specific parts of the page, as opposed to throughout the page layout, are called spot colors. These are used to add emphasis or impact to your design without the huge expense of four-color printing. For example, you may want the banner of your newsletter to be printed in a color, while the rest of the document remains black and white. The color, if used properly, will add some communication impact to your newsletter.

THE FOCOLTONE SYSTEM

Next there is the *FocolTone* color model. It is a color system designed exclusively for process printing. The FocolTone colors represent all available process color combinations and can be reproduced as process tint percentages or single spot colors. FocolTone lists 763 color combinations. A complete reference set including swatch book and large format chart with CMYK screen percentages and mixing formulae are available from the company. See *Appendix B* for address information.

The concept behind FocolTone is that of a mixture intended to reproduce colors accurately regardless of printing conditions. The system's combination of colors, coupled with a software program for printers, compensate for a variety of printing problems. One major problem for the printer is dot gain. The software calculates for printer problems such as dot gain for standard paper and newsprint. It is available in both Mac and PC disk formats, provided directly to the printer for solutions to these special color problems.

THE TRUMATCH COLOR SYSTEM

Perhaps the most promising new color system available in electronic publishing comes from TruMatch, Inc. It is quickly becoming the new standard in achieving predictable four-color printing when the prepress work is handled by PostScript imagesetters.

The *TruMatch* system is the first to digitally match your screen color with your proofer color and a printer swatch. It enables you to compensate by adjusting the monitor to find a lighter or darker color value without having to change any of the color cast values (i.e., hue, saturation, chroma, or brightness). This gives a remarkable rendition of the color value through the precision of imagesetters and the ability to output screen percentages in increments of 1%.

An advantage of TruMatch is that you can output color separations at your local service bureau with digital accuracy. This gives the designer another option over traditional color separation techniques.

HSB COLOR

HSB is a color system invented by three physicists,Harry, Steve, and Bill, hence the name. Just kidding. They were really artists, not physicists! Actually, HSB is the old standby of hue, saturation, and brightness. These are three of those elusive quantifiers making color what it is today.

HSB is more popular with artists than designers or printers, in part because of the way they mix colors. HSB is more for the enjoyment of screen color and has little to do with printer's colors of magenta, cyan, yellow, and black. In order for a printer to have proper separations, the HSB must translate to CMYK for separations.

RGB COLOR

Bill decided to strike out on his own, so he left the HSB group and formed the *RGB* color system. He called it that because he looked at it when finished and said to himself, "Real Good, Bill!"

If you believe that, there's no hope for you! Actually, the RGB color system is the one you probably see each time you look at a color monitor (such as a television set). It represents the colors of light in your cathode ray tube: red, green, and blue. In the spectra of light, red, green, and blue when mixed give the full color spectrum, or at least as much of the spectrum as your monitor will allow.

NOTE

No matter what color system you choose to select in QuarkXPress, chances are your monitor only uses only three colors, red, green and blue. You can't change physics by a menu selection.

RGB is known as an *additive* color system. When added together they make the appropriate colors of the total color spectrum available for use on your monitor. Mix equal percentages of red, green, and blue on your screen and the result is white.

CMYK COLOR

CMYK represents the *subtractive* color system that printers use. CMYK is an acronym for cyan, magenta, yellow, and black. How K became black is anyone's guess!

Ink color is subtractive because it absorbs light. When the primary colors of cyan, magenta, and yellow are mixed together equally, they make black. Secondary colors are mixed from primary colors. Green is mixed from cyan and yellow; red is magenta and yellow, while magenta and cyan make blue.

EDITING AND CALIBRATING COLOR

As mentioned, color is a rather subjective art. It has many variables as well as applications. Many of these variables come from the equipment you are using. To use QuarkXPress effectively, try to have a minimum of an 8-bit color graphic capability on your computer. 24-bit is more appropriate, but that involves more cost in color graphics and memory for your computer.

NOTE

Default values and selections are always made while a document is not open. Values and selections made with a document open typically are specific to that document and do not affect default (global) values.

One of the ways you can "control" color is through QuarkXPress's color edit capabilities. You can gain access to these through the Default Colors dialog box (Edit ➤ Colors). This is a color inventory of all current colors in QuarkXPress. From this dialog box, you may choose to add or edit colors through the Edit Color dialog box. If you are not in a document the dialog box is called Default Colors (see Figure 17.1). These are colors that will appear in all documents.

FIGURE 17.1
This illustration depicts the sequence and dialog boxes involved for color modification in QuarkX-Press. The Default Colors dialog box is shown when no document is open.

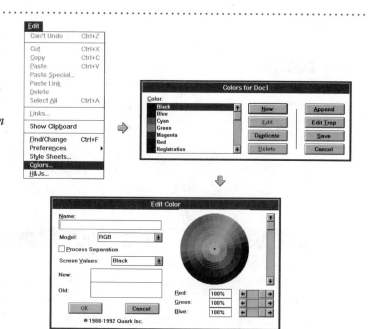

THE COLORS DIALOG BOX

The Default Colors dialog box appears when you select Edit ➤ Colors. It displays the active document or default colors palette (see Figure 17.2). You can do the following in this dialog box:

▸ Edit an existing color from the palette

▸ Add a new color for the palette

FIGURE 17.2
The Default Colors dialog box—if a document is open, its color palette will show.

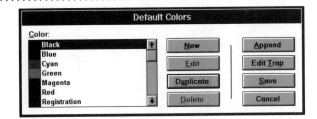

> ▸ Duplicate a color from within the same color palette
>
> ▸ Delete a color from the palette
>
> ▸ Append colors from other QuarkXPress documents
>
> ▸ Specify trapping values for specific colors
>
> ▸ Save changes to the palette
>
> ▸ Cancel all activities and leave color unchanged

TIP

Dialog box changes, once made, cannot be undone like errors in your document. Make sure you are happy with your changes before you close the dialog box. When you want to save, click the Save *option; to cancel and make no changes, click* Cancel.

ADDING A NEW COLOR TO THE PALETTE

Clicking **New** brings the Edit Color dialog box. This enables you to select a new color in one of the six color models, as listed above. To choose one of the six color systems select the pop-up menu from the Model field (see Figure 17.3).

Once a color model is selected, the dialog box changes to reflect the particular color chart or wheel for that model. Figure 17.4 illustrates all six models and how the dialog box changes to enable you to select a color. In those models with a color wheel—RGB, HSB and CMYK—you can either select from the wheel or

FIGURE 17.3
Select from one of six color models in the Edit Color dialog box.

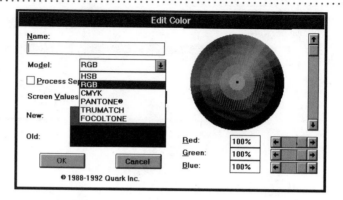

numerically key in your setting from the values below. To select a new color from the color wheel, click anywhere on the wheel. The color will be noted as a color swatch in the New field to the left of the wheel. You change the intensity of color by using the vertical scroll bar.

TIP

As you become more experienced in QuarkXPress, you will rely on numerical data more so than visual esthetics. If you select a color from the color wheel, jot a note as to its numerical value. This way you can recreate it again without too much difficulty. If you lose the note, look up the value from any document, via the Append option, explained below.

Below the color wheel in the RGB, HSB, and CMYK models are numerical value fields (and horizontal scroll bars). As you change the color wheel, the appropriate numerical value changes in these fields. An alternative is to change the value and have the color wheel reflect its change. Alter the numerical field by typing in your new value or using the horizontal scroll bars.

FIGURE 17.4

This illustration compares all six color modes (HSB, RGB, CMYK, Pantone, TruMatch and FocolTone) and their methods.

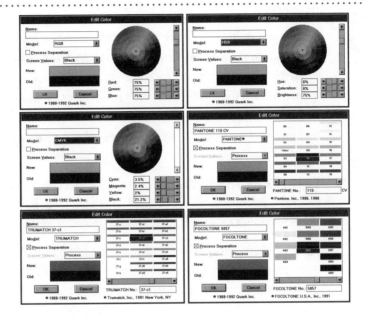

Other options in this dialog box include Process Separation check box and the Screen Values pop up menu. Selecting the Process Separation check box instructs QuarkXPress to separate a color into cyan, magenta, yellow, and black plates when you click Make Separations in the Print dialog box (File ➤ Print). Leave unchecked and QuarkXPress will print the color as a spot color only. You select the plate to place this spot color within. To do this, select Separations in the Print dialog box; then from the submenu next to Separations, select the spot color (plate) to print.

Once all changes and options are acceptable, you can give it a file name in the Name field and press **OK** to apply. Your new color appears in the color palette inventory. If changes were made on the global (default) color palette, they can be seen in any document. If you made the changes in a specific document, they will apply to that document only.

327

WARNING

The New, Edit, *and* Duplicate *options in the Default Colors dialog box all appear to be identical. Be careful, they are not! You can easily change an existing color if you select the Edit button instead of New or Duplicate. It is too easy to make a mistake here and no Undo is available. Also beware of Delete; if you click this button, the color will be removed without warning.*

EDITING IN THE DEFAULT COLORS DIALOG BOX

The **Edit** option is the default option within the Default Colors dialog box. That is, if you press Enter, you will be at the Edit option.

Edit enables you to alter a color from your existing color palette. To properly use this option, first select (by clicking on) a color from the color palette shown in the Default Colors dialog box. Then press Enter or click on the Edit button. This leads you into the Edit Color dialog box again. All procedures are the same as indicated for the New option above. The only difference is that the color swatch will show both a new color choice and the original color (chosen in the previous dialog box). You can give this new color a name in the Name field. This works with all selectable colors except for standard selections of Registration, Black, Cyan, Magenta, White, or Yellow. In Edit mode, your name replaces the name of the color you chose to edit.

THE DUPLICATE OPTION IN THE DEFAULT COLORS DIALOG BOX

The Duplicate option works like those above, with the exception of the Name field. Immediately upon opening the Colors dialog box, select the color you wish to copy and click on the Duplicate option. A new dialog box for Edit Colors appears. In the name field, it reads *Copy of* your color name.

The Duplicate option is available so you can make subtle changes to existing colors while using them as a reference, keeping the original color unchanged. To remove a color from the color palette, identify the color and press the Delete option. The color disappears.

THE APPEND OPTION

The Append option enables you to import another document's color (from its color palette) to your active document's color palette. Click on this option and the Append Colors dialog box appears (see Figure 17.5). This is a "search through everything you've got to select a file" dialog box, which you probably have experienced often in the Windows environment. Once you have selected the file, the Edit Colors dialog box appears and you select the color from that document's color palette to import.

WARNING

Some people have a bad habit of adding colors to the palette for frivolous reasons (e.g., they might want to see their type in a blue pastel on a yellow background). Do not waste memory adding changes that are not essential to production. All these kind of changes slow processing and add to the activity of the program.

You might use this option when you are working on related documents and want to edit colors in certain documents, but not make them global options. Also, if you add a color to only a few documents, you save the memory overhead of bringing up the new colors in all documents, many of which might not use them.

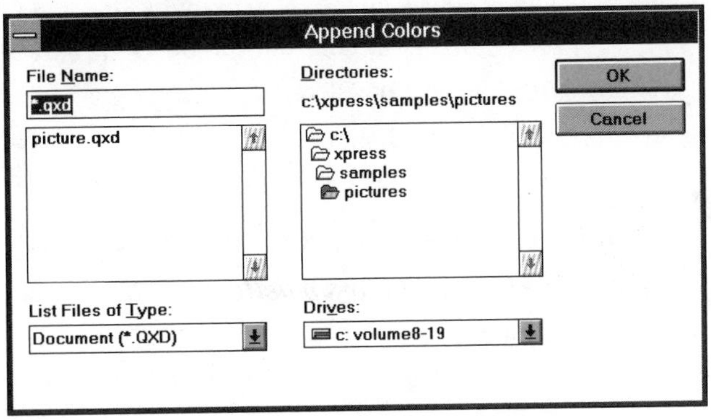

FIGURE 17.5

The Append Colors dialog box appears when you select Append from the Default Colors dialog box.

Append Colors		
File **N**ame: **.qxd** picture.qxd	**D**irectories: c:\xpress\samples\pictures c:\ xpress samples pictures	OK Cancel
List Files of **T**ype: Document (*.QXD)	Dri**v**es: c: volume8-19	

THE EDIT TRAP OPTION

The Edit Trap option enables you to select from a variety of trapping options for color separation purposes. Full discussion of this option is deferred until *Chapter 19*, which presents a comprehensive discussion on the topic of trapping in QuarkXPress.

NOTE

In the Edit Colors dialog box, you have the options of Save *and* Cancel. *To enter your changes, click on Save. To cancel all activity and make no changes click on Cancel.*

OTHER COLOR MENU AND PALETTE SELECTIONS

In addition to the Colors and Edit Colors dialog box, there are other areas of color manipulation in QuarkXPress to identify. These include specific color menu and palette selections for items within the QuarkXPress document.

APPLYING COLOR TO A TEXT ITEM

You can apply color to a text item's foreground or background in a number of ways. One such method is through the menu selection for color.

You must first have an active text box in your document, preferably with text inside. Highlight the text with the Content tool (click and drag over the range of type characters). You will apply color only to the type characters here. This is foreground color in the text box item.

NOTE

Another way to alter colors is through use of the Colors palette. See the section on the Colors palette later in this chapter.

Once highlighted, select Style ➤ Color. This brings up the color palette for the document, including default colors for all documents (global). Change the color for your selected type range from the submenu color palette and it changes the color of the type in your document item. You may also use the same technique to apply Shade to type characters (Style ➤ Shade). You can shade in any color, including black. You may select a shade for this color as well (see Figure 17.6).

NOTE

Two other ways to color the background of an item include use of the Item ➤ Modify specifications dialog box and through the Colors palette (View ➤ Show Colors).

It enables you to designate the background color of the document item from the assorted document colors or from the default (global) colors.

ADDING COLOR AND SHADE TO PICTURE BOXES

Adding color to a picture box is similar to adding it to a text box. You can place color in the foreground or background. In picture boxes, however, a large determinant of color rendition is the type of graphic placed in the item box. Remember,

FIGURE 17.6

You can select color and shade combinations for Background areas of the text.

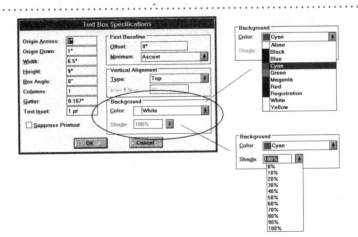

you have a variety of formats to deal with here. Also, how the box is sized around the graphic has a lot to do with showing or not showing background color.

NOTE

PICT images will not allow changes in color, shade, or halftone screen value, as they are essentially "snapshots."

Figure 17.7 depicts a rough bitmapped image inside an active picture box. Since it is active, it can be manipulated for foreground and background color and shade. To alter the item's foreground color and shade, select the appropriate option from the Style menu (Style ➤ Color or Style ➤ Shade).

NOTE

Grouped items also have color and shade potential for the background only. You cannot color or shade the foreground of items that are grouped, but you can modify the background. Other manipulations for grouped items are similar to those for ungrouped items.

FIGURE 17.7

QuarkXPress enables you to color and shade certain graphic formats (here a bitmapped graphic is illustrated).

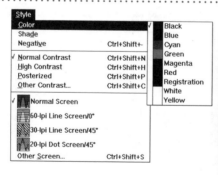

To alter background color for the picture box, select Item ➤ Modify and then choose either the color or shade option. This gives the Picture Box Specifications dialog box. Just as with text boxes, select the appropriate color and shade from the submenus as desired.

APPLYING COLOR TO LINES

Lines may not receive as much attention as text or picture boxes, but you can manipulate them in many ways. Draw a line with one of the line drawing tools, the Orthogonal Line tool or the Line tool.

An active line can be colored and shaded through the foreground only. This makes sense, because lines really have no background, since they are not contained in boxes. You can change a line's color and shade through the Style menu (see Figure 17.8) or through the Line Specifications dialog box (Item ➤ Modify).

The Line Specifications dialog box (Item ➤ Modify) enables you to modify the line, including its color and shade (see Figure 17.9). Other modifications deal with line width, type, arrows, location, and rotation.

FIGURE 17.8

Menu options for a line item include color and shade applications.

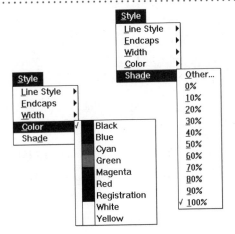

FIGURE 17.9

The Line Specifications dialog box enables you to alter color as well as all other aspects of the active line.

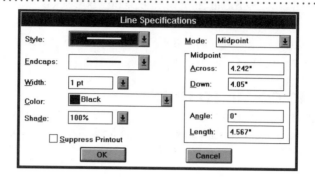

THE COLOR PALETTE

One of the palettes we haven't explored much is the Color palette (View ➤ Show Colors). Like other palettes, you may show, hide, relocate, and resize it as needed.

The top part of the palette consists of a row of icons representing coloration and shade for the item frame, foreground, and background. In addition, there is a shade control (see Figure 17.10). As the item type changes, the foreground icon alters appropriately. The foreground icon changes to reflect the active item. Figure 17.10 indicates alternate icons for each item type. Icons not applicable (e.g., the background icon for line item) are dimmed. If nothing in your document is selected, the entire color palette is grayed out.

Another function of the Color palette is that of color blends. To create a blend like the one depicted in Figure 17.11, follow these steps:

1. Create a text box and key in some text (modifying it if you like).

2. With the Colors palette showing and the text box active, click on the background icon.

3. Select Linear Blend from the pop-up submenu.

4. Select the #1 button option to choose the first color in the blend. The example has white as the first color.

FIGURE 17.10

The Color palette (View ➤ Show Colors) can be used to modify Text Box, Line, or Picture Box Foreground colors.

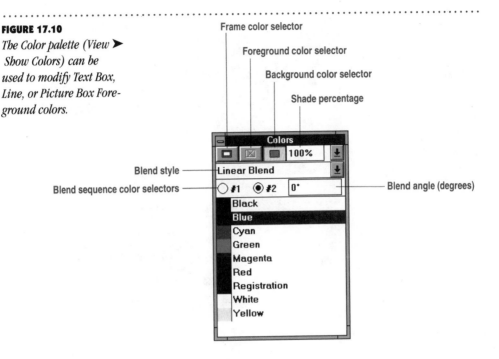

Frame color selector

Foreground color selector

Background color selector

Shade percentage

Blend style

Blend sequence color selectors

Blend angle (degrees)

5. Select the #2 button and choose a second color in the blend sequence. The example has cyan as the second blend color.

6. The example also chose a 15° rotation of the blend. This is subtle, yet tasteful, as rotations go.

7. Click outside the text box to deactivate it and watch QuarkXPress perform the blend. Note how the Color palette is dimmed when nothing is selected.

NOTE

The Solid blend is another type of blend, but it is not shown in Figure 17.11. You should experiment with the Solid blend and compare results with that of the Linear Blend style.

FIGURE 17.11

*The background color
blend potential illustrated
in progression: 1) select
the background icon;
2) choose linear blend;
3) select first color;
4) select second color;
5) select angle of blend;
6) deselect the item
and blend occurs.*

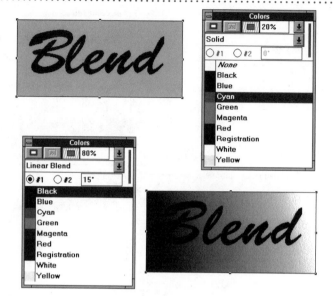

Color palette applications can color the foreground, background, or frame of an item, or all three in combination. You can also apply shade values to any color chosen. The Color palette is one-stop shopping for all your color needs!

CONTRAST AND HALFTONE OF PICTURE BOXES

Two last manipulation areas, applicable only to picture boxes, are control over Contrast and Halftone. They were held back to incorporate in the Color Concepts of the book because they are manipulations similar in nature to color manipulation. You can also add these concepts with color for very interesting results as you will see in the examples.

CONTRAST POSSIBILITIES FOR PICTURE BOXES

Under the Style menu, you can manipulate various picture images for contrast, in particular, TIFF images. Your selections include rendering the image Negative (see Figure 17.12) and adjusting contrast to Normal, High, and Posterized (see Figure 17.13).

FIGURE 17.12

An picture box changed to Negative

You may also select Other Contrast to visit the Picture Contrast Specifications dialog box (see Figure 17.14).

The tools in this dialog box are described here:

- The Hand tool moves the entire contrast curve on the graph.

- The Pencil tool makes freehand adjustments to the curve.

- The Line tool makes linear adjustments to the curve.

- The Posterizer tool places handles in the middle of the 10% increments of the curve. Not the same as the Posterizer Contrast tool.

- The Spike tool places handles on the 10% incremental marks on the curve.

- The Normal Contrast tool resets the contrast to a normal 45° line.

FIGURE 17.13

*The options of High
Contrast and Posterized
images*

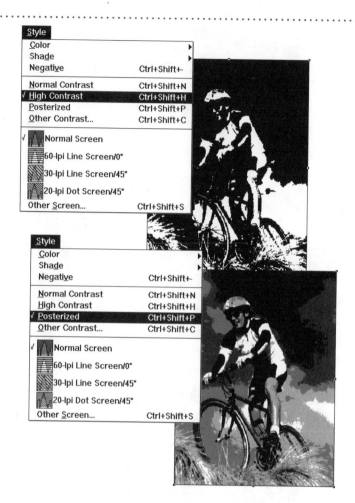

- The High Contrast tool creates a curve with two levels: 0% and 100%.

- The Posterized Contrast tool creates a curve with six levels: 0%, 20%, 40%, 60%, 80%, and 100%.

- The Inversion tool flips the vertically.

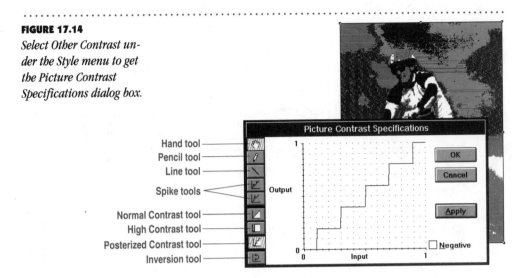

FIGURE 17.14

Select Other Contrast under the Style menu to get the Picture Contrast Specifications dialog box.

When you activate a picture box containing a color bitmapped or TIFF image and choose Other Contrast, the Picture Contrast Specifications dialog box includes your choice of color model. You can modify contrast for an individual color component or a combination of color components for the selected model (see Figure 17.14).

DEFINING HALFTONE SCREENS

Traditionally, the lithographic camera operator would have to photograph a continuous tone print using a contact screen to create a halftone. A halftone is an image consisting of a series of black-and-white dots of various sizes, that when printed, give the illusion of a continuous tone photograph. Since the press does not print with shades of gray, the only way to create the illusion of gray tones is through halftoning techniques.

Talk to any professional designer working in the area of high-resolution screen photographs in QuarkXPress and they may tell you that they still prefer to take photos out to the traditional color separation shop. Although the technology is growing rapidly, many designers feel they should not be in the color separation or half-tone business; others are more qualified to deal with these areas.

QuarkXPress has halftone capabilities built in, so you can import a scanned TIFF, RIFF, or EPS image and apply your own halftone screen for imagesetter output. Standard screen choices are listed under the Style menu. Standard screen choices include Normal Screen, 60—Line Line Screen/0°, 30—Line Line Screen/45°, and 20—Line Dot Screen/45°. There is a difference in final appearance of each screened photograph. Different situations and design considerations determine your choice here.

WARNING

Check with your printing sales representative to see what kind of screen value would be best for the product you want to print. There are many variables to creating a good screened image, the least of which is probably how the image looks on your monitor. Don't judge halftone quality by what you see on the screen.

You may also wish to create a halftone screen from the custom area of this menu, the Other Screen (Ctrl+Shift+S). Figure 17.15 illustrates the Picture Screening Specifications dialog box. Here, you can specify the line frequency in lines per inch (lpi) and screen angle. Pattern "dot" choices include the traditional Dot, the Line, Ellipse, Square, and Ordered Dither. The Ordered Dither is not a traditional printer's halftone dot; rather it is a new method developed to print photographs with screens on low-resolution printers, such as your desktop laser printer. You should not submit this for print quality.

FIGURE 17.15

Customize your screen options with the Picture Screening Specifications dialog box (Ctrl+Shift+S).

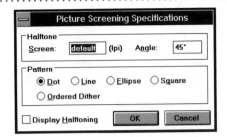

Picture Screening Specifications

Halftone
Screen: default (lpi) Angle: 45°

Pattern
⦿ Dot ○ Line ○ Ellipse ○ Square
○ Ordered Dither

☐ Display Halftoning [OK] [Cancel]

TIP

Don't display the halftone on your screen as you work because it simply takes more time for QuarkXPress to draw and takes away from productivity.

Also on this dialog box is a check box enabling you to display the halftone photo on your screen as you work. Perhaps a handy feature if the client is standing over your shoulder as you work, but rather useless otherwise.

PRINTING

PostScript Printing

FAST

To have a high-quality output image   348

you must output in PostScript. This page description language allows you to
draw any image on the page and print in the highest resolution (capable of
the output machine).

To speed up your QuarkXPress output   349

there are several things you can watch for, including your "network" connections. A connection solution incorporating Ethernet matched with the proper
cabling structure may improve speed over older-style serial or parallel
printer cables.

To speed printing scanned images   349

that you have in your QuarkXPress document, scan the picture at a resolution just over twice the final output resolution.

To have higher quality and control in color   351

you should utilize the PostScript 2 page description language printers whenever possible.

To use QuarkXPress in the office environment 353

consider your output options. Often a desktop laser printer gives excellent results for the type of work you do, at other times only an imagesetter output is acceptable.

To gain the highest possible output quality 355

you need to print with an imagesetter. If you business doesn't have one, you should call a *service bureau* (these service bureaus used to be the typesetting shops, but their roles have changed with the technological revolution of desktop publishing).

To make life easier for people at the service bureau 358

you may want to consider omitting the TIFF and EPS images from your QuarkXPress document. Print these separately and the work will go much smoother. The OPI options in print setup will help here.

Today, the accepted standard page description language in desktop and electronic publishing is PostScript software from Adobe Systems Incorporated. It is in use by more than 240 products from over 40 manufacturers. This product, perhaps more than any other, has revolutionized prepress technology.

WHAT IS POSTSCRIPT?

PostScript is the name of a computer language that describes how pages image on laser output devices. It can describe any page, and any element on the page. This was a seminal advancement over previous typesetting machines, or non-laser machines that could output only alphanumeric characters. The laser allows programs such as PostScript to draw any image on the page. The PostScript language is communicated by applications such as QuarkXPress when they want to tell a printer or imagesetter what to print.

PostScript is not the only page description language. It is the most popular, though, because it outshines other languages in capability and versatility. It includes provisions for using outline typefaces and halftone images. It also is the only language currently in use for imagesetters at the service bureau, an important part of the print production environment.

TIP

In order to maximize your system and productivity, you must keep abreast of all technological improvements in hardware and software manipulation—in particular, how to optimize Windows performance.

The PC with DOS/Windows is not optimized for producing PostScript quickly. To improve output speed, the following is suggested:

1. Use a dedicated machine to handle printing when possible.

2. Connect the printing computer directly to the printer with no others on the network.

3. Use Ethernet or some other fast communication channel.

4. Avoid placing EPS and TIFF files in the document on the network server.

5. Scan grayscale and color images at a resolution just over twice the final output resolution.

6. Scan line art at resolutions lower than final output.

7. Remove all initial programs and utilities not needed for your QuarkXPress/Windows operation.

8. Join the QuarkXPress Users International organization for ongoing tips and hints from users around the world (see information in *Appendix A*).

One of the most convenient aspects of PostScript is that the typical user does not have to be a programmer to take advantage of its power. Instead, applications make intelligent decisions, based on user input, and place the appropriate PostScript commands into action. These commands generate from a special part of the application software called a *driver*. This software driver program runs over 55 PostScript printers and imagesetters shipping today.

POSTSCRIPT AS AN INTERPRETER

The PostScript Interpreter, a program residing usually at the printer, receives PostScript language signals from the application program. A variety of configurations for the interpreter are available, including dedicated PostScript interpreter boards within a connected computer, a special PostScript interpreter board placed in the printer or imagesetter, or a separate stand-alone box containing the interpreter connected to the printer (see the section called *The Raster Image Processor*).

NOTE

Although imagesetters are capable of setting quality at 2540 dots per inch (dpi), they may be set by the operator for lower quality. Visually, few people can tell a quality difference between 1400 dpi and 2540 dpi. Imagesetters that output type at nearly 1400 dpi run twice as fast as those at 2540 dpi. Productivity!

Regardless of its physical makeup, the interpreter receives signals from the application program and constructs a representation of the page to draw in the laser printer. While printing, it takes into account the capabilities of the output machine. The output machine can range in quality from the desktop laser printer at 300 dots per inch (dpi) to a 2540 dpi imagesetter. The interpreter outputs the desired page according to the machine's maximum quality standards (as set by the user).

THE RASTER IMAGE PROCESSOR (RIP)

Often, the interpreter program resides on a circuit board or cartridge inside the output machine. Some imagesetters have an external interpreter inside a Raster Image Processor (RIP). It may be an external box or an attached computer. The RIP is often what determines the speed of output.

RIP technology is extremely fast-paced in its evolution. It is also the most problematic component of the PostScript system. If any problems occur in image output, most often they originate in the RIP. Many people are perplexed with RIP technology because it is relatively new and constantly changing. No one has had years of experience with any particular RIP.

A key component in the imagesetter RIP is the hard disk drive. It performs a variety of functions for page description. It involves inputting, manipulating, and storing a great deal of data. It is common for a color file to have 30 to 35 Mb of material. Efficiency is extremely critical in data loads of this size.

In addition, the hard disk stores the PostScript Interpreter software, printer fonts, and font cache, and on some RIPs, a screen cache. The hard disk with its PostScript interpreter is the center of all this data. Managing the data requires efficiency and working toward more efficient systems keeps companies competitive in the Imagesetter/RIP business.

As you keep abreast of changes, the most widely publicized are the new RIPs. They are part of an extremely fast moving technology, changing nearly every day.

POSTSCRIPT LEVEL 1 AND LEVEL 2

The page description language as described in this chapter is known as *PostScript Level 1*, or more simply just PostScript. It has been a powerful description language, and if Adobe has its way, will continue to dominate. To keep above the competition and evolve PostScript Level 1, Adobe has introduced *PostScript Level 2*. It involves more efficient ways to describe the appearance of a page. These include improved font switching, text composition, compressed image transmission, and better caching of the text and graphics that describe the appearance of forms and patterns. A powerful upgrade strategy is that any page you can print on a Post-Script Level 2 printer can print or display on the current installed base of Post-Script products. You can seamlessly integrate the newest PostScript printers and imagesetters.

POSTSCRIPT LEVEL 2

PostScript Level 2 extends the boundaries of Level 1. It incorporates several Post-Script language enhancements made over the last few years, such as color printing, Japanese language printing, and Display PostScript. Level 2 products include support for:

- The cyan, magenta, yellow, and black (CMYK) color model

- Color images (RGB and CMYK)

- Non-roman character sets and encodings (Japanese, Chinese, etc.)

- Optimized text and graphics operators from the Display PostScript system

- Forms and form caching

- Patterns and pattern caching

- Device-independent color

- Data compression and decompression filters

- Improved halftoning algorithms for color separations

- Improved memory management

- Resources management

- Improved support for printer-specific features.

NOTE

When products list as Roman and Non-Roman, these designations refer to the alphabet style. For example, the Roman alphabet, as used in the United States, differs from Kanji characters used in Asia.

WHAT KIND OF PRODUCTS USE POSTSCRIPT?

There are several products using PostScript; these are classified in distinct categories. Products that might enhance your business's output include:

- Black-and-white printers: Roman

- Black-and-white printers: Non-Roman

- Color printers: Roman and Non-Roman

- Film recorders

- Imagesetters/typesetters: Roman and Non-Roman

- Stand-alone RIPs: Roman and Non-Roman

- Software RIPs

For a complete list of these and other products and more information on Post-Script, contact Adobe Systems Incorporated (see *Appendix B*).

PRINTING CAPABILITIES OF QUARKXPRESS

Typically, the QuarkXPress user will prepare documents for printing for one of two categories of output: the laser printer or the imagesetter. There are a few distinct steps to perform in preparing documents for one of these.

PREPARING YOUR DOCUMENT FOR LASER PRINTING

Although QuarkXPress is a production tool in print publication, you may use it as a short-run communication tool in the office environment. For this, imagesetting output is inappropriate. Rather, the best way to produce the "quality" of communique appropriate is through the desktop laser printer. These come in a variety of quality standards ranging from 300 dpi black-and-white to over 1000 dpi. Some machines print in color or grayscale, and some non-laser machines can accept PostScript output. You can use any of these devices to proof your work before sending it to an imagesetter, or in many cases, to produce the end product.

THE PRINTER SETUP DIALOG BOX

To print the document, you must perform a few preparatory steps. Save the finished document to the hard disk, floppy disk, or network for later retrieval. Then select File ➤ Printer Setup to get the Printer Setup dialog box. This dialog box allows you to specify the printer type you have connected as well as to control various output features (see Figure 18.1).

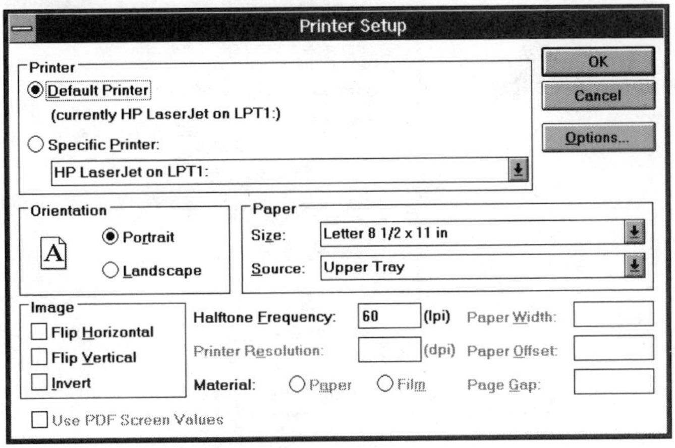

FIGURE 18.1

The Printer Setup dialog box enables you to select the printer type for output.

TIP

Remember to save early and often. Before printing and before closing the document, save it! You will find that electronic publishing is not yet an exact science; an ounce of prevention is worth a pound of cure.

One key area in the Printer Setup dialog box is the selection of printer types. QuarkXPress enables you to print on a variety of output machines, many of which are in the drop-down menu in Figure 18.2. If your printer is not listed, try alternate printers. Often printers with different names have the same tech specs as the ones listed. If you still have no luck, contact Quark and they can suggest an another solution.

Also, you may select a screen value, the default is 60 lines per inch (lpi). This is acceptable quality for laser printer. Higher resolution may be wasted on a 300 dpi printer.

The third QuarkXPress-specific option in this dialog box programs paper size. Select from the drop-down menu selections in Paper Size of letter, legal, A4, and so on. Sizes unavailable to your chosen printer will not be listed.

FIGURE 18.2

The drop-down menu in the Printer Setup dialog box lists several output printers.

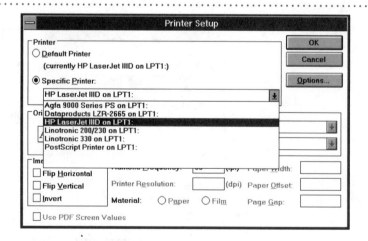

NOTE

There is a difference between lines per inch (lpi) and dots per inch (dpi). Lines per inch is an older judgment of quality for the printer industry. It represents the coarseness or refinement of the halftone screen. Newsprint prints on about 85 lpi. On the opposite end, fine, high gloss paper such as on annual reports may require 200 lpi screen quality. In dots per inch, 300 is near the low end and 2540 is imagesetter quality.

You see other information fields dimmed because they apply to imagesetters. Select an imagesetter and they become pertinent. When you have finished making your selections, click OK.

IMAGESETTER SETTINGS

Preparing a document for printing on an imagesetter is very similar to any other laser printer until you reach the Printer Setup dialog box (see Figure 18.3). Once chosen, the imagesetter will open other field values, as shown. Check with your service bureau. If you have an imagesetter in your company, check the manufacturers manual for that machine.

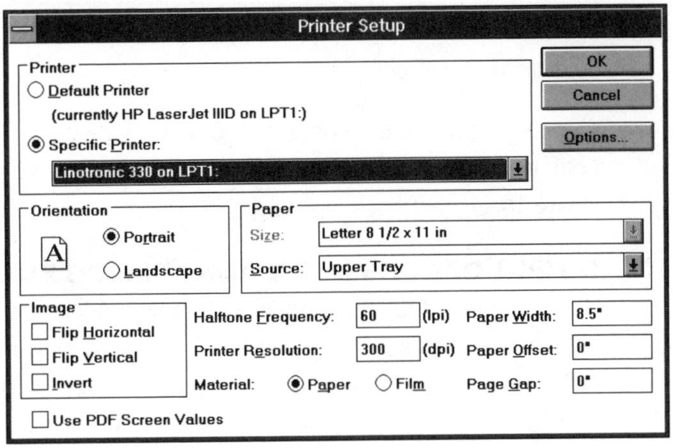

FIGURE 18.3

Choose an imagesetter from the Printer Type list and you will have a new assortment of fields to fill. Check with your service bureau or imagesetter manual for specifications on their machine.

Printer Setup

Printer
- ○ Default Printer (currently HP LaserJet IIID on LPT1:)
- ● Specific Printer: Linotronic 330 on LPT1:

OK / Cancel / Options...

Orientation: ● Portrait ○ Landscape

Paper — Size: Letter 8 1/2 x 11 in — Source: Upper Tray

Image: ☐ Flip Horizontal ☐ Flip Vertical ☐ Invert — ☐ Use PDF Screen Values

Halftone Frequency: 60 (lpi) Printer Resolution: 300 (dpi) Material: ● Paper ○ Film

Paper Width: 8.5" Paper Offset: 0" Page Gap: 0"

TIP

If you want the high quality output of an imagesetter but don't own one, contact a service bureau. Service bureaus, also called typesetting shops, will output your document from stored floppy disk to the imagesetter. Call first for information on page options for their equipment.

PRINT MANAGEMENT

The next area to check is that of the printer setup, under the File menu. It's important to double-check, because if it is incorrectly set up, your document won't print. Make sure you have a proper physical connection to the printer and set software appropriately. You may also have to use this dialog box to select from different printers. See your Windows manuals for a complete description on printing and the Print Manager dialog box.

THE PRINT DIALOG BOX

The Print dialog box (File ➤ Print or Ctrl+P) contains four primary options for QuarkXPress 3.1. They are:

Blank Pages

OPI

Print Status

Print Master Pages

All other options in the Print dialog box are endemic to Windows printing. Those options unique to QuarkXPress include the Output, Tiling, and Color sections (see Figure 18.4).

OUTPUT OPTIONS IN THE PRINT DIALOG BOX

Output options define the printed look of your document. The Normal, Rough, and Thumbnails options define the size and quality of your output. The default is Normal. If you want to see a less refined, quicker print, choose Rough. If you want some cute little drawings that you can't read at all, pick Thumbnails.

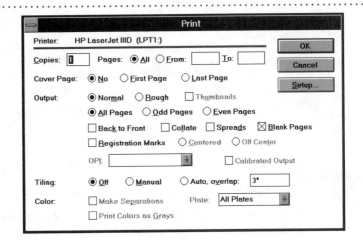

TIP

Use the Odd Pages, Even Pages options for your document to print on both sides of the paper. Run the job on Odd Pages, then take the stack, flip it and run it through again, checking Even Pages. It takes a little practice to get the system down, but you can put together great dummy publications or one-of-a-kind reports this way.

The All Pages, Odd Pages, and Even Pages options do what they imply. To print all pages in sequence, select All Pages. To print only odd numbered pages (usually right side pages in a spread), pick Odd Pages. Even Pages are for left facing pages of a spread.

The Back to Front option is handy for moving from one printer to another. Today's work environment may force you to move from one computer to another. Consequently, you may work on several styles of printers. This option saves the aggravation of having to reshuffle the papers when all document pages print first to last page. Use it with Collate to help sort sequential pages. Spreads allows you to print left and right hand pages together as one spread.

The Blank Pages feature is relatively new to QuarkXPress (Mac) and a nice option to include in the Windows version. At first, it may not seem very intelligent to pay for printing blank pages at a service bureau. Before the document goes to the service bureau you may want to make that dummy, using the desktop laser printer. But this option allows you to keep your sanity when creating a comprehensive layout.

NOTE

Many QuarkXPress users feel more comfortable with their own form of registration and trim marks. They choose to draw their own marks, rather than use those in the software. Also, at the last QUI conference some people noted that the registration marks were off one pixel, which was not acceptable in their work.

Click on the Registration Marks option and your document will print with trim and registration marks. You have the option of placing these marks on center or off center.

WARNING

Check with your service bureau or printer to see what setting they suggest in OPI.

The OPI pop-up menu allows you to specify the way pictures and Open Prepress Interface (OPI) comments are output. The choice depends on which way you plan to output the document and on whether you have high-resolution files with pictures in the document. OPI is available only when you select a PostScript output device. Options include Omit Tiff, Omit TIFF & EPS, and Include Images.

Omit TIFF & EPS suppresses the printout of images in both the TIFF and EPS picture format. OPI comments for both formats are in the output data. You should choose this option when going out to a device that replaces TIFF and EPS comments with those of higher resolution images. Sending PostScript images to color separation devices like a Scitex or Crossfield will require replacing low-resolution images with high-resolution ones.

Omit TIFF suppresses the printout of TIFF pictures but TIFF OPI comments remain in the output data. EPS pictures print normally, but EPS OPI comments are not included. Choose this option when outputting to an OPI system that replaces TIFF pictures (most systems use this method).

Include Images prints pictures in TIFF and EPS formats as usual. OPI comments are included for TIFF but not EPS data. If the high-resolution image is not found, the system will default to using the associated PICT image in substitution.

Also included in this dialog box is Calibrated Output. To use the calibrated settings built into QuarkXPress for most printers, check this option. Unchecked, the output matches other noncalibrated applications. The default is checked.

If a master page (or facing master pages) displays in the document window, all controls in the Page Setup dialog box are available and all controls in the Print dialog box are available, except All, From, and To.

Printing for Color

To have high resolution color in your PC 369

you must have a high-resolution color graphics card in the computer. This should be connected to an appropriate color monitor. A proper match between monitor, graphics card, and your needs is necessary.

To help align each color when printing 370

you should include registration marks. These can be generated manually by drawing them with QuarkXPress or through automation by selecting the Trim Marks option in the Print dialog box (File ➤ Print).

To have a good working relationship with the printer 372

you should communicate your needs prior to the completion of the QuarkXPress document. Often, printers hate for "computer artists" to generate their own traps and separations and will insist on reworking your document, wasting both time and money.

To edit trapping in QuarkXPress 373

select the Edit Trap button in the Colors dialog box (Edit ➤ Colors).

Printing for color is perhaps the most controversial aspect of electronic publishing. For years, the work was divided among many experts: the typesetting shop set the type; the artist generated the artwork; photographers photographed; camera operators converted it all to film, etc. Now you are in the midst of a one-stop prepress software environment capable of manipulating virtually all prepress specializations from one workstation.

Although QuarkXPress is on the leading edge in color capabilities, some people are still reluctant to jump into color. More than a few professionals take the approach that color separation is a specialty best left to the color separation shop. It involves years of experience and expensive equipment to perform properly. Others see this new desktop technology as the stepping stone to one-man (or one-woman) prepress; there is no need to pay hundreds of dollars to separation specialists for a QuarkXPress job you can output at the local service bureau.

This chapter attempts to just lay it on the line, presenting QuarkXPress in its base form. Certain XTensions can launch QuarkXPress into another realm in color, but, that's another chapter—*Chapter 20* to be exact!

GETTING COLOR INTO THE SYSTEM

There are several ways of getting color into your QuarkXPress document. These depend on what type of color image you need. Color ranges from spot color (single colors in a specific area or areas of the document page) to full-color photography. The simplest way to deal with color in QuarkXPress is to use the techniques introduced in this book for applying color to your layout. This may include changing type to a specific color, or applying color and shade to item boxes or frames. If you need to import more complex work, such as a scanned piece of artwork or a photograph, there are a few alternatives.

BRINGING COLOR IN WITH A DESKTOP SCANNER

One of the most common ways people import color images to computers is the desktop or *flatbed* scanner. Scanner technology, like all other computer technology, has emerged fairly recently for the electronic publishing field. Anyone who started in this five years ago may have a collection of scanners, from the original desktop page scanners that always destroyed the copy, to flatbed black-and-white, color, grayscale, and now 24-bit scanners. Technology is moving at a frantic pace. Fortunately, the cost of desktop equipment is relatively low compared with traditional printer's equipment.

The desktop scanner ranges in price from a few hundred dollars for hand-held scanners to a few thousand dollars for medium quality, 8-bit color scanners. For a few thousand dollars more (nearly fifteen thousand more), you can get into the high level of desktop scanners. These are flatbed or drum-type scanners that take images and convert them into 24-bit color digital files. Naturally, the lower costing machines are more prevalent.

NOTE

ZSoft PhotoFinish was used to edit the screen captures used in this book.

These machines all scan on a flat *bed*, so you can place the artwork or photograph over a glass, similar to making a photocopy. Appropriate software in the computer operates and manipulates the scan. Once the image is in the computer, you can manipulate the image through the scanning software or through certain photo retouching software packages like Adobe Photoshop.

There is another type of scanner to consider if you are in a buying mood. The second type, the *slide* scanner, is also popular, although not as popular as the flatbed style. With this device you scan a 35-mm photographic slide and alter the image with photo retouching software. There is something about transmitted light that has an edge over reflected light for scanner quality. The slide scanners have been available longer, and therefore have a quality edge over flatbed scanners.

NOTE

If you buy a desktop scanner and place it next to your desktop computer, which in turn rests next to the desktop printer, how large a desk do you need?

A third kind of scanner emerging in the marketplace is the *drum* scanner. It looks like a shrunken color separation scanner that may be in the printer's shop. In theory it works like the more expensive color separation scanner. To operate it, you mount a color film transparency, or print, on a glass drum that looks like a tube. A mechanism inside transmits light and analyzes every particle of the image as the drum rotates around at a high rate of speed. This digitizes the information and stores it on the computer for analysis and manipulation. The entire unit rests on a desktop. Desktop drum scanners have an input resolution of up to 4000 dpi.

Technology is changing so quickly that you must do your own investigating into price and quality. What may be the best quality or emerging standard today may be obsolete in two years. The best way to keep abreast of technological advances is to attend trade shows and conferences. A less expensive method is to subscribe to trade journals and magazines.

CAPTURED VIDEO AND STILL VIDEO

Another method of color image input is through the technology of video. This comes in two flavors: captured video and still video.

Captured video consists of a video card and software inside your computer. This video card has connections to a video tape player. As you play the tape, the software controls a utility that can capture one of the video frames. The software then digitizes the captured image, making it suitable for manipulation like any other color image. Motion video captures have a tendency, as of this writing, to be of lower quality than still video captures, due to their scan-line capability. This may change if high-definition television (HDTV) becomes a standard.

Still video is similar to (but still rather distinct from) captured video. In still video, you use the same video capture board and software. You can directly connect the configured computer to a still video camera with record and play capabilities.

The still video camera resembles a traditional hand held 35-mm camera for film. You place a tiny floppy disk in the camera, though, rather than film. The image is stored on the floppy disk. Cameras range from rather inexpensive (a few hundred dollars) to extremely expensive (several thousand dollars) with complete interchangeable lenses from such well-knowns as Canon and Nikon. Naturally, the more expensive cameras have greater scan resolution. These cameras also have an external player—a video disk player you connect to the computer's video capture card.

These still video cameras are remarkable. You can connect them to a telephone modem and transmit digital image. In Desert Storm, the military used these cameras to record images and send the pictures back to Washington for analysis the same day. This helped with daily strategy in the war.

MORE ON COLOR COMPUTER EQUIPMENT

What does it take to run color on your desktop? The answer is: a great deal of money! To be properly equipped and competitive in this market today, you should plan to spend from $20,000 to $30,000. Costs include a quality scanner or scanners, a souped-up computer, and a color printer or proofing device.

TIP

Buy lotsa memory! If you intend to work with color, you're getting into the big leagues. You need the right tools to make it work. You should have a fast computer; typically the 486DX is about as slow as you want to have. It should have a minimum of 8 Mb of RAM, a large hard drive, and a removable cartridge drive. And while you've got the checkbook out, buy an accelerated high-resolution color graphics board with a two-page, high-resolution monitor.

All too often, people see the false potential for jumping into the desktop publishing market by looking at clone prices in the newspaper. They think that desktop computers and software can do it all. For the price of a clone and a software application, they think they can do everything that a troop of prepress craftsmen can. Obviously, it doesn't work like that.

NOTE

Cash buys equipment, not skill! You still have to know what you are doing. As the lower cost of PC clones and Windows now enable many to be in the graphic communications industries, more people will be creating work that ranges from terrible to excellent. There is a great deal to be said for natural talent, but don't overlook formal education or mentoring with an experienced craftsperson in this industry.

THE COMPUTER

Since you already have a general idea on color input devices, as described above, you can jump ahead to the computer. This may be more appropriately named the "color workstation." There are several companies marketing packaged systems that they call color workstations. The packages include all necessary hardware, storage, and software to be in this business.

If you want to build a system yourself you can do it through standard computer equipment and peripherals. Start with a solid computer platform, such as an IBM or IBM clone with the Intel 486DX microchip, which you can expand later. Typically, the 486DX has potential to be upgraded to the DX2 configuration, doubling its clock speed. PC prices being what they are today, you should consider the 33mhz 486DX arrangement, with plans to upgrade to the DX2-66mhz chip later. The P5 (Pentium) chip due out in 1993 is suggested to be far superior to the 486DX in every way. Look for this to be a better alternative soon.

This fast computer should also have a high RAM memory potential. You should install a minimum of 8 Mb of memory. It is not uncommon for people working in this field to have 20, 32, or even 64 Mb of RAM memory in their systems. Remember, an uncompressed, (desktop) high-resolution color picture may consume about 8 Mb of memory. You also have the advantage of using virtual memory in Windows 3.1, but reading and writing to a hard disk drive is much slower than using RAM memory.

TIP

In shopping for removable storage systems, check with your service bureau. If you are sending large files to the service bureau for color separation, it makes sense to purchase the same style of unit they use.

To store the large files you'll undoubtedly be using, you should also have a large hard disk, accompanied by a removable cartridge, tape or disk system. Most service bureaus support the Syquest style of removable 44 or 88 Mb cartridge at this time. However, there are emerging technologies of optical disk and cartridge systems storing in excess of a gigabyte (1000 Mb) of material.

To see the high quality image on your computer, you need a monitor and graphics card capable of displaying accelerated 1024×768 quality. The ideal setup is to buy this configuration with a two-page monitor or perhaps two monitors. In Quark-XPress, you would probably find it more productive to have a standard monitor (SVGA 14″) to the side of your document layout monitor. This standard monitor could then house all your palettes. Two graphics cards in PC enable you to use two monitors; you can switch back and forth with a sweep of the cursor.

PREPARING FOR COLOR OUTPUT

Along with the color capabilities outlined in the previous two chapters, Quark-XPress excels in desktop publishing in an area called trapping. What is this mysterious concept so new to electronic publishing? Basically, it is manipulating the colors of objects so that there will not be too little or too much overlap of two colors side by side.

TRAPPING WITH DESKTOP COMPUTER TECHNOLOGY

Here is a good prank to play on your local printer. Call your print sales rep and say you have a color job prepared on the computer, complete with separations and trapping. Insist on highest quality and quick turn around. If your printer is like most you will hear dead silence on the other end of the line.

Generally, computer-prepared color has not been well received by the production community. Primarily, it has a bad track record because of calls like the one described above. Printers say that only about 5% of all color composed on the desktop computer is correctly done. Designers skilled in graphic layout have tried color separation and trapping fundamentals through an inexpensive computer program. True, today's programs can perform great work, but like anything else, skill makes the product as much as the tool. If you don't know about stripping, camera work, and separations, you probably will be out of your element in electronic separation and trapping.

But what the heck, maybe it is getting foolproof! QuarkXPress and its many XTension developers would like you to do separations on the computer. So now we get to the capabilities of separation, and more specifically in this chapter, trapping, in QuarkXPress.

WHAT EXACTLY IS TRAPPING ANYWAY?

Just what is trapping and why is it so controversial on the desktop computer? Trapping is a manipulation process in color work that overcomes the limitations of printing with the transparent inks that are, for the most part, used in process color printing. It is the combination of those transparencies that give the color spectrum for full-color printing. If you want a specific color to highlight, you may choose to have it print alone on the paper, not to overlap. As Figure 19.1 depicts, if you hold back ink in certain areas, such as for the type characters, then fill with a different colored ink, registration has to be perfect! Anything less is recognized as a blatant error in printing. Printers hate this because it makes them look bad, even if it is the person doing the prepress work (i.e., you) who is in error. A certain amount of press misregister is attributable to paper shrinkage, plate misalignment or other reasons. Proper trapping hides this due to a precise overlap that barely covers where the two colors meet.

NOTE

Registration is when each color image in the multi-color printing process is in exact alignment and position, relative to other colors of the print. In four-color work, cyan, magenta, yellow and black must be in exact position printed on the same sheet of paper to give full-color printing properly. Printers use the registration mark target (the circle with lines crossing) to help align each color as it prints on the press.

FIGURE 19.1
Using shades instead of colors (because the book is not printed in color), the illustration shows trapping problems.

TRAPPING OPTIONS AND CORRECTIONS

There are three options in trapping: traditional, high-end, and desktop. Printers and prepress shops often must originate or duplicate (repair) separations and traps made by desktop publishers. This is nothing new. These people have been in that business since day one. The biggest frustration they have is redoing someone else's work—usually the desktop designer's.

In traditional shops, printers may ask clients to go back and correct faulty traps (although it's highly unlikely they will succeed the second time) or they can correct it themselves. Most often they opt for the latter because they know how to control quality.

NOTE

*Outline type was generated through choke and spread techniques
on the camera before the font was available on phototype.*

In a traditional trap, the printer (lithographic camera operator or stripper) creates the *chokes* and *spreads*. These are trapping terms meaning to enlarge colors a bit to meet and overlap the next color they meet (spread) or reduce them slightly (choke). This is a technique that has been around for decades.

A popular way to hide the white paper when two colors meet is to spread or choke colors so that they overlay slightly. When adjacent colors have a slight overlap of the proper amount, they give the optical illusion of just touching and help hide misregistration. Other names for chokes and spreads include *shrinks* and *grips* and *fatties* and *thinnies*.

Another form of trapping is through high-end equipment. These machines are laser scanner systems costing up to a million dollars. These systems can be deadly accurate, as well as perform a variety of special effects. Ask an owner of one of these systems if your $700 PC software can trap as well as his equipment!

Most printers would rather generate their own traps from the start. So if you plan to work with a particular printer, camera operator or color separator, talk to them first before blindly plowing ahead.

TRAPPING WITH QUARKXPRESS

If you decide that traditional or high-end color separation is not appropriate for your needs, you may want to consider color separation and trapping on the desktop computer. This section gives an overview of trapping potential in QuarkXPress.

TIP

*Some colors are more difficult to trap to than others; for example,
gold is difficult. Good communication with your printer during
the job preparation can help you avoid generating unprintable
areas. A little planning goes far.*

To print the colors you have in your QuarkXPress document, a printing plate is made for each spot or process color separation. When multiple plates (inks) are used on a press job, each one has to print in perfect registration. If not, in places where one ink meets another, a thin white line (the white of the paper) will show through. This is undesirable!

To deal with trapping problems in QuarkXPress, select Edit ➤ Colors. The Colors dialog box displays (see Figure 19.2). Remember, if you are in a document, the Colors for Document dialog box is specific to colors in that document. If you are not in a document, default or global changes will occur as you change color attributes in the Colors dialog box.

NOTE

There are three types of trapping in QuarkXPress; automatic, color-specific, *and* custom.

Highlight a color you wish to trap and click on the Edit Trap button. This takes you to another dialog box, the Trap Specifications for color dialog box (where color is your specified color). As shown in Figure 19.3, the Trap Specifications dialog box allows you to pick the color your chosen color will trap to. It spreads to the background color you select here. If, for example, yellow type is to appear over a blue background, you would have selected to Edit Trap for Yellow; on the Trap Specifications screen, your color (background) choice would be Blue.

FIGURE 19.2

The Colors for Document dialog box (Edit ➤ Colors) has an option for Edit Trap.

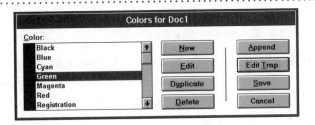

FIGURE 19.3
*The Trap Specifications
dialog box for your cho-
sen color to trap to the
background color*

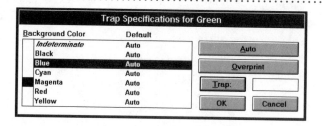

NOTE

*A foreground color (also known as an object color) can trap
relative to its background color in two ways: (1) Spreads—the
color item enlarges slightly to overlap the background color; (2)
Chokes—the area of the background where the object should go
(called the* knockout *area) reduces slightly so that the background
color overlaps the foreground color.*

Once you select the background color to trap toward, you can apply the trap in an
automatic or manual technique. The preferred method is manual, because of the
control you have over trap values. In QuarkXPress 3.1, you select manual by typing
in a trapping value, thereby creating one uniform spread or choke around the colored object. Certain problems may arise when objects protrude slightly out of the
background area. Other problems may occur where there are more than three colors involved (see Figure 19.4). Trapping is meant to have one color work with another (two colors total); when you have three or more colors, the formula gets
rather complex and confusing.

QuarkXPress's *automatic* trapping, the default method, is based on the relative
luminance (value or darkness) of foreground and background colors. You can
specify how QuarkXPress applies automatic trapping through the Trap options in
the Application Preferences dialog box (Edit ➤ Preferences ➤ Application). Figure 19.5 illustrates the Application Preferences dialog box.

FIGURE 19.4

You may have trapping problems when odd overlaps or odd color combinations occur.

FIGURE 19.5

The Application Preferences dialog box.

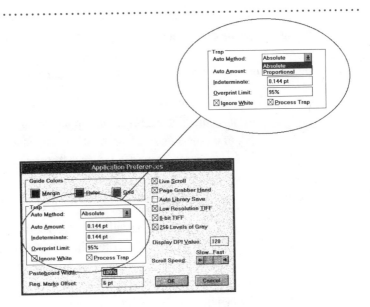

AUTOMATIC TRAPPING

To specify the method that QuarkXPress uses to determine the trapping relationship, choose an option from the Auto Method pop-up menu in the Trap options of the Application Preferences dialog box. *Absolute* traps the value in the Auto Amount field, according to the darker foreground or background color. The background color chokes by Auto Amount if the foreground color is darker; it spreads if the color is lighter.

Choose *Proportional* to trap using a fraction of the value in the Auto Amount field. This is based on the difference between luminance (darkness) of the color. The formula is:

Auto Amount x (foreground color darkness—background color darkness)

The background color chokes by the resulting amount if the foreground object color is darker; the foreground color spreads by the amount if the object color is lighter.

To control the amount of automatic choke applied (Auto Amount + or Auto Amount −), enter a value between 0 and 36 pt, in increments as fine as 0.001 pt in the Auto Amount value field. You can also enter the word *overprint*, which results in foreground and background colors with an Auto relationship.

The Indeterminate value controls the amount of trap applied to objects in front of multiple-color or conflicting trap-relationship backgrounds. Values range from − 36 pt to 36 pt., in increments as fine as 0.001 pt. You may also type *overprint* in the field. This results in foreground colors with Auto relationship to the Indeterminate background color.

The Overprint Limit option enables you to specify a shade above or below which an object color will overprint its background, enter a value between 0% and 100%, in increments as fine as 0.1%. The value entered here affects black when black is an object color set to Auto in the Trap Specifications dialog box. It also affects any object color specified Overprint as the color-specific trapping relationship in this dialog box.

Remember, the advice was to leave color separation to the specialists!

Check Ignore White to specify that an object in front of multiple backgrounds (including white) not take white into account while trapping. Unchecked, all items overprint a white background color. Overprint is considered an infinite choke. If an object (foreground) color is in front of both a white background and background color as specified to spread, it will trap to the Indeterminate color.

THE PROCESS TRAP OPTION
OF THE APPLICATION PREFERENCES DIALOG BOX

Check the Process Trap option to have QuarkXPress trap process separation plates individually when a page contains overlapping process colors. QuarkXPress compares the darkness of each process component of the foreground (object) color relative to its background color darkness. So if, for example, two shades of magenta are compared, then like comparisons are made for the other printer separation plates: yellow, cyan, and black.

Check Process Trap with overlapping process colors and an absolute trapping relationship and QuarkXPress divides the absolute value in half and applies it to the darker component of each plate. This provides a smoother trap while providing the same area of overlap.

If touching process colors have proportional automatic trapping, the amount of trap is determined by multiplying the Auto Amount value (specified in the Application Preferences dialog box) by the difference in darkness between the object color and the background color. This trap value then applies as explained above for colors with absolute trapping relationships.

EXAMPLE	OBJECT	BACKGROUND	ABSOLUTE TRAP	PROPORTIONAL TRAP
C	70%	30%	+1/2 trap amount	Auto Amount (70%–30%)/2
M	30%	50%	−1/2 trap amount	Auto Amount (30%–50%)/2

EXAMPLE	OBJECT	BACKGROUND	ABSOLUTE TRAP	PROPORTIONAL TRAP
Y	70%	80%	−1/2 trap amount	Auto Amount (70%–80%)/2
K	20%	15%	+1/2 trap amount	Auto Amount (20%–15%)/2

NOTE

When Process Trap is checked, trapping values in the Trap Specification palette may not be implemented as you expect when you print process separations: the trap value specified will be divided among plates.

When Process Trap is unchecked, QuarkXPress traps all process components equally using the trapping value associated with the object color relative to the background color.

NOTE

For small text (less than or equal to 24 points) and small objects (dimensions less than or equal to 10 points), QuarkXPress attempts to preserve the object shape during process trapping. It does this by disallowing spreads or chokes when the object's shape would be compromised. QuarkXPress does this by comparing the darkness of the object on each plate to the darkness of its entire background and only spreading if that plate is less than or equal to half the darkness of its background. Conversely, choking will occur only when the background plate component is less than or equal to half the darkness of the object.

COLOR-SPECIFIC TRAPPING IN QUARKXPRESS

To specify trapping values for specific objects relative to specific colored backgrounds, use the Colors dialog box (Edit ➤ Colors). Select the color to trap as the foreground or object color, and click the Edit Trap button. The Trap Specifications dialog box displays. The Default column lists trap values for each color, as defined in the Application Preferences dialog box. Overprint indicates that the object color (with an applied shade greater than that specified in the Overprint limit field of the Application Preferences dialog box) will not be knocked out of the background color's separation plate. A numeric value indicates a custom Trap value.

NOTE

A term describing a background with multiple colors in QuarkXPress is Indeterminate color. A color picture would be an example of Indeterminate color because of its multi-color background. QuarkXPress traps foreground colors to a specified background color in an Indeterminate color environment.

To specify trapping between the selected foreground color and the background color, select from one of the background colors listed. To select more than one background color, hold down the Shift key while clicking on background color names to select. The Auto, Overprint, and Trap buttons become active.

Specify auto trapping between the foreground color and selected background color(s) by clicking on Auto.

To ensure that applied foreground color items are not knocked out of the selected background color's separation plate, click Overprint. Only object colors with an applied shade greater than that specified in Overprint Limit field of the Application Preferences dialog box will overprint.

To specify a trap value between the foreground color and selected background color(s), enter a value in the Trap field and click Trap. Enter values from −36 pt to 36 pt, in increments as fine as 0.001 pt. A negative trap value chokes the object color's knockout area on the background color's separation plate; a positive value spreads object colors so they overlap the background color.

PRINTING
FOR COLOR
....

CH. 19

THE TRAP INFORMATION PALETTE

The Show/Hide Trap Information option under the View menu displays a palette you can use to specify trapping relationships for adjacent colors on an object-by-object basis. Bring up the Trap Information palette as you would any other palette listed under the View menu. Then move it and close it also as you do other palettes. See Figure 19.6 for a representation of the Trap Information palette.

The Trap Information palette consists of pop-up menu areas that vary, depending on the type of active item involved. They display six options for trapping color applied to the active item to its background color or adjacent color. The palette also enables you to trap text or a picture to its background color, or trap a frame to its background color. Options include Default, Overprint, Knockout, Auto Amount (+), Auto Amount (−), and Custom. The Default option enables you to trap the current active object color against its background. The trap value is displayed in the field to the right of the pop-up menu. Select Auto to trap determined by the Auto Amount and Auto Method settings in the Applications Preference dialog box.

FIGURE 19.6

The Trap Information palette (View ➤ Show Trap Information)

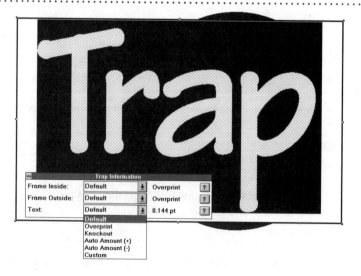

The Overprint option is chosen if you want to specify the current object color not knock out of its background. This allows the foreground color to print over the background color directly and may yield unexpected results if the printer uses typical transparent inks. Choosing Overprint, overrides the Overprint Limit value entered in the Applications Preference dialog box. To specify the current object color knock out of its background color (printing on the white paper, rather than the background color ink), with no trapping, choose Knockout. Select the Auto Amount (+) or (−) options to select a spread or choke preference. Choose Auto Amount (+) for the value displayed to the right of the pop-up menu is positive, indicating that the object color will be spread. If you choose Auto Amount (−), the value displayed to the right of the pop-up menu is negative, indicating that the background color will be choked. Specify your own trapping value for an active item by choosing Custom from the pop-up menu. Enter a value in the field to the right of the pop-up menu from −36pt to 36pt in increments as fine as .001-point. Information is available clicking on the question mark button. This is a type of on-line help built into this palette. To close the information window, click on the OK button.

PRINTING A COLOR DOCUMENT

Like everything else, there are a variety of ways to do a color print of your document. You might want to buy a color printer for around $10,000. There are two basic varieties. First, there is the thermal wax transfer; this takes colored wax sheets and bakes each color image down on the page; e.g., yellow, magenta, cyan, and black. Currently this takes about a minute per color. This means that a letter size document with full color will proof in about four minutes. The cost and speed of production prevent this from being much more than a proofing system at this time. Another type of machine used more often for photographic rendition is the dye sublimation printer. Originally intended as an output device for still video, it can be used to print document pages. However, output size is more in line with photographic paper standards than for printing paper standard sizes. For example, you can print a dye sublimation print in 8″×10″, but not 8½×11″. This may change as the dye sublimation printer gains wider acceptance in the desktop market.

NOTE

Rendering color on the computer monitor differs from rendition color on the proof. And both are different from color on the printed paper. An absolute must when doing prepress work for color printing is to have a proof made after the film is run in the imagesetter. Buy a Chromalin or some comparable high quality proof. Average price for the proof is about $50.

These methods provide the designer and client with comprehensive layouts or proofs of the layout. They are nowhere near accurate enough to provide a color separation proof. This must be done using output negative film in more traditional methods. There are a variety of techniques used here also such as ColorKey, Matchkey, and Chromalin. These tend to be more accurate than the color printer proof, but they still take some imagination compared with color on the printed page. This type of proof is more the standard in the industry than other techniques mentioned.

The ultimate color proof always has been and always will be the press proof. This is a proof that is run on the press, using the exact negatives, printing plates, inks, and paper used for the job. This is also the most expensive kind of proof, for obvious reasons.

Now that you have the knowledge to buy the right equipment, use the software properly and call the right specialists for help, you should want for nothing. Enjoy!

The Trap Information palette lets you customize on an object-by-object basis the way in which trapping is performed when you print separations. This palette is a movable window, always displayed in front of document windows. Its position is saved when you exit the program.

Use Show Trap Information (View menu) to display the palette. When the palette is displayed, the menu entry changes to Hide Trap Information. The Trap Information palette changes to show pertinent information for active items. Up to three pieces of trapping information can be displayed on the palette, depending on the active items and the currently selected tool. These include: Background, Text, Picture, Line, Frame Inside, and Frame Outside. Directly to the right of each title is a drop-down list; it enables you to select a trapping method for that component. Methods include: Default (uses the method specified in the Trap area of Application Preferences), Overprint (object shape is not knocked out of the background color plates), Knockout (exactly cuts out the object on plates that don't contain the object color), Auto Amount (+) (spreads the background by the Auto Amount as specified in the Trap area of Application Preferences), Auto Amount (−) (chokes the object by the Auto Amount as specified in the Trap area of Application Preferences), and Custom (allows a custom trapping value to be entered to spread (+) or choke (−). To the right of the drop-down list is the result of the selected trapping method. If Default is selected, a help icon (a button with a question mark on it) is displayed to the right. Click on this icon to view an explanation of the way in which QuarkXPress arrived at the displayed trapping value. If Custom is selected, an edit field is available for entering the custom value. The Control menu box on the left edge of the palette's title bar can be used to hide the Trap Information palette.

To spread the contents of a picture box in a framed box: Set the Frame Inside value to choke the knockout of the frame. This causes the picture and the background to spread.

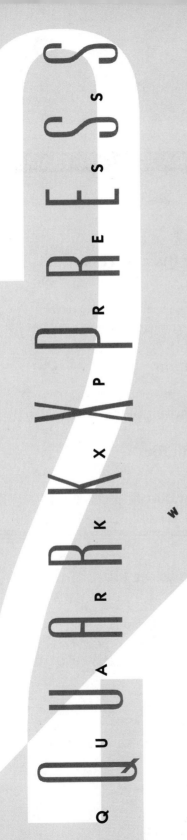

XChange and XTensions

To search and replace colors in the QuarkXPress document 390

use the ColorManager XTension from CompuSense. It enables you to replace colors regardless of location, including text, lines, frames, or backgrounds.

To utilize a higher level of hyphenation 390

use the Dashes XTension from CompuSense. It has algorithms that provide a 99% success rate in hyphenation, and works with foreign languages as well!

To record a header with all pertinent file information for your document 392

use the File Manager XTension. It has information about the creator, the project the document belongs to, creation and last modification dates, and the file revision status.

To see text hidden from view in an overset text box 394

get Overset! This XTension to QuarkXPress saves you time fitting text to boxes. When you click on an overset mark within a text box, Overset! creates a temporary text box that allows you to view overset copy.

XTensions are the livelihood of the QuarkXPress application. They are programs that enable the user to keep current on features to make their application run smoother. XTensions are the programs that help keep QuarkXPress the leader in electronic publishing.

WHAT ARE XTENSIONS?

QuarkXTensions technology lets you add software *modules* to expand the features and capabilities of QuarkXPress for specialized publishing tasks. This capability lets you add front- or back-end applications and integrate them with the rich functionality of QuarkXPress. Common applications include links to databases, pagination systems, automation of common processes, special color separation tools, and scanner drivers. Using QuarkXPress as the core of a publishing system and strengthening its capabilities with XTensions is a cost-effective way to solve complex publishing problems.

WHERE DO XTENSIONS COME FROM?

Like QuarkXPress itself, some XTensions come directly from specialists at Quark. However, independent and group developers from all parts of the world write XTensions also. People are writing and releasing XTension modules faster than the information can reach the QuarkXPress user. That is why QuarkXPress users around the world rely on the premier XTension clearinghouse, *XChange*. This company provides the QuarkXPress user base with quality XTension modules in a one-stop shopping environment. All XTensions listed in this book are available through XChange and suggested prices are shown to give you an idea of relative costs. Prices are subject to change. Check with XChange for a complete list of their inventory and pricing considerations, including site license prices.

Although QuarkXPress 3.1 for Windows is relatively new, there are over 100 XTensions available for the Macintosh version of QuarkXPress. It stands to reason that many of these developers will soon be reworking the code to adapt to a Windows format. The fact that Microsoft allows developers to use a simpler language such as Visual Basic to write for Windows should also be a plus for developers with less sophisticated programming skills. Look for many more XTensions for the Windows version of QuarkXPress in the near future.

HOW TO REACH XCHANGE

Contact XChange by telephone, fax, or through one of the major on-line services:

Sales *800-788-7557*

Sales (outside the continental U.S.) *303-229-0656*

FAX *303-229-9773*

Developer Relations *303-225-2484*

CompuServe *75300,2336*

AppleLink *W.Buckingham*

America OnLine *XChange*

XChange OnLine is the product information, suggestion and correspondence link. Their staff monitor the DTP Vendor Forum on CompuServe (DTPVEN) daily and try to respond to requests for information within 24 hours. In addition, members of the XTension of the Month Club get access to a private library of XTension demos, updates, and more. CompuServe offers special sign-up bonus to new members registered through XChange. See *Appendix A* for more details on CompuServe.

COLOR USAGE

(*Vision's Edge, Inc.* $30.00/$45.00 Int'l.) This utility lists the colors in a given document in a dialog box that indicates where and how the color applies. Colors sort by page number, with more information on process separation. Color Usage shows background or line color, frame, picture, and text character color. When you select a color from the dialog list, the RGB, CMYK, and screen color sample will display on your computer's monitor.

COLORMANAGER

(*CompuSense* $149.00/$219.00 Int'l.) ColorManager weds power and simplicity in a "must have" XTension if you do any color work in QuarkXPress. This program allows you to identify, control, and easily maintain any color used within your document. It provides a tool simplifying production of any color job.

ColorManager enables you to search for and replace colors. You can replace them regardless of location, including text, lines, frames, or backgrounds. Another option is the ability to specify the color's shade percentage, even while searching. This XTension allows you to make global changes of all color occurrences or individual occurrences.

This XTension adds a new menu called Color to the menu bar with various selections. The first option is Color Usage, allowing search, replace, and manipulation of colors in the current document. Custom and process colors in high resolution EPS files track in the EPSF Usage feature. It allows users to locate, select, and open the EPS file they want to check. A preview of the graphic is also available. For custom colors, you can determine if that color already exists in the current document. If not, you can create it within the ColorManager.

The EPSF Report option will provide users with a printed report on all EPS files in a selected document, listing for each the custom colors. It presents a dialog box similar to that for a new QuarkXPress document. You can specify the report's name, page size, and position of its margin guides. Also, you can specify if the report should print immediately after compilation or save for later examination.

The final two features are the Screen Angles and File Mover options. The Screen Angles option allows users to specify custom CMYK screen angles to four decimal points for printing. Finally, the File Mover feature enables you to save a file to any destination disk or folder. The file and all its linked files will transfer to the specified location.

DASHES

(*CompuSense* $200.00) The Dashes XTension provides high quality Hyphenation for your QuarkXPress text. Its aim and purpose is to provide a tool that improves the appearance and readability of a user's page by inserting inconspicuous hyphens, so as not to disturb the flow of meaning in the story.

The internal hyphenation code that is used in this XTension has been licensed from Circle Noetic Services, thus you are guaranteed to receive the same high standard of hyphen breaks as is provided by their renowned Dashes DA (for the Macintosh platform). Features include:

- Allows you to insert discretionary hyphens into a selection of text, the current text box, or the complete document.

- When inserting hyphens, the Auto Hyphenation Rules that you specify from within QuarkXPress (Edit ➤ H&Js) are fully obeyed.

- Allows you to remove discretionary hyphens from a selection of text, the current text box, or the complete document.

- If you are unhappy with the way the XTension hyphenates a word, you can enter it into your own Dashes exception dictionary.

- Each Dashes hyphen has a stylistic ranking associated with it, this allows you to exclude hyphens that are not up to the stylistic quality you specify.

- Allows you to import and export hyphenation exception lists into and out of the XTension.

- Will correctly hyphenate words that contain ligatures.

- All the hyphens inserted are stored as discretionary hyphens within the document, thus the document will not reflow due to hyphenation exceptions when opened or printed on another machine.

- Will correctly hyphenate the document, regardless of the System or Program language.

- Dashes XTension is a linguistically based algorithm. It puts in over 99% of the possible hyphens with over 99% accuracy in all languages offered.

FILE MANAGER

(*CompuSense* $149.00/$219.00 Int'l.) File Manager allows users to easily label, categorize, search for, move, and otherwise control all their QuarkXPress documents. It is a powerful yet simple to use add-on software module. File Manager includes the following features:

▶ The ability to create a new document allows the user to choose the page size from one of the many pre-defined standard page sets.

▶ Allows the user to create and maintain her own libraries of non-standard, commonly used page sizes and other page parameters.

▶ The File Mover is an option allowing you to select a file and specify a destination disk and or folder where you want to copy the file. The file and all its linked files transfer.

▶ When moving or copying a file, the user may move the QuarkXPress Preferences file and the fonts at the same time.

▶ An Error Log maintains a record of all screen and printer fonts that could not be located or moved.

▶ The Document Manager is a high performance publication tool that provides management and tracking capabilities for all your QuarkXPress documents.

▶ The user can create a header file for each document with information about the creator, the project the document belongs to, creation, and last modification dates and the file revision status.

▶ It is possible to modify the header files at any time.

▶ The user can specify defaults for the Creator and Project name in the header file. It is also possible to define the number and names of the various document revision status elements.

▶ The Document search utility provides high speed searching for files based on document name and/or document header data.

FLEXSCALE

(*Vision's Edge, Inc.* $59.00/$89.00 Int'l.) Another utility, this XTension allows a document to scale upon output to a printer. You can assign vertical and horizontal scaling percentages independent from one another to create rudimentary flexography. The document can be scaled between 50% and 150% vertically and horizontally. To activate this XTension, the user simply holds down the Alt key while selecting the Print command. Then the desired scaling percentages are entered into the FlexScale dialog. The scaling percentages are accurate to two decimal places, i.e. 102.87%. After selecting the Print button, the printing process continues normally, except that the output is scaled (see Figure 20.1)

FIGURE 20.1

A dialog box from the FlexScale XTension

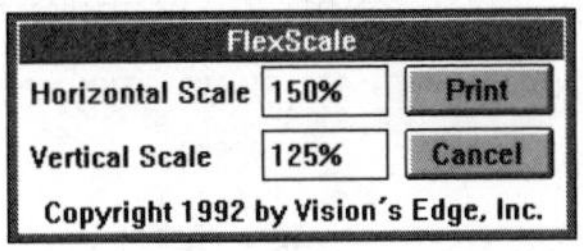

FlexScale

Horizontal Scale 150%   Print

Vertical Scale 125%   Cancel

Copyright 1992 by Vision's Edge, Inc.

THE MISSING LINK

(*Visions Edge, Inc.* $69.00/$99.00 Int'l.) This XTension deserves a commendation! How often have you wished you could "freeze" the links in a text chain to facilitate special editing, drag-copying from document to document, or placement in a library?

Your wish is granted, and then some, with The Missing Link. It adds a new preference dialog, accessed through the Unlink Tool. Here the user decides if The Missing Link unlinks the original text boxes, duplicates them in position, or duplicates and offsets them.

Also included with The Missing Link is the ability to link text boxes/chains that already contain text to other boxes/chains that contain text. The user has the option of telling The Missing Link to keep paragraphs intact as it creates the link between boxes. Single or multiple text boxes can be broken out of a text chain to create a new text chain, without disturbing the rest of the chain (see Figure 20.2)

FIGURE 20.2

*A dialog box from the
Missing Link XTension*

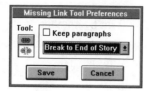

OVERSET!

(*North Atlantic Publishing Systems, Inc.* $69.00/Int'l.) Overset! saves you time fitting text to boxes. When you click on an overset mark within a text box, Overset! creates a temporary text box that allows you to view overset copy. You can then edit your copy or adjust your text box size to get the fit you want. The temporary text box will disappear when the text fits. If there is no actual copy, the temporary text box will turn on and off, signaling that the overset mark is due to a return. When you store a document, the temporary text box automatically disappears. Now you can get to an exact fit with ease!

PINPOINTXT

(*Cheshire Group* $79.50/$119.00 Int'l.) If you've ever had trouble printing a QuarkXPress document, PinPointXT is an absolute necessity. This easy to use XTension enables you to select Error Reporting from the Utilities menu. It tracks and reports any errors in your document, including the exact location of the error, using the QuarkXPress document coordinates. You can move right to the spot and pinpoint exactly where the problem occurred. Then use the convenient dictionary to look up and solve your printing problem. The dictionary is written in plain and clear language with the user in mind. It includes basic error handling tips and explains every possible PostScript error (see Figure 20.3)

FIGURE 20.3

*A dialog box from the
PinPointXT XTension*

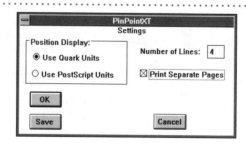

PROTABSXT

(*European American Graphics* $245.00/$365.00 Int'l.) ProTabsXT adds enhancement to QuarkXPress with professional typesetting capabilities. This XTension lets you break the 20-tab barrier in QuarkXPress, straddle and balance columns, and more. Features include:

- Automatically calculates the widths of tab columns and gutters to ensure alignment and fit.

- Allows automatic calculation of fixed and variable-width columns.

- Allows alignment of column heads over the longest column line.

- Straddle text across any or all columns and gutters.

- Automatically generate vertical and horizontal rules across all combinations of columns, gutters, and rows.

- Autovert command generates automatic vertical rules.

- Tab style sheets allow you to save your setting for use in future documents.

Tables are entirely self-contained, and can be moved, resized, cut, or pasted. Columns and rules will recalculate automatically, based on the new available areas.

Since ProTabsXT constructs its own combination of columns and gutters within its user-defined box, the number of available columns is twice QuarkXPress's maximum of 20. It returns the precision of tabular control familiar to typesetting professionals.

RESIZE XT

(*Vision's Edge, Inc.* $60.00/$90.00 Int'l.) If you have ever labored to scale each element of a layout to fit a new format, you know how much time such a project consumes. Just realigning all the items to maintain the aspect ratio of the original layout can be unbelievably cumbersome.

You could save the page as an EPS, and scale it to the proper size, but the resulting graphic is of course uneditable. That means if there are any document page edits, it is resaved as an EPS. Also, if the layout is very complex, or has imported graphics, the EPS from Save Page as EPS can be quite large.

Resize XT allows all elements of any group that could include the entire contents of a page or spread, to scale from 20% to 400%. Scaling of line weights, graphics, text and tabs can all be specified independently. The resulting collection of elements remains completely editable; every item is placed in the correct position, maintaining proper aspect ratio of the original layout.

SONAR BOOKENDS

(*Virginia Systems, Inc.* $129.95/$195.95 Int'l.) With Sonar Bookends, anyone can easily make an index and table of contents for a QuarkXPress document in a matter of minutes. Features include:

- Automatic indexing of keywords: An index consisting of all words can be made in seconds. Common words or unimportant words can be automatically eliminated.

- Indexing of word/phrase lists: An index can be made of a user-supplied list of words and phrases.

- Support for multiple-level indexes: Hierarchical indexes are supported with an unlimited number of levels.

- Flexible formatting: Page numbers can be separated with either commas or tabs. Chapter references can also be included in the index.

- Indexes can be printed or saved: The index can be printed directly or brought back into QuarkXPress for further editing.

SONAR TOC

(*Virginia Systems, Inc.* $99.00—requires Sonar Bookends—$149.00 Int'l.) Sonar TOC extends Sonar Bookends' indexing and table of contents creation capabilities with style sheets. Product highlights include:

- Fast and easy table of contents (TOC) generation: Simply tell Sonar TOC which style sheets are for headers, subheaders, sub-subheaders, etc., and it will produce a multilevel table of contents in seconds.

- Table of contents supports multiple sections: The page numbers in the table of contents appear just as they do at the bottom of each page in the document, including Roman numerals and prefix information.

- Indexing made even easier: Anything marked using style sheets can pass to Sonar Bookends for indexing. This feature is especially useful when indexing a catalog.

SPELLBOUND

(*CompuSense* $199.00 per language/$300.00 Int'l.) The SpellBound spell checker XTension enables you to check the spelling of a single word, of an active story, of an entire document, or of the text on master pages. It provides the following functionality and features not found in the internal QuarkXPress spellchecker.

- Allows multiple auxiliary dictionaries (up to five) to be open at any one time.

- Provides for an exception dictionary. This is useful if you wish to implement house styles or ensure words are always spelled in a certain manner (e.g., *disk* instead of *disc*).

- Detects capitalization errors (e.g.., will flag a word such as *mexico* as wrong and suggest *Mexico*).

- Uses a comprehensive, phonetically based algorithm, when looking for alternative spellings to words.

- Has a more precise definition of word boundaries. This allows you to spell check words such as *Ph.D.* and *QuarkXPress*.

- Allows you to use the spell checker as a "Guesser"; you may interactively type in your guess and do a lookup on this. This same feature allows you to highlight portions of compound words and get spelling suggestions on the constituent words.

- Distinguishes between words with the same spelling but with different capitalization. When replacing a misspelled word, you may choose to replace only words with the same capitalization as the present word or all occurrences.

- Gives you the choice of *casting* capitalization of the replacement word to that original or not.

- Allows you to edit any of the open auxiliary or exception dictionaries, while doing a spell check.

- Allows you to enter non-alphabetic characters into the auxiliary or exception dictionaries. Note: if non-standard characters are entered into an English auxiliary dictionary, then the dictionary cannot be used with the Internal QuarkXPress spell checker.

- Will spell check words containing certain ligatures.

TIMESTAMP

(*Vision's Edge, Inc.* $39.00/$59.00 Int'l.) The TimeStamp XTension allows you to apply unlimited time stamps to any document. Automatically updated whenever the document is saved, the time stamps enable you to easily and accurately determine a document's last revision (see Figure 20.4)

FIGURE 20.4

A dialog box from the TimeStamp XTension

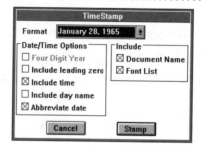

Features include:

- Unlimited time stamps per document.

- Time stamps are automatically updated with every save.

- Five different date formats, with the flexibility to alter many aspects of each format.

- Ability to include the time along with the date.

- Ability to include the choose name in any time stamp.

- TimeStamp frames can be placed on master pages to allow quick time-stamping of all pages.

Appendices

QUARKXPRESS

QuarkXPress
Windows

QuarkXPress
Resources

here are several areas from which to draw resources, including trade organizations, software developers, hardware manufacturers, etc. The appendix offers a few of the more important contacts for further document processing in QuarkXPress.

POSTSCRIPT PRODUCTS

The following companies manufacture hardware or software that use the Adobe PostScript page description language.

Adobe Systems Incorporated
1585 Charleston Road
P.O. Box 7900
Mountain View, CA 94039-7900
(415) 961- 4400

Agfa Corporation
200 Ballardvale Street
Wilmington, MA 01887
(508) 658-5600

**Agfa Corporation Business
Imaging Systems**
One Ramland Road
Orangeburg, NY 10962-2693
(800) 288-4039
(914) 365-0190

Agfa-Gevaert N.V.
Septestraat 27
B-2510 Mortsel
Belgium
32-3-444-2111

Agfa-Gevaert Japan, Ltd.
8-1, Higashiyama, 3-chome
Meguro-ku
Tokyo 153
Japan
81-3-5704- 3071

AST Research Incorporated
16215 Alton Parkway
P.O. Box 19658
Irvine, CA 92713-9658
(714) 727-4141

Autologic
1050 Rancho Conejo Boulevard
Newsbury Park, CA 91320
(805) 498-9611

Berthold AG
Stammhaus Berlin
Teltowkanalstrasse 1- 4
D-1000 Berlin 46
49-30-7795-116

Birmy Graphics Corporation
255 East Drive
Suite H
Melbourne, FL 32904
(407) 768-6766

Cactus
17 Industrial Road
Fairfield, NY 07004
(201) 575-8810

Canon, Inc.
Shinjuku Dai-ichi Semei
Building
7-1 Nishi-Shinjuku 2-chome
Tokyo 163
Japan
81-3-3348-2121

Canon USA
One Canon Plaza
Lake Success, NY 11042- 1113
(516) 488-6700

Dataproducts Australia
Pacific View Business Park
Unit 2/10 Rodborough Road
French's Forest, NSW 2086
Australia

Dataproducts Corporation
6200 Canoga Avenue
Woodland Hills, CA 91367
(818) 887-8000

Dataproducts Limited
Clonshaugh Industrial Estate
Dublin 17
Ireland
353-1-474-855

Diconix
3100 Research Boulevard
P.O. Box 3100
Dayton, OH 45420
(513) 259-3100

Digital Equipment Corporation
146 Main Street
Maynard, MA 01754-2571
(800) DEC-INFO
(800) 343- 4040

**Digital Equipment
Corporation**
Sunshine 60 Building, 55th
Floor
1-1 Higashi-Ikebukuro 3-chome
Toshima-ku
Tokyo 170
Japan
81-3-3989-7212

Digital F/X
755 Ravendale Drive
Mountain View, CA 94043
(415) 961-2800

Eastman Kodak Company
343 State Street
Rochester, NY 14650
(800) 242-2424

E.I. du Ponte de Numours
600 Eagle Run Road
Newark, DE 19714-6099
(302) 774-1000

Electronics for Imaging, Inc.
950 Elm Avenue 300
San Bruno, CA 94066
(415) 742-3400

Epson America, Inc.
20770 Madrona Avenue
Torrance, CA 90503
(800) 289-3776

Epson Europe B.V.
Prof. J.H. Bavincklaan 5
NL-1183 AT Amstelveen
The Netherlands
31-20-5475-222

Fujitsu America, Inc.
3055 Orchard Drive
San Jose, CA 95134-2022
(408) 432-1300
(800) 626-4686

Fujitsu Limited
Marunouchi Center Building
6-1 Marunouchi 1-chome
Chiyoda-ku
Tokyo 100
Japan
81-3-3216- 3211

GCC Technologies
580 Winter Street
Waltham, MA 02154
(800) 422-7777
(617) 890-0880

Gestetner Lasers Pty Limited
12 Rodborough Road
French's Forest, NSW 2086
Australia
61-2-975- 0555

Hewlett-Packard
11311 Chinden Boulevard
P.O. Box 15
Boise, ID 83707-0015
(208) 323-6000

Hewlett-Packard GmbH
Herrenberger Strasse 130
D-7030 Boblingen
Germany
49-7031-140

**International Business
Machines**
US Marketing and Services
Dept. 805
900 King Street
Rye Brook, NY 10573
(800) IBM-2468

**International Business
Machines (Europe)**
Tour Pascal-La Defense 7 Sud
Cedex 40
F-92075 Paris La Defense
France
33-1-4767-6000

Lexmark International, Inc.
740 New Circle Road
Lexington, KY 40511
(606) 232-2000

Linotype-Hell AG
Mergenthaler Allee 55-75
D-6236 Eschborn bei
Frankfurt
Germany
49-6196-980

Linotype-Hell Company
425 Oser Avenue
Hauppauge, NY 11788
(513) 434-2000

Linotype-Hell Limited
Bath Road, Cheltenham
Gloucestershire, GL53 7LR
United Kingdom
44-242-222-333

**Mannesmann Scangraphic
GmbH**
Rissener Strasse 112-114
D-2000 Wedel/Hamburg
Germany
49-4103-801-106

The Monotype Corporation plc
Salfords, Redhill
Surrey, RH1 5JP
England
44-737-768-644

Monotype Incorporated
2500 Brickvale Avenue
Elk Grove Village, IL 60007
(708) 350-5600

NEC Corporation
33-1, Shiba 5-chome
Minato-ku
Tokyo 108
Japan
81-3-3454-1111

NEC Technologies, Inc.
1414 Massachusetts Avenue
Boxborough, MA 01719
(800) 343-4418

NEC GmbH
Klausenberger Strasse 4
D-8000 Munchen 80
Germany
49-89-93-0060

Oce Graphics France S.A.
1, rue Jean Lemoine-B.P. 113
F-94003 Creteil Cedex
France
33-1-4898-8000

Oki Electric Industry Co, Ltd.
7-12 Toranomon 1-chome
Minato-ku
Tokyo 105
Japan
81-3-3501-3351

Oki Europe Limited
347/353 Chiswick High Road
London, W4 4HS
United Kingdom
44-81-742-2001

Okidata
532 Fellowship Road
Mt. Laurel, NJ 08054
(800) OKI-DATA

Optronics
An Integraph Division
7 Stuart Road
Chelmsford, MA 01824
(508) 256-4511

**Panasonic Communication
& Systems Co.**
Computer Products Division
Two Panasonic Way
Secaucus, NJ 07094
(800) 447-4700

Panasonic Europe Limited
Panasonic House
Willoughby Road
Bracknell
Berkshire, RG124FP
United Kingdom
44-344-853-901

QMS, Incorporated
1 Magnum Pass
Mobile, AL 36618
(205) 633-4300

**QMS Eastern Hemisphere
Operations**
117 Boulevard Magenta
F-75010 Paris
France
33-1-4526-0193

QMS Japan KK
4-3-7 Babadori
Utsunomiya
Tochigi
Japan 320
81-286-27-1185

Ricoh Company Limited
15-5 Minami Aoyama 1-chome
Minato-ku
Tokyo 107
Japan
81-3-3479-2905

Ricoh Corporation
Peripheral Products Division
3001 Orchard Parkway
San Jose, CA 95134
(408) 432-8800

Ricoh Europe B.V.
Hansa Allee 201
D-4000 Dusseldorf 11
Germany
49-211-528-50

Scitex America Corporation
8 Oak Park Drive
Bedford, MA 01730
(617) 275-5150

Scitex Corporation, Ltd.
P.O. Box 330
46103 Herzlia B
Israel
972-52-529222

Scitex Europe S.A.
Avenue Louise 120
B-1050 Brussels
Belgium
32-2-642-1511

Silicon Graphics Incorporated
2011 N. Shoreline Boulevard
Mountain View, CA 94039-7311
(415) 960-1980

Silicon Graphics GmbH
18, Avenue Louis Casai
CH-1209 Geneva
Switzerland
41-22-798-75-25

Texas Instruments, Incorporated
Peripheral Products Division
P.O. Box 202230
Austin, TX 78720-2230
(800) 527-3500

Texas Instruments
Manton Lane
Bedford, MK41 7PA
United Kingdom
44-234-270-111

Tektronix
26600 SW Parkway
Wilsonville, OR 97070
(800) 835-6100

Tektronix Europe Limited
Fourth Avenue
Globe Park
Marlow, Bucks SL7 1YD
United Kingdom
44-628-486-000

Varityper
11 Mt. Pleasant Avenue
East Hanover, NJ 07936
(800) 631-8134

Volt Autologic Ltd.
Alban Park, Hatfield Road
St. Albans
Hertfordshire, AL4 OJJ
England
44-727-834-132

Wang Laboratories, Inc.
One Industrial Avenue
Lowell, MA 01851
(508) 459-5000

Xerox Corporation
800 Long Ridge Drive
Stamford, CT 06904
(203) 968-3378

XTENSION DEVELOPMENT

In order to contact a private developer of XTensions or to request information on how you can become a registered XTension developer, contact:

United States Developer Desk
Quark, Inc.
1800 Grant Street
Denver, CO 80203
303-377-6327 fax
AppleLink D1590

International Quark-XTension Developer Desk
Q.S.S.
Kilbarry House
Dublin Hill
Cork, Ireland
021-300171 fax
AppleLink D2351

COMPUSERVE

The CompuServe Information Service offers a group of basic services for a standard monthly fee of $7.95. Services outside this group of basic services are offered on a pay-as-you-go basis and referred to as *extended* services.

Reading electronic mail from all incoming sources (except Internet) is free. Also, up to sixty three-page electronic mail messages can be sent free each month.

Perhaps the most important information for those in electronic publishing is found in electronic forums. These forums bring together thousands of members sharing ideas and information about careers, hobbies, health, lifestyles, computer technology, etc. CompuServe has a desktop publishing forum available giving you outstanding information in this field. You can also download freeware and shareware XTensions, fonts and other software programs through CompuServe. If you want to ask a manufacturer directly about a product, chances are they have an address on CompuServe. More than 180 software and hardware companies provide support for their products through online forums.

To find out more call a customer service representative at (614) 457-8650 or write to CompuServe Corporate Headquarters, 5000 Arlington Centre Boulevard, P.O.Box 20212, Columbus, OH 43220.

ORGANIZATIONS

There are many trade organizations—both local and international—that may be helpful to your efforts in desktop publishing. Two such organizations that you should put on your *Must Join* list are:

QuarkXPress Users International
P.O. Box 170
Salem, NH 03079
(603) 898-2822
(603) 898-3393 fax

Typographers International Association (TIA)
2233 Wisconsin Avenue, NW
Suite 235
Washington, DC 20007
USA
(202) 965-3400
(202) 965-3522 fax

QUARKXPRESS

QUARKXPRESS
LIBRARY

This appendix is a gallery of important and commonly used QuarkXPress elements. It includes palettes, menus, and dialog boxes.

THE QUARKXPRESS ENVIRONMENT

The main elements of the QuarkXPress environment are contained in the document window (shown in Figure B.1). These include:

Ruler origin box: Enables you to reposition and reset the ruler origin.

Control menu box: Use to close the current window.

Document name: Tells the name of the file.

Title bar: Click and drag to move the document window

Maximize button: Forces the application to fill the entire screen.

Minimize button: Reduces the application to an active icon.

Pasteboard: A nonprinting work area surrounding pages.

Scroll bars/boxes/arrows: The position of the scroll boxes within the scroll bars indicates the position of the document page(s) within the document window. You can click the arrows or in the bar, or drag the box, to move about in the document.

Border: Click and drag the border to resize the document window.

Size box: Use to reduce or enlarge the window to a specific size.

Page number indicator: Displays the number of the page currently displayed in the document window.

FIGURE B.1

The document window

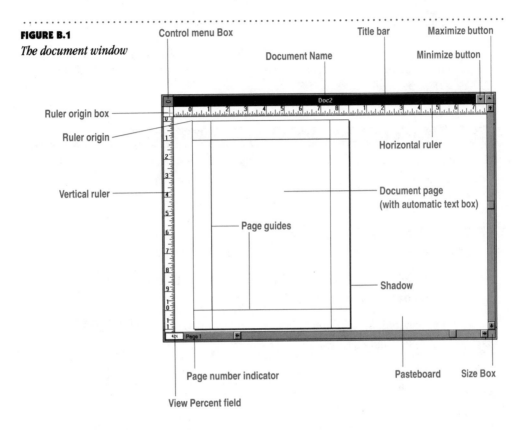

View Percent field: Indicates the magnification or reduction of the page view. Enter values in this field from 10% to 400%. Press the Enter key to implement the value.

Ruler origin: The point at which the rulers measure 0 across and 0 down.

Page guides: Nonprinting lines that indicate a page's margins and columns. (Page guides are dotted lines on black-and-white and grayscale monitors).

Vertical ruler: shows distance down.

Horizontal ruler: shows distance across.

Document page: This is where you place the item boxes that will make up your page layout.

Shadow: Indicates the border between the pasteboard and the page.

Automatic text box: The text box that QuarkXPress places on the first page of the document if you select the Automatic Text Box option in the New dialog box (File ➤ New).

THE PALETTES

QuarkXPress includes seven "floating" palettes (that means you can click and drag to move them wherever you want) that you can either hide or show from the View menu.

THE TOOL PALETTE

The Tool palette (shown in Figure B.2) includes the following:

Item tool: Enables you to move, group, ungroup, cut, copy, and paste items (text boxes, picture boxes, lines, and groups).

Content tool: Enables you to import, edit, cut, copy, paste, and modify box contents (text and pictures).

FIGURE B.2

The Tool palette

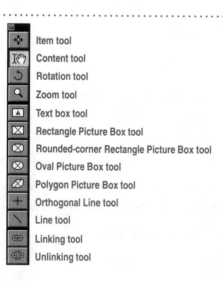

Rotation tool: Enables you to rotate items manually.

Zoom tool: Enables you to reduce or enlarge the view in your document window.

Text Box tool: Enables you to create a new text box.

Rectangle Picture Box tool: Enables you to create rectangular picture boxes.

Rounded-corner Rectangle Picture Box tool: Enables you to create rectangular picture boxes with rounded corners.

Oval Picture Box tool: Enables you to create oval and circular picture boxes.

Polygon Picture Box tool: Enables you to create polygon picture boxes. (A polygon is a shape with three or more sides).

Orthogonal Line tool: Enables you to create horizontal and vertical lines.

Line tool: Enables you to create lines of any angle.

Linking tool: Enables you to create text chains to flow text from text box to text box.

Unlinking tool: Enables you to break links between text boxes.

THE DOCUMENT LAYOUT PALETTE

The Document Layout palette (View ➤ Show Document Layout), shown in Figure B.3, enables you to create, name, delete, arrange, and apply master pages; insert, delete, and move document pages; navigate through document pages and master pages; and create multi-page spreads.

THE LIBRARY PALETTE

A Library palette (Utilities ➤ Library), shown in Figure B.4, enables you to store and retrieve frequently used Items (text boxes, picture boxes, lines and groups).

THE MEASUREMENTS PALETTE

The Measurements palette (View ➤ Show Measurements), shown in Figure B.5, allows you to view and edit specific item contents. Information categories within the Measurements palette change as the item highlighted changes; i.e., text size element vs. drop cap element.

FIGURE B.3

The Document Layout palette

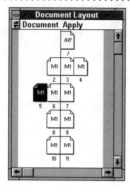

FIGURE B.4

The Library Palette

FIGURE B.5

The Measurements palette

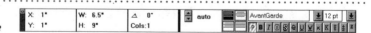

THE COLORS PALETTE

The Colors palette (View ➤ Show Colors), shown in Figure B.6, enables you to apply color and shade to box backgrounds, lines, frames, text, and pictures. You can also use the Colors palette to specify one- or two-color blends for box backgrounds. You can use this palette to open a Colors dialog box by holding down the Ctrl key and clicking on the color name.

FIGURE B.6

The Colors palette

THE TRAP INFORMATION PALETTE

You can implement or override automatic and color specific trapping settings on an item-by-item basis through the Trap Information palette (View ➤ Show Trap Information), as shown in Figure B.7. Specifications for custom trapping can vary from −36 to 36 points.

FIGURE B.7

The Trap Information palette

Trap Information		
Frame Inside:	Overprint	Overprint
Frame Outside:	Custom	0.235 pt
Picture:	Default	Knockout

THE STYLE SHEETS PALETTE

The Style Sheets palette (View ➤ Show Style Sheets), shown in Figure B.8, may be used to view or select a style sheet name to apply to selected text. You can also open the Style Sheets dialog box by holding down the Ctrl key and clicking on a style sheet name.

FIGURE B.8

The Style Sheets palette

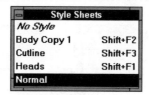

THE MENUS

This section shows the sundry QuarkXPress menus, listing the commands found on each. Remember the following principles:

▸ To drop a menu, click on its title in the menu bar; alternately, press Alt, followed by the underlined letter in the menu name.

▸ If a command is dimmed, it is not available.

▸ A check mark to the left of a menu command indicates that an attribute is applied or a function is in effect.

Each menu includes one or more of the following elements:

Keyboard equivalents: These enable you to choose a menu command using the keyboard. Press the keys listed to the right of the menu entry or press Alt, followed by the underlined letter in the menu name, followed by the underlined letter in the menu name.

Submenu indicator: An arrowhead displayed to the right of an command indicates that choosing that command displays a submenu from which you can choose a command. You can use the right arrows to scroll through the list. To select a fill, click on its name or use the up or down arrow keys. Double-click on a file name to open the file

Submenus: A submenu displays a list of commands related to the menu command that displays it. Choosing a submenu command either performs an action or opens a dialog box.

Ellipsis (...): These indicate that choosing the command displays a dialog box.

THE FILE MENU

The File menu (shown in Figure B.9) includes commands that relate to entire documents (files). Groups of related commands are separated by lines in the menu.

FIGURE B.9

The File menu

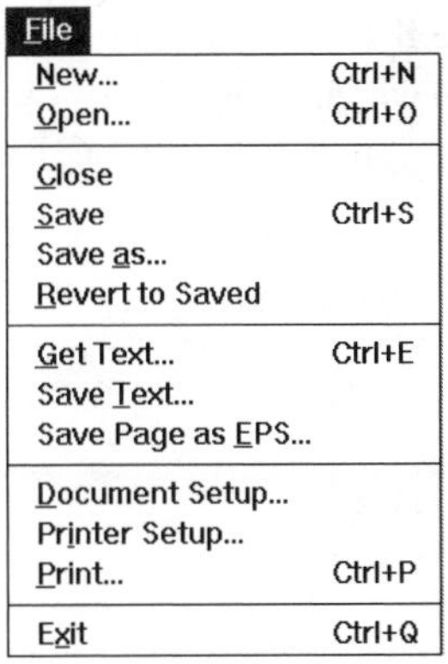

File	
New...	Ctrl+N
Open...	Ctrl+O
Close	
Save	Ctrl+S
Save as...	
Revert to Saved	
Get Text...	Ctrl+E
Save Text...	
Save Page as EPS...	
Document Setup...	
Printer Setup...	
Print...	Ctrl+P
Exit	Ctrl+Q

The first group enables you to create and open documents. The second group enables you to close, save, and make a copy of a document, and to undo your last set of changes to a document. The third group enables you to import text and pictures into documents, save text in a variety of formats, and save document pages as EPS pictures. The fourth group enables you to change a document's page size while it is active and to control the way in which the document prints out. The last command enables you to exit the program.

THE EDIT MENU

The Edit menu (shown in Figure B.10) includes commands for editing text, pictures, and items, for changing QuarkXPress default specifications, and for controlling text formatting features. Groups of related features are separated by lines.

The first command enables you to undo certain actions. The second group enables you to edit text and pictures or items, depending on whether the Content tool or the Item tool is selected in the Tool palette. The third group enables you to customize the way files import into QuarkXPress are updated via OLE (Object Linking and Embedding). The fourth group enables you to display a window that shows the contents of the Clipboard. The fifth group includes commands that enable you to search for and replace text and character attributes; to define application, general, typographic, and tool default specifications; and to create and edit style sheets, colors, and hyphenation and justification specifications.

THE VIEW MENU

The View menu (shown in Figure B.11) includes commands for controlling what you see on-screen and the way in which items and pages are displayed. Groups of related commands are separated by lines.

FIGURE B.10
The Edit menu

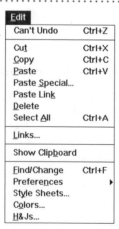

FIGURE B.11

The View menu

View	
<u>F</u>it in Window	Ctrl+0
<u>5</u>0%	
<u>7</u>5%	
√ <u>A</u>ctual Size	Ctrl+1
<u>2</u>00%	
T<u>h</u>umbnails	
Show <u>G</u>uides	
Show <u>B</u>aseline Grid	
<u>S</u>nap to Guides	
Show <u>R</u>ulers	Ctrl+R
Show <u>I</u>nvisibles	Ctrl+I
Hide <u>T</u>ools	
Show <u>M</u>easurements	
Show <u>D</u>ocument Layout	
Show St<u>y</u>le Sheets	
Show <u>C</u>olors	
Show Tra<u>p</u> Information	

The first group enables you to specify the size of the document view. The second group enables you to control the way in which visual layout aids are displayed and operate. The third group enables you to display or hide palettes that provide tools, field, and icons for working with items, text, pictures, document and master pages, style sheets, colors, and trapping.

THE STYLE MENU

The commands in the Style menu vary according to the active item: a text box, a picture box, or a line. The Style menu for text (shown in Figure B.12) includes commands for specifying character attributes and paragraph formats. These commands are available when the Content tool is selected and a text box is active. Groups of related commands are separated by lines.

The first group enables you to apply and modify character attributes. You can specify font, size, type style, color, shade, and scale for characters, as well as inter-character spacing and the position of characters relative to their baselines. The second group enables you to apply and modify paragraph formats. You can specify alignment, leading, indents, rules, and several other paragraph formats, and you can apply a style sheet to selected paragraphs.

FIGURE B.12

The Style menu for text

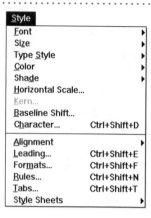

The Style menu for pictures (shown in Figure B.13) enables you to change the color and shade of a picture, to create a negative of a picture, to adjust the contrast of a picture, and to control the way in which QuarkXPress creates an electronic halftone of the picture. Groups of related commands are separated by lines.

Using the Style menu, you can modify pictures in TIFF (Tagged Image File Format), metafile color, grayscale, line art, color bitmaps, or black and white bitmaps. EPS

FIGURE B.13

The Style menu for pictures

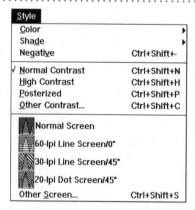

(Encapsulated Postscript) pictures cannot be modified through the Style menu; use the original application for creating EPS documents to modify them.

The Style menu for lines (shown in Figure B.14) includes commands that enable you to specify line style, endcaps, width, color, and shade.

FIGURE B.14
The Style menu for lines

THE ITEM MENU

The Item menu (shown in Figure B.15) includes commands for working with all items; i.e., text boxes, picture, lines and groups. Groups of related commands are separated by lines.

FIGURE B.15
The Item menu

Item	
Modify...	Ctrl+M
Frame...	Ctrl+B
Runaround...	Ctrl+T
Duplicate	Ctrl+D
Step and Repeat...	
Delete	Ctrl+K
Group	Ctrl+G
Ungroup	Ctrl+U
Constrain	
Lock	Ctrl+L
Send Backward	
Send To Back	
Bring Forward	
Bring To Front	
Space/Align...	
Picture Box Shape	▶
Reshape Polygon	

The first group enables you to make specifications for boxes, lines, and groups, to place frames on boxes, and to control the way in which text flows in relation to items. The second group enables you to make one or more duplicates of an item and to remove items from a document. The third group enables you to create groups in which multiple items act as one and to prevent items from being moved or resized accidentally. The fourth group enables you to change the stacking order of items on a page and to control the spacing and alignment of items. The last group enables you to change the shape of a picture box at any time and to reshape polygon picture boxes.

THE PAGE MENU

The Page menu (shown in Figure B.16) includes commands for arranging pages in a document and for navigating through a document. Groups of related commands are separated by lines.

FIGURE B.16

The Page menu

The first group enables you to insert, delete, and move pages within a document. The second group enables you to modify the placement of page builds on master pages and to change the numbering system of a document range of pages in a document. The third group enables you to navigate through a document. The last command enables you to display a master page or a document page.

THE UTILITIES MENU

The Utilities menu (shown in Figure B.17) includes commands for checking spelling and hyphenation, for creating and opening libraries, and for listing fonts and pictures used in the document. The Utilities menu also displays commands for XTensions to QuarkXPress placed in the program directory before launching the program.

FIGURE B.17

The Utilities menu

Utilities
Check Spelling ▶
Auxiliary Dictionary...
Edit Auxiliary...
Suggested Hyphenation... Ctrl+H
Hyphenation Exceptions...
Library...
Font Usage...
Picture Usage...
Tracking Edit...
Kerning Table Edit...
Read Registration...

DIALOG BOXES

A typical QuarkXPress dialog box is shown in Figure B.18. A dialog box is displayed on-screen when you choose a command that is followed by an ellipsis (for example, Modify, under the Item menu).

All dialog boxes contain one or more of the following elements:

Field: Enables you to enter specific values. You can add values to or subtract values from values in dialog box fields that control item specifications.

Dialog box name: Gives a good clue as to its function.

Area: QuarkXPress places a border around and assigns a name to an area that contains related fields, buttons, and/or drop-down lists. An area name can include a check box. The fields and controls in such an area become active when you check the box.

Field   Dialog box name

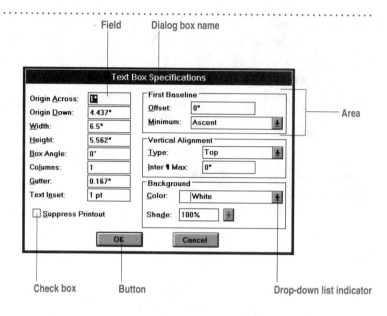

Area

Check box   Button   Drop-down list indicator

Drop-down list indicator: A drop-down list is a space-saving method of providing several options. Click and hold on the arrow to display the list.

Button: clicking a button does one of three things: it performs an operation, selects an option, or opens and closes a dialog box. To perform an operation or open a dialog box, move the arrow pointer over the button and click. If the button is surrounded by a thick border, pressing the Return key will perform the same operation as clicking the button. To select an option, click the button representing the option you want.

Check box: These represent options that you can turn on and off by clicking with the mouse. A checked box indicates that an option is turned on.

INDEX

NOTE TO THE READER

Page numbers in **boldface** refer to primary discussions of a topic; page numbers in *italic* refer to figures or tabular material.

A

About QuarkXPress command (Help menu), **56–58**
absolute leading, **218**
absolute page numbers, 115, 123–124
accent marks, specifying height, 264
activating. *See also* selecting
  QuarkXPress, 4, 6–11
  text boxes, 17
active applications, 12
active picture box, 280
Actual Size option (View menu), **15**, **51**, 127
add-ons. *See also* XTensions
  third-party XTensions, 42
Adobe PostScript. *See* PostScript
Adobe Type Manager. *See* ATM (Adobe Type Manager)
A4 size paper, 63, 354
aligning
  objects, 54
  text, 52, 176–178
    on single characters, 203
    with style sheets, 199–200
    vertically, 211, 220–222, 264–265
Alignment ➤ Centered option (Style menu), **24**
Alignment option (Style menu), **176–177**
Alt+F4, for closing documents, 45
Alt key combinations, 418
America OnLine, for XChange, 389
Ami Pro, format available from
    WordPerfect 5.1, 147
anchoring
  items on master pages, 126

items to text, 91–92, 266
Append Colors dialog box, **329**, *329*
Apple File Exchange, for text file translation, 149–151
AppleLink, for XChange, 389
Application option (Edit ➤ Preferences menu), **94**
Application Preferences dialog box, specifying automatic trapping, **374**, *375*, **376–378**
applications
  caution on cutting and pasting between, 45
  caution on running multiple, 10
  determining active, 12
  exiting, 44–45
  toggling between, 13
areas (on dialog boxes), **425**, *426*
ascenders, *265*
ASCII format, **149**
  available from WordPerfect 5.1, 147
  importing, 151–156
  saving text files in, 43
aspect ratio, **292**
ATM (Adobe Type Manager)
  assortment of font sizes, 165
  for improved screen quality, 134, 241
  for mixing font formats, 252, 253
  recommended for PostScript fonts, *166*, 166
Auto Constrain option, **91–92**
AUTOEXEC.BAT file, launching QuarkXPress from, 4
auto hyphenation, 271
Auto Image runaround mode, 308–309, *309*, *310*
auto leading, **215–217**
automatic indexing, with Sonar Bookends XTension, 387, 396

E

SYBEX

FREE BROCHURE!

Complete this form today, and we'll send you a full-color brochure of Sybex bestsellers.

Please supply the name of the Sybex book purchased.

_____

How would you rate it?

_____ Excellent   _____ Very Good   _____ Average   _____ Poor

Why did you select this particular book?

_____ Recommended to me by a friend
_____ Recommended to me by store personnel
_____ Saw an advertisement in _____
_____ Author's reputation
_____ Saw in Sybex catalog
_____ Required textbook
_____ Sybex reputation
_____ Read book review in _____
_____ In-store display
_____ Other _____

Where did you buy it?

_____ Bookstore
_____ Computer Store or Software Store
_____ Catalog (name: _____)
_____ Direct from Sybex
_____ Other: _____

Did you buy this book with your personal funds?

_____ Yes   _____ No

About how many computer books do you buy each year?

_____ 1-3   _____ 3-5   _____ 5-7   _____ 7-9   _____ 10+

About how many Sybex books do you own?

_____ 1-3   _____ 3-5   _____ 5-7   _____ 7-9   _____ 10+

Please indicate your level of experience with the software covered in this book:

_____ Beginner   _____ Intermediate   _____ Advanced

Which types of software packages do you use regularly?

_____ Accounting	_____ Databases	_____ Networks
_____ Amiga	_____ Desktop Publishing	_____ Operating Systems
_____ Apple/Mac	_____ File Utilities	_____ Spreadsheets
_____ CAD	_____ Money Management	_____ Word Processing
_____ Communications	_____ Languages	_____ Other _____ (please specify)

Which of the following best describes your job title?

_____ Administrative/Secretarial   _____ President/CEO

_____ Director   _____ Manager/Supervisor

_____ Engineer/Technician   _____ Other _____

(please specify)

Comments on the weaknesses/strengths of this book: _____

_____

_____

_____

_____

Name _____

Street _____

City/State/Zip _____

Phone _____

PLEASE FOLD, SEAL, AND MAIL TO SYBEX

SYBEX, INC.
Department M
2021 CHALLENGER DR.
ALAMEDA, CALIFORNIA USA
94501

SYBEX

SEAL

MENU MANAGEMENT

FILE MENU

Get Text/Get Picture	Ctrl+E
New	Ctrl+N
Open	Ctrl+O
Printer setup	Ctrl+Alt+P
Print	Ctrl+P
Quit	Ctrl+Q
Save as	Ctrl+Alt+S
Save	Ctrl+S

EDIT MENU

Copy	Ctrl+C
Cut	Ctrl+X
Find/change	Ctrl+F
General preferences	Ctrl+Y
Paste	Ctrl+V
Select All	Ctrl+A
Typographic preferences	Ctrl+Alt+Y
Undo	Ctrl+Z

ITEM MENU

Activate hidden items	Ctrl+Alt+Shift+click at overlap
Bring item forward 1 level	Alt+Item Menu Bring Forward
Constrain to square/circle rotation to 0/45/90°	Shift drag
Delete	Ctrl+K
Duplicate	Ctrl+D
Frame	Ctrl+B
Group	Ctrl+G
Lock/unlock	Ctrl+L

Modify (specifications dialog box)	Ctrl+M
Resize line, constrain to same angle	Alt+Shift drag
Runaround	Ctrl+T
Send item Backward 1 level	Alt+Item Menu Send Back
Step and repeat	Ctrl+Alt+D
Ungroup	Ctrl+U

UTILITIES MENU

Check spelling of story	Ctrl+Alt+W
Check spelling of word	Ctrl+W
Suggested hyphenation	Ctrl+H

VIEW MENU

Actual size	Ctrl+1
Apply/exit	Enter
Display tool palette/next tool	Ctrl+Tab
Fit in window	Ctrl+0 (zero)
Keep a selected tool	Alt+select tool
Measurements palette	Ctrl+Alt+M
Next field	Tab
Open section dialog box	click on page number area
Open style sheets dialog box	Ctrl+click on style sheet name
Previous field	Shift Tab
Show invisibles	Ctrl+L
Show rulers	Ctrl+R
Tool preferences	double click (on tool)
Undo changes	Ctrl+Z